Racket and Paddle Games

SPORTS, GAMES, AND PASTIMES INFORMATION GUIDE SERIES

Series Editor: Ronald M. Ziegler, Humanities Reference Librarian, Holland Reference Library, Washington State University, Pullman

Also in this series:

BICYCLES AND BICYCLING—*Edited by Barbara A. Schultz and Mark P. Schultz*

CAMPING AND BACKPACKING—*Edited by Cecil F. Clotfelter and Mary L. Clotfelter*

GAMBLING—*Edited by Jack I. Gardner*

GOLF—*Edited by Joseph S.F. Murdoch and Janet Seagle*

HORSEMANSHIP—*Edited by Ellen B. Wells*

MOTORSPORTS—*Edited by Susan Ebershoff-Coles and Charla Ann Leibenguth*

PRIVATE AVIATION—*Edited by Floyd Nester Reister*

WILDERNESS WATERWAYS—*Edited by Ronald M. Ziegler*

WOMEN IN SPORT—*Edited by Mary L. Remley*

The above series is part of the
GALE INFORMATION GUIDE LIBRARY

The Library consists of a number of separate series of guides covering major areas in the social sciences, humanities, and current affairs.

General Editor: Paul Wasserman, Professor and former Dean, School of Library and Information Services, University of Maryland

Managing Editor: Denise Allard Adzigian, Gale Research Company

Racket and Paddle Games

A GUIDE TO INFORMATION SOURCES

Volume 9 in the Sports, Games, and Pastimes Information Guide Series

David A. Peele

Reference Librarian
College of Staten Island Library
New York

Gale Research Company
Book Tower, Detroit, Michigan 48226

Library of Congress Cataloging in Classification Data

Peele, David A
    Racket and paddle games, a guide to information
sources.

    (Sports, games, and pastimes information guide
series ; v. 9) (Gale information guide library)
    Includes indexes.
    1. Racket games—Bibliography. 2. Racket games—
Information services. I. Title. II. Series.
Z7514.R32P44 [GV990]   016.79634   80-23977
ISBN 0-8103-1480-0

VITA

David Peele is a reference librarian at the College of Staten Island Library in New York City. He received a B.A. from Swarthmore College, 1950; M.S. in library science from Western Reserve University, 1951; and M.A. from Swarthmore College , 1954. He reviews books on racket sports for CHOICE and LIBRARY JOURNAL. He has published several articles on library topics under his own name, and others under the pseudonym Elsie Dinsmore. Peele is a member of the American Library Association, Library Association of the City University of New York, and United States Tennis Association.

CONTENTS

Contents

Contents

ACKNOWLEDGMENTS

I express my gratitude and appreciation to the many publishers who supplied free copies of the books annotated here, as well as to the several persons who supplied leads to information sources, with special thanks to Fred Weymuller for his help in that regard; and to my wife Marla for gathering most of the information about audiovisual materials, assigning grade levels to juvenile books, and putting up with my daily 5:30 a.m. rising to read yet another racket sport book. Thanks also to Denise Allard Adzigian and Claudia Dembinski at Gale Research, whose careful work made the book a lot better than it otherwise would have been.

SERIES EDITOR'S PREFACE

This book is the ninth volume in the Sports, Games, and Pastimes Information Guide Series. The series embraces a diversity of literature on leisure activities. It may be axiomatic that when an individual is attracted to a sport or pastime, he or she longs to learn more about it, making a fertile spawning bed for specialized publications on the subject. Such publication possibilities do not languish unnoticed for long.

As a result, an announcement that there is a proliferation of sports and recreation literature hardly qualifies as news. However, to those not associated with recreation research, subject-area collection building, and the publication of reference works in the field, it may be less obvious that there has not been a concurrent development in sports and recreation bibliography to accurately record this growth. This series of information guides represents an acknowledgment of the need for bibliographic control, and an attempt to impose that control through the identification of books and other information sources within a wide range of sports, games, and pastimes. Volumes in this series will attempt to provide librarians, researchers, practitioners, and others with selective annotated lists of books and other pertinent information.

In RACKET AND PADDLE GAMES, David A. Peele has gathered over nine hundred information sources in tennis, racquetball, table tennis, and the various additional sports in which rackets or paddles are used.

Within chapters on individual racket sports are found further topical subdivisions such as listings of books, audiovisual materials, periodicals, associations, equipment, and much more. The extent of Peele's knowledge of racket sports and associated reference sources is evident throughout the work, but never more obviously than in his list of "Recommended Purchases for Libraries and Individuals."

This volume answers a bibliographic and informational need for an authoritative reference work in the field of racket and paddle sports.

Ronald Ziegler, series editor
Washington State University

INTRODUCTION

From the late 1960s through the 1970s, the sport[1] of tennis experienced a great boom in the United States. Several factors contributed to that explosion of interest. One was the beginning of open tennis in 1968 with consequent over-the-table rather than under-the table payments. Second, televised tennis grew, with two matches in particular attracting special interest--the dramatic five-set struggle between Rod Laver and Ken Rosewall in the World Championship of Tennis finals in 1972 that extended into prime time and drew twenty-one million viewers (see 326 and 624), and the Billie Jean King-Bobby Riggs Astrospectacle in September 1973 watched by thirty-seven million,[2] nearly fifty million,[3] or over sixty million[4] depending on your source (see 307). Third, the general spread of the idea that lifelong exercise is good for one and the fact that fat racket sport players are rarely seen made more and more people take up the game. The late 1970s also saw increasing participation in squash racquets and even more of the same in racquetball, both of which are easier to learn at the elementary level than tennis and have the built-in advantage of walls, so that not too much time is spent chasing missed balls. Platform tennis received television exposure for the first time during the same years; "ping pong diplomacy" helped table tennis; and the end of the decade saw badminton begin to shake itself out of the doldrums where it had been bogged down for so long.

A result of this enthusiasm has been a multitude of books, films, and organizations that relate to racket sports. The person who goes to a well-stocked bookstore, for example, will find whole shelves of titles, particularly in tennis.

---

1. Although not synonyms, the words "sport" and "game" have been used interchangeably throughout this book.
2. Grace Lichtenstein, A LONG WAY BABY (New York: William Morrow, 1974), p. 254. (See 457.)
3. Linda Dannenberg, "The Rise and Fall of a Phoenix." In WORLD OF TENNIS 74 (New York: Popular Library, 1974), p. 242. (See 817.)
4. Dennis Van der Meer, TENNIS CLINIC (New York: Hawthorn, 1974), p. 89. (See 866.)

Introduction

This book's purpose is to provide a bibliographic and information guide to these materials. Major games each have a chapter devoted to them, and chapter 9 gives brief information about minor games--"minor" being one about which there is not a body of in-print books as of the publication date of this volume--and spin-offs from the major ones.

A few words on some of the subheads used may be helpful.

(1) Associations, Foundations, Organizations. Only a close reading of periodicals devoted to each game will enable one to keep up with the frequent name and address changes. TENNIS WEEK (see 875) occasionally publishes a "Directory" of organizations in its issues, but it must be used with care. For example, a news story in the 8 November 1979 issue on page 9 indicated that the International Racquetball Association had changed its name to the American Amateur Racquetball Association, but the former was still being listed in the "Directory" section as late as February 1980. National organizations and international organizations with headquarters in North America are included; local, regional, and international organizations with headquarters outside North America are not. The author would welcome correspondence about any omissions. In some cases the phrase "Did not respond to correspondence" is written after the name of an organization. In all such instances a minimum of two letters was sent with return address included. The letter was not returned to the editor and no response was forthcoming. The presumption has been, therefore, that the letter was received, but the organization chose not to respond. Information about such organizations has been obtained from sources other than the organization itself.

(2) Audiovisual Materials. Producers' catalogs, national associations for each game, the EDUCATIONAL FILM LOCATOR (New York: Consortium of University Film Centers and the R.R. Bowker Co., 1979), the GUIDE TO FREE-LOAN SPORTS FILMS (Alexandria, Va.: Serina Press, 2d ed., 1976), and the indexes produced by the National Information Center for Educational Media (NICEM) were the sources used to gather this information. NICEM must be used with some care. The subject indexing is not thorough, and one must not only search under, for example, "Tennis," but also under such related headings as "Physical Education." The listed film distributors often go out of business or move and leave no forwarding address. For that reason no NICEM item has been included unless its existence could be confirmed in another source. Another problem has been that sources were not always complete in their bibliographic data, principally in not giving a date for a film, and readers will note that that information is not always provided.

(3) Books. Books included here are almost all those listed in the R.R. Bowker publication, SUBJECT GUIDE TO BOOKS IN PRINT, 1979-1980. As in the case of films careful cross-checking was necessary. Some books on the game of racquetball, for example, are listed where one would expect to find them under "Racquetball." Completely different titles on the same sport are found under "Paddle Tennis" and "Racket Games." The continued use of the first of those two is not accurate. The SUBJECT GUIDE lists under it, in addition to the aforementioned racquetball titles, books on platform tennis. Platform tennis

and paddle tennis are different games; the confusion arose because the former is sometimes called "paddle." By continuing to use paddle tennis for books on platform tennis, the Library of Congress is perpetuating the error.

Many other recently out-of-print titles plus some privately published and vanity press books are annotated here. The emphasis is on titles published since 1968 in the United States and Canada, with a few pre-1968 titles also included.

In addition to standard bibliographic information provided for all entries cited in this guide, the International Standard Book Number (ISBN) and the Library of Congress card number (LC) have been given for books and audiovisual materials for which they could be found with a minimum search. This information should be helpful to libraries considering purchase. For books that have more than one edition (trade edition, paperback edition, etc.) the ISBN used is always for the library edition. For books that were published simultaneously in the United States and Canada, bibliographic data is given for the former only.

(4) Camps. For badminton, racquetball, squash racquets, and table tennis, actual camp names and addresses are given. This was done because names of camps in those sports are not easily found. Even if the camp has changed name or location, this information should provide a starting point. Camps are ephemeral for those sports, and the best sources for information are the national associations and the periodicals--and in the latter one may find camp information only in an advertisement or buried in a news article. For tennis, names and addresses are not given. Updated camp information is readily available in some standard sources, and those sources are listed in that section of chapter 8.

(5) Periodicals. An all-purpose annotation for racket sport magazines might read "Instructional articles, biographies, interviews with leading players, comments on the game, tournament announcements and results, and new product information and news are provided." In all periodical citations where the words "standard annotation" appear in the description, that is what is meant.

As periodicals librarians know, magazines in every subject field appear and disappear, sometimes without notice even to their subscribers. The major long-lasting national racket sport periodicals are provided; if the author has missed some of the minor ones it may well be because they moved with no forwarding address.

Chapter 1

RACKET GAMES IN GENERAL

ASSOCIATIONS, FOUNDATIONS, ORGANIZATIONS

1   NATIONAL LEFT-HANDERS RACQUET SPORTS ASSOCIATION. c/o
Charlene Grafton, 3042 Rosa del Villa, Gulf Breeze, Fla. 32561.

> The purpose of this organization is to be "a clearing house for
> information related to being left-handed in a right-handed
> world and its implications through the racquet sports." (Quote
> from TENNIS magazine (see 31), February 1980, "Sideline
> Slants," p. 14).

1A PROFESSIONAL STRINGERS ASSOCIATION. 2209 South Thirty-second
Avenue, Omaha, Nebr. 68105.

> This association was organized to promote good workmanship
> and to offer a forum for the exchange of ideas. It publishes
> a monthly newsletter and serves as a clearinghouse for new
> product information and as a place where members can get
> questions answered.

2   TENNIS CORPORATION OF AMERICA. 2020 West Fullerton Avenue,
Chicago, Ill. 60647.

> The largest owner and operator of indoor racquetball, squash
> racquets, and tennis facilities in the United States, this or-
> ganization performs feasibility studies on the setting up of such
> facilities for interested parties.

3   TENNISEARCH. 1208 Providence Road, Charlotte, N.C. 28207.

> This is a personnel-search organization that aims to match
> qualified persons with openings for club managers, teachers,
> and management people for sporting goods manufacturers in
> racket sports.

4   TRAVELERS TENNIS AND RACQUETBALL. New Market Mall, Paines-
      ville, Ohio 44077.

> This is an organization that allows members who travel to use
> the facilities like members at clubs in North and Central
> America where the two sports are played. Various discounts
> for such items as car rentals are included in the membership
> fee.

5   UNITED RACQUETSPORTS FOR WOMEN. P.O. Box 230, New York,
      N.Y. 10461.

> This organization, founded in 1979, hopes eventually to repre-
> sent women's interests in all racket sports (during the first year
> the emphasis was on paddleball and racquetball). Membership
> includes a subscription to THE WALLBANGER NEWS (see 34)
> and reduced entry fees for organization-sponsored tournaments.

6   UNITED STATES RACQUET STRINGERS ASSOCIATION. 108 Spinnaker
      Court, Del Mar, Calif. 92014.

> Similar in purpose to the Professional Stringers Association
> (see 1A), this organization publishes an annual string rating
> survey and holds seminars on stringing.

BOOKS

Those interested in writing the racket game book that will be seminal, or at
least definitive, should consult a copy of the latest edition of the R.R. Bowker
annual publication LITERARY MARKET PLACE. This reference book contains a
list of publishers classified by fields of activity. Check under "Sports" to find
those that might be receptive to racket game books.

For those searching for secondhand or out-of-print material, the following guides
to North American Specialty stores might prove useful. Readers should check
under "Sports" as well as "Tennis" in the indexes. The guides are: (1) AB
BOOKMAN'S YEARBOOK. P.O. Box AB, Clifton, N.J. 07015. (In keeping
with the nature of the antiquarian book trade, the 1976 edition of the AB
BOOKMAN YEARBOOK was published in 1978.) (2) BOOKDEALERS IN NORTH
AMERICA. This is revised every three years and published by Sheppard Press in
London. (3) BUY BOOKS WHERE--SELL BOOKS WHERE. This is compiled by
and available from Ruth Robinson, Route 7, Box 162A, Morgantown, W. Va.
26505. (4) DIRECTORY OF AMERICAN BOOK SPECIALISTS. 3d ed. New
York: Continental, 1976-77.

The editor has either visited or written to most of the sources listed in the
above four titles. The following short list represents those found most useful
for racket sports in particular: (1) Gwynned Valley Book Store, Plymouth Road
at the Reading Railroad Station, Gwynned Valley, Pa. 19437. It is open 365

days a year. (2) Joseph O'Gara, 1311 East Fifty-seventh Street, Chicago, Ill. 60637. While in the neighborhood go two blocks further to Powell's Book Shop, 1503 East Fifty-seventh Street, Chicago, Ill. 60637. (3) Kay Book and Magazine Supermarket, 620 Prospect Avenue, Cleveland, Ohio 44115. (4) Nicklas and Parker, 24 Lake Street, Cooperstown, N.Y. 13326. (5) Strand Book Store, 828 Broadway, New York, N.Y. 10003. (6) E. Tatro, 60 Goff Road, Wethersfield, Conn. 06109, sells books by mail only. Write, expressing your interest to be put on a mailing list.

Annotations for specific books follow.

7   Diagram Group. ENJOYING RACQUET SPORTS. New York: Padding-
     ton, 1978. 160 p. Photos., dgrms., dwgs. Paperbound. ISBN 0-448-
     22192-6. LC 77-14284.

     This is an outline of the rules, court dimensions, equipment
     requirements, strokes, and elementary tactics of the racket
     games. Clear drawings illustrate points made.

7A   FitzGibbon, Herbert, and Bairstow, Jeffrey. THE COMPLETE RACQUET
     SPORTS PLAYER. New York: Simon and Schuster, 1979. 221 p. Pho-
     tos., dgrms., dwgs. ISBN 0-671-24740-9. LC 79-22199.

     The authors designed this book for the racket sport player in
     one sport who is considering trying another. Only the major
     games are considered--badminton, platform tennis, racquetball,
     squash racquets, tennis--and the emphasis throughout is on a
     comparison of those games in terms of such topics as grips,
     strokes, strategies, and competition. The rules of the five
     games are given.

8   Gimmy, Arthur. TENNIS CLUBS AND RACQUET SPORT PROJECTS: A
     GUIDE TO APPRAISAL, MARKET ANALYSIS, DEVELOPMENT AND FI-
     NANCING. Chicago: American Institute of Real Estate Appraisers,
     1978. 94 p. Photos., bibliog. ISBN 0-911780-45-9.

     Gimmy collects data helpful to those analyzing a proposed
     racket club. Supply and demand as well as site and manage-
     ment are considered, case studies are presented, and how to
     appraise both indoor and outdoor clubs is discussed.

9   Harrah, Barbara. SPORTS BOOKS FOR CHILDREN: AN ANNOTATED
     BIBLIOGRAPHY. Metuchen, N.J.: Scarecrow, 1978. 526 p. ISBN
     0-8108-1154-5. LC 78-18510.

     This book covers all sports, and is worthy of inclusion here
     for what it does in the area of racket sports. It is a bib-
     liography of books in print as of January 1977 for children from
     grades three to twelve. Descriptive annotations and grade levels
     are given for each title. Fiction is included. Readers will
     note that many books considered adult level in this book are

listed. This is not so much a difference of opinion as rein-
forcement of a point made in this book (see p. 203) that
clearly written books intended for adults can also be under-
stood by children.

10   Hendershot, Claude. A HANDBOOK OF SPORT COURT CONSTRUC-
TION: RACQUETBALL HANDBALL SQUASH RACQUETS. Sunbury, Ohio:
Sunbury, 1978. 176 p. Paperbound.

After Gimmy (see 8), one should read this handbook, which
is a guide for architects, contractors, and developers to such
factors in construction as sound problems, floors, lighting,
heating, ventilating, air conditioning, and how to install the
necessary walls for these games. The emphasis is on racquetball. There is no index.

11   Lawrence, A. Paul. A MANUAL FOR RACKET STRINGERS. San Diego,
Calif.: Ektelon, 1976. 50 p. Dwgs. Paperbound. LC 76-27193.

This is a how-to-do-it guide with a clear text. It includes
information on how to take off and put on grips. Compare
with Pray (see 14).

12   MacLean, Norman. PLATFORM TENNIS, RACQUET BALL & PADDLE
BALL. New York: Drake, 1977. 128 p. Photos., dgrms., dwgs.
Paperbound. ISBN 0-8473-1463-4. LC 76-43416.

This is a combination of history and of how to play. The his-
tory--a brief overview of founders, rules, and champions
through 1976--includes not only the title sports but also court
tennis, racquets, squash racquets, squash tennis, and lawn
tennis. The instruction is brief with a chapter on each of
the title games. Information on how to construct a platform
tennis court is also given.

13   National Association for Girls and Women in Sport. NAGWS GUIDE:
TENNIS, BADMINTON, SQUASH. Washington, D.C.: American Alliance for Health, Physical Education and Recreation, 1972-- . Biannual. Photos., dgrms., bibliog. Paperbound.

This is a compilation of articles about tennis, badminton, and
squash, covering instruction, history, and organizational matters. Current rules are included, and each new edition has
a revised bibliography of books, magazines, and films.

14   Pray, Rick. STRINGING RACQUETS FOR PROFIT. Rev. ed. San Diego,
Calif.: Associated Tennis Suppliers, 1976. 212 p. Photos., line dwgs.
Three-ring binder. LC 76-17210.

A far more detailed book than Lawrence's (see 11), this one
has very large, clear drawings, as well as a text on basic

and advanced stringing. Nearly half the book is devoted to business techniques--attracting customers, how to price, keeping books, purchase and inventory control, and so forth.

15 RULES OF THE GAME: RACQUET SPORTS. New York: Crown, 1977. 95 p. Photos., dgrms. Spiral bound. ISBN 0-517-52993-9. LC 77-73666.

This is a spin-off from the book RULES OF THE GAME (New York: Two Continents, 1974) giving rules and court dimensions for racket games and jai alai. The dimensions of the table tennis table and tennis court are in such small print that they are virtually unreadable, and the conclusion of a sentence in the racquetball rule for hinders is left out.

16 Spomer, John. RACQUET AND PADDLE SPORTS FACTS. Chicago: National Sporting Goods Association, 1975. 36 p. Photos., dgrms. Paperbound.

This is an information guide for the manufacturing of equipment for all racket sports, except tennis. For each game, court, racket, and ball specifications are given in detail. There is also a brief section on accessories, such as nets, posts, and their requirements.

17 Squires, Dick. THE OTHER RACQUET SPORTS. New York: McGraw Hill, 1978. 273 p. Photos., dgrms. ISBN 0-07-060532-7. LC 78-18537.

This is a combination reference, personal opinion, and auto-biographical storybook about racket games other than tennis. For each sport a glossary, a history, court dimensions and equipment, how-to-play information, and present and future prospects are included. The author interviews a leading player and recounts a match with him.

18 Turner, Pearl. INDEX TO OUTDOOR SPORTS, GAMES AND ACTIVITIES. Westwood, Mass.: F.W. Faxon, 1978. 409 p. ISBN 0-87305-105-X. LC 77-07295.

This is for all games, not just racket sports, and is worthy of inclusion here for what it does for the latter. Included is a bibliography of books arranged by sport with a detailed subject breakdown; for example, "Paddleball," with subheads "Equipment," "Rules," and "Teaching." Books published between 1970 and 1975 on the various sports are listed, and WORLD TENNIS magazine (see 876) is also indexed for the same period.

EQUIPMENT

The main source of information for purchasing racket game equipment is the following:

19   Sporting Goods Dealer. THE SPORTING GOODS DEALER'S DIRECTORY. St. Louis, Mo.: 1899-- . Annual. Paperbound.

> This is a directory of product manufacturers in sports. "Product" is broadly defined. Under badminton, for example, the following are only some of the subheads used: "Accessories," "Books," "Grips, Racket," "Holders, Eyeglasses," and "Tape Court Marking." Under each of these subheads the names of manufacturers are listed, and their complete addresses are supplied in the back of the directory.

The magazines connected with the various games are good sources of new product information. See also the annotations in the periodicals section of this chapter, pp. 11-12, for TENNIS INDUSTRY (see 32) and TENNIS RACQUET TRADE (see 33). For women who may have difficulty in finding small racket handles, for example, the Women's Sports Center, 555 Washington Street, Wellesley, Mass. 02181, supplies equipment tailored for women players.

Finding specialists is sometimes a problem, particularly in the case of shoes. At any public tennis court, you can hear someone say, "I have very [wide, narrow] feet, and I can't find comfortable sneakers." For such complaints, the editor offers the following suggestions. If the problem is wide feet, try writing to the following manufacturers to ask for the name of the closest local seller. Hitchcock Shoes, 165 Beal Street, Higham, Mass. 02043; Kaepa, P.O. Box 250, Horseshoe Bay Boulevard, Marble Falls, Tex. 78654; or Riddell, 1001 East Touhy, Des Plaines, Ill. 60018. The Thom McAn Jox model can also be found in wide sizes. For narrow or wide shoe needs try either the Lawson Hill Leather and Shoe Company, 580 Winter Street, Waltham, Mass. 02154, or New Balance Athletic Shoes, 38-42 Everett Street, Boston, Mass. 02134.

See also the "Equipment" section of chapter 8, "Tennis," in this book (see p. 183).

INJURIES

Racket sports have a few things in common: much running, stopping short, changing direction, and clenched grips on (as well as numerous incorrect ways to swing) rackets. "Racquetball wrist," "tennis elbow," and what to do if one is hit in the eye by a speeding flying object are common problems. The two essential library purchases are:

20   ENCYCLOPEDIA OF SPORT SCIENCES AND MEDICINE. New York: Macmillan, 1971. 1,707 p. ISBN 0-02-300300-6. LC 70-87898.

> This is a vast tome on the state of medical knowledge about sports. It includes sections on the measurement and evaluation of activity drills for the various sports; chronic, acute, and subacute injury; clinical examination, location and treatment of injuries; and much more.

21   Mirkin, Gabe, and Hoffman, Marshall. THE SPORTSMEDICINE BOOK. Boston: Little, Brown, 1978. 225 p. ISBN 0-316-57434-1. LC 78-14908.

> Breezy in tone, this work covers topics such as myths ("You should take salt tablets"); drugs, sex, and their effect on performance; and exercising in extreme weather. Lists of names and addresses of members of the American Orthopaedic Society for Sports Medicine and of the American Academy of Podiatric Sports Medicine are provided.

The various periodicals connected with the games cover medical matters, with tennis elbow common enough to break into general magazines as well: for example, "Tennis Elbow Anyone" in CONSUMER REPORTS, May 1978, pp. 226-28. As Mirkin and Hoffman state, there are good reasons to use the advice of a sports medicine specialist.

LIBRARIES

Institutions and individuals collecting materials on racket sports tend to do so for several sports. For that reason, information will be given here about all large collections, even in those cases where the material is entirely about tennis.

It is certainly true that some places and persons have been missed in the list that follows. Salespersons in the Brattle Book Shop in Boston spoke highly of "the fabulous Bud Collins collection." But three letters to Collins at three different addresses produced no response, so that collection must go unrecorded here. Those who were left out due to the editor's ignorance, however, are invited to communicate with him at the address given below (p. 10).

Because of the difficulty of obtaining information about the quantity of sports books, three institutional sources are not placed in the following section. The Library of Congress in Washington, D.C., and the National Library of Canada are the unofficial and official bibliographic centers for the two countries, and as national depositories they are bound to have a substantial number of items. The New York Public Library's collection in its main building at Fifth Avenue and Forty-second Street in Manhattan is also a fine one, particularly in tennis.

Another excellent source is SUBJECT COLLECTIONS, edited by Lee Ash (New York: R.R. Bowker, 5th ed., 1979). The collections listed by Ash under "Tennis" are here, but it is also useful to look at the libraries listed under "Sports" and its various subdivisions. Many of them are likely to have good collections on the racket sports.

The general rule for all individual collectors given below is that they do not loan materials. Individuals interested in seeing the collections may write for an appointment. All figures are approximate, with each collector making continuing additions.

INSTITUTIONAL COLLECTIONS

22 INTERNATIONAL TENNIS HALL OF FAME LIBRARY. 194 Bellevue Avenue, Newport, R.I. 02840.

> This collection covers court tennis and tennis exclusively, and it includes more than five hundred books. This is a principal source for old films about the game.

23 RACQUET AND TENNIS CLUB LIBRARY. 370 Park Avenue, New York, N.Y. 10022.

> Material in all the racket games, with a particular attempt to be comprehensive in court tennis, is included in the sixteen thousand books and back runs of periodicals. G.K. Hall in Boston published a two-volume book catalog of the collection in 1970, titled A DICTIONARY CATALOG OF THE LIBRARY OF SPORTS IN THE RACQUET AND TENNIS CLUB.

24 ST. JOHN'S UNIVERSITY LIBRARY. Jamaica, N.Y. 11439.

> The library houses the William Fischer Lawn Tennis Collection. Books, back runs of periodicals, and several file drawers of pamphlets, programs, yearbooks, and clippings about tennis are included in the two thousand items.

25 SPORT INFORMATION RESOURCE CENTRE. 333 River Road, Ottawa, Ontario K1L 8B9.

> All racket sports are included, with books, theses, and journal articles in the collection. There is no actual count, but an informed estimator put the collection at thirteen hundred items.

26 UNIVERSITY OF ILLINOIS AT URBANA CHAMPAIGN LIBRARY. Urbana, Ill. 61801.

> The material is housed in the Applied Life Studies Library and the stacks of the main library. All racket sports are covered,

and the collection includes six hundred books and two hundred microfilms.

27   UNIVERSITY OF NOTRE DAME LIBRARY. Notre Dame, Ind. 46556.

The INSPORT (International Sports and Games Research) collection is housed here. All racket sports are included. Much of the material in this recently established collection of materials in all sports is uncatalogued, but the collections' curator estimates that there are hundreds of hardcover books and thousands of paperbacks, pamphlets, programs, and ephemera that are devoted to racket games.

INDIVIDUAL COLLECTIONS

George Alexander. 4901 Spaulding Street, Boise, Idaho 83705.

All racket sports, with prime emphasis on court tennis and tennis, are in this collection of over eight hundred books. There is a strong section of early rule books and annuals and back runs of periodicals.

John Blum. c/o Ferons, 47 East Forty-fourth Street, New York, N.Y. 10017.

All racket sports are included in this collection of about 350 titles, which includes some back periodicals and a few rare items.

John P. Campbell. 690 First Avenue, Chula Vista, Calif. 92010.

Close to three hundred books and one hundred "ephemera and miscellaneous junk" are included in this tennis-only collection.

William Clothier. 215 South Sixteenth Street, Philadelphia, Pa. 19102.

Tennis and court tennis are the strengths in this collection of over one hundred books and back runs of early periodicals and yearbooks.

William Cole. 43 Rinewalt Street, Williamsville, N.Y. 14231.

All racket sports with a main emphasis on psychology are included, as well as periodical back runs and a clipping file. The collection comprises over 150 books.

Sheldon Katz. 211 Roanoak Avenue, Riverhead, N.Y. 11901.

Two hundred fifty books covering tennis only are in this collection.

Don Leary. Balboa Bay Club, 1221 West Coast Highway, Newport Beach, Calif. 92660.

> Tennis is the only subject in this collection of over three hundred books, with particular emphasis on instruction. There are also some back runs of periodicals.

George Mars. 611 Park Avenue, Baltimore, Md. 21201.

> Court tennis, racquets, squash racquets, squash tennis, and tennis are covered. Mostly older books and many prints are included in this collection of five hundred items.

David Peele. 111 West Ninety-fourth Street, New York, N.Y. 10025.

> All racket sports are included. Particular strengths are tennis fiction and books for children in this collection of over eight hundred items.

John Rooney. 325 East 201st Street, New York, N.Y. 10458.

> Several hundred titles are in this collection covering tennis only.

Fred Weymuller. Genesee Valley Club, 421 East Avenue, Rochester, N.Y. 14607.

> All racket sports are covered. Many old prints and back periodicals are included in this collection of five hundred books.

Gary Wilensky. 429 East Fifty-second Street, New York, N.Y. 10022.

> This collection of seven hundred and fifteen hundred back periodical issues primarily covers tennis.

PERIODICALS

In addition to the titles cited below and those in the individual sports chapters to follow, many racket sport articles are published in the JOURNAL OF PHYSICAL EDUCATION AND RECREATION, a periodical that is indexed in both CURRENT INDEX TO JOURNALS IN EDUCATION and the EDUCATION INDEX. The term "tennis" was put into the Educational Resources Information Center (ERIC) system in June 1975, and "squash racquets" was entered in 1978. Indexes to sport materials in periodicals have multiplied in recent years. The 8 times per year SPORT AND RECREATION INDEX published by the SPORT INFORMATION RESOURCE CENTRE (see 25) began in 1974. It states that it " . . . indexes all the major sport and recreation journals," and that the centre runs computer searches on specific subjects for a fee. Two new U.S. tools began publication in 1978: PHYSICAL EDUCATION INDEX (Ben Oak Publishing Company, Box 474, Cape Girardeau, Mo. 63701) and the PHYSICAL EDUCATION/ SPORTS INDEX (Marathon Press, Box 8140, Albany, N.Y. 12203). Bill Katz wrote a scathing review of the former in LIBRARY JOURNAL, 1 January 1979, p. 89; and its publishers wrote an equally scathing reply that was not published but they will send it to anyone who writes to them. Early issues of these indexes covered the major U.S. periodicals in racquetball and tennis.

Annotations for specific magazines follow.

28 PADDLE WORLD. Circle Publications. 37 Quade Street, Glens Falls, N.Y. 12801, 1975-- . Bimonthly.

> This magazine covers platform tennis, paddleball, and paddle tennis. The standard annotation (see p. xvii) applies here

29 RACQUET. Reflex Sports. 342 Madison Avenue, New York, N.Y. 10017, 1976-September-October 1979. Bimonthly.

> The editor tried to create what he called "a literate stylish sports journal," with a few results, but a main emphasis on reflective articles on the games and in-depth portraits of players. After a three-year run the title died.

30 RACQUETS CANADA. Canadian Athletic Program Service. 63 Yonge Street, Toronto, Ontario M4Y 2A2, 1971-- . 7 per year.

> All games are covered, but tennis is the mainstay in this journal that emphasizes sports in Canada. The standard annotation (see p. xvii) applies.

31 TENNIS: MAGAZINE OF THE RACQUET SPORTS. Tennis Features. 495 Westport Avenue, Norwalk, Conn. 06856, 1965-- . Monthly.

> In spite of the subtitle, games other than tennis are not given much coverage here. The prime subject is tennis and the coverage is thorough. In addition to the standard annotation items (see p. xvii) there is an annual listing of tennis camps, an annual review and records of the previous year, and a review of new books.

32 TENNIS INDUSTRY. Industry Publishers. 915 Northeast 125th Street, North Miami, Fla., 1972-- . 11 per year.

> Prior to October 1977, this covered tennis only, but racquetball has been included. All aspects of the industry are explored: for example, courts, equipment, and accessories, with the emphasis on how to sell more.

33 TENNIS RACQUET TRADE. Circle Publications. 37 Quade Street, Glens Falls, N.Y. 12801, 1972--. 10 per year.

> This covers business news of the racket sports--new product

information, manufacturer's directories, people in the business, and so forth.

34 THE WALLBANGER NEWS. Wallbanger News. P.O. Box 295, Gracie Station, N.Y. 10028, 1978-- . Bimonthly.

This publication began as a publication devoted to one-wall paddleball. In late 1978, it expanded to include coverage of sports in which one does bang a wall--racquetball and squash racquets--as well as paddle tennis and platform tennis. The NEWS is presented in newspaper format, primarily covering news items and tournament information.

SYMPOSIUM

A National Symposium on the Racquet Sports was held in 1979 and 1980 and gives promise of becoming an annual event. The prime purpose is to afford an opportunity for those interested in teaching methodologies and research in the games to get together to discuss the latest information. Write to Jack Groppel, 116 Illini Hall, 725 South Wright Street, University of Illinois, Champaign, Ill. 61820.

TOURNAMENTS

The World Racquets Championship inaugurated a television special in 1977, when leading figures in racket games were invited to compete for a "King of the Racquets" title. Players are allowed to participate only in sports in which they have not made their reputations. For example, Marty Hogan, racquetball champion in 1978 and 1979, could not compete in that sport. The sports are subject to change from year to year, but the usual ones are badminton, racquetball, squash racquets, table tennis, and tennis. Hilary Hilton, platform tennis champion, played in the 1978 tournament on equal terms with the men--no "Challenge of the Sexes" handicap for her in any of the matches.

On the practical level, a question that sometimes arises in running tournaments is how to organize them, particularly when an odd number of players has entered. The United States Tennis Association's OFFICIAL YEARBOOK (see 812) illustrates how to do this for a single elimination tournament, and INSIDE BADMINTON by Finston and Remsberg (see 74) shows how it works for single elimination, double elimination, drop flight, and ABCD tournaments (pp. 75-77).

A subsection on tournaments will not appear in future chapters except for chapter 8, "Tennis." The national associations for each sport provide information for major competitions, and periodicals and state and local associations are the best sources for information about lesser tournaments.

Chapter 2

BADMINTON

In the standard account of how badminton got its name, the Duke of Beaufort was entertaining guests at his country seat, Badminton Park, in Gloustershire in the early 1870s. When it rained, the guests wanted something to do, so they used children's battledores and shuttlecocks and stretched a cord across a room. The doors to that room opened in at the middle, so the original court was narrower at the net than at the back. At about the same time an Eastern game called poona, using woolen balls rather than shuttlecocks but otherwise similar, was being played in India by army officers who brought the game home with them to Bath, Southampton, and other military centers where the game took root.

Currently badminton is in a state of flux, but things are looking better. The one U.S. periodical, BADMINTON USA (see 89) folded in 1976, but was shakily resurrected in 1978 with two very thin issues, and appears to be on the road to recovery with a more substantial September 1979 issue. Open badminton (professionals and amateurs competing in the same tournament) was approved by the International Badminton Federation in June 1979. The game has shared a place in the racket sport boom. An article on page 136 of TENNIS magazine (see 31) for February 1977 under the title "Badminton" stated there were an estimated twenty thousand players at a serious level in 1977 compared to five thousand in 1971.

Badminton in Canada is alive and flourishing. Each province has its own association, and at least one of them, the Ontario Badminton Association, is active as a book and film center and newsletter publisher.

ASSOCIATIONS, FOUNDATIONS, ORGANIZATIONS

35 CANADIAN BADMINTON ASSOCIATION.

36 CANADIAN BADMINTON COACHES ASSOCIATION.

37 CANADIAN BADMINTON UMPIRES ASSOCIATION.

   The address for each of the above three associations is 333

River Road, Vanier, Ontario KlL 8B9. The Badminton Association is the governing body for the game in Canada. It arranges Canadian and any other international or open tournaments held in the country. The Coaches Association, open to all coaches qualified in one of the official levels of coaching certification approved by the Badminton Association, provides a platform for members to express their views on coaching matters. The object of the Umpires Association is to maintain and improve the standards of officiating and to certify all umpires who serve in matches under the Badminton Association's jurisdiction.

38 UNITED STATES BADMINTON ASSOCIATION. P.O. Box 237, Swartz Creek, Mich. 48473.

This association, the governing body for the game in the United States, arranges the national championships, upholds the rules of the game and the status of the players, and assists in the development of clubs.

39 UNITED STATES BADMINTON PLAYERS ASSOCIATION. 200 Hudson Terrace, Yonkers, N.Y. 10701.

An association representing the interests of badminton players at all levels, it aims to give professionals a voice in decisions made by world governing bodies, identifies colleges that compete and provide financial assistance for players, and involves itself in promotional efforts with anyone willing to promote--corporations, television networks, and so on.

Local associations exist in the Canadian provinces and in many cities in the United States. The United States Badminton Association (see 38) publishes a directory of clubs, and a fine list of such organizations for the New York City area appeared in the NEW YORK TIMES, 6 March 1978, sec. C, p. 12.

AUDIOVISUAL MATERIALS

It should be noted that only the names or acronyms of distributors are given in the annotations below. An alphabetical list of distributors' full names with addresses can be found in the appendix to this book, pp. 205-10.

40 ADVANCED BADMINTON. 16mm. film or 3/4-inch videocassette. Color. Sound. 22 minutes. 1970. Also available in Spanish. Purchase: AIMS. Rental: AIMS (16 mm. film only); University of Idaho (16mm. film, English only); University of Illinois (16mm. film, English only). ISBN 0-699-00281-8. LC 77-706472.

Wynn Rogers and other champion players demonstrate advanced badminton techniques in singles, doubles, and mixed doubles.

41   ALL-ENGLAND CHAMPIONSHIPS, 1975. 16mm. film or videocassette
(film in color, videocassette in black and white). Silent. Purchase:
Coaching Association of Canada. Rental: Ontario Badminton Association (16mm. film with men's singles and doubles and women's singles
only).

   This film shows matches in the men's and women's singles,
   doubles, and the mixed doubles.

42   BADMINTON. 16mm. film or videocassette. Color. Sound. 14 minutes. 1968. Purchase: National Film Board of Canada. Rental: University of California (16mm. film only); National Film Board of Canada.
LC FiA68-1366.

   This film aims to encourage more people to take up the game.
   It explains the rules and shows a championship doubles match.

43   BADMINTON. Three 16mm. films or super 8mm. cassettes. Color.
Sound. 1976. Purchase: AAHPERD; Athletic Institute.

   National champions Cindy Baker, Judi Kelley, Chris Kinard,
   and Charlie Coakley demonstrate fundamentals of the game.
   Contents: (1) GRIP, FOOTWORK, SERVES. 16 minutes.
   LC 76-701202. (2) BASIC STROKES. 17 minutes. LC 76-
   701203. (3) BASIC STRATEGY AND DRILLS. 18 minutes.
   LC 76-701204.

44   BADMINTON. Two 16mm. films, super 8mm. films, or videocassettes.
Color. Sound. Purchase: Champions on Film.

   Contents: (1) THE SERVE, OVERHEAD, FOREHAND AND
   BACKHAND STROKES, BASIC 'PISTOL' GRIP, BODY MECH-
   ANICS OF THE SHOTS. (2) UNDERHAND NET STROKES,
   DRIVES, AND AROUND THE HEAD SHOTS. The films em-
   phasize body position, racket position and footwork, which
   are analyzed in slow motion and freeze frame shots.

45   BADMINTON. Thirteen super 8mm. cartridges. Color. Silent. 4 minutes each. 1968. Purchase: AAHPERD; Athletic Institute; A.W. Peller;
Mason. LC FiA68-2482.

   James Poole, Margaret Varner, and James and Janette Breen
   demonstrate correct techniques in regular and slow motion.
   Contents: (1) GRIP AND COCKING. (2) FOOTWORK.
   (3) HIGH DEEP SERVE. (4) LOW SHORT SERVE. (5) DRIVE
   SERVE. (6) FLICK SERVE. (7) FOREHAND OVERHEAD
   SHOTS, DEFENSIVE AND ATTACKING CLEAR. (8) FORE-
   HAND OVERHEAD SHOTS, SMASH AND DROP. (9) BACK-
   HAND OVERHEAD SHOTS, DEFENSIVE AND ATTACKING
   CLEAR. (10) BACKHAND OVERHEAD SHOTS, SMASH AND
   DROP. (11) DRIVE SHOTS, UNDERHAND CLEAR SHOTS.
   (12) NET SHOTS. (13) AROUND-THE-HEAD SHOTS, CLEAR,
   SMASH, DROP.

46   BADMINTON. Six super 8mm. cartridges. Color. Silent. 3 minutes each. 1969. Purchase: Champions on Film.

These are the basic fundamentals of badminton as taught by James Poole. Contents: (1) THE SERVE. (2) OVERHEAD FOREHAND STROKES. (3) OVERHEAD BACKHAND STROKES. (4) UNDERHAND NET STROKES. (5) DRIVES AND AROUND-THE-HEAD STROKES. (6) FOOTWORK. See also 79.

47   BADMINTON FUNDAMENTALS. 16mm. film. Color and black and white. Sound. 11 minutes. 1950. Rental: University of Colorado; University of Idaho; University of Illinois; Indiana University; University of Iowa; Kent State University; University of Michigan; University of Minnesota; University of Nebraska at Lincoln; University of Utah; University of Wisconsin at La Crosse. ISBN 0-388-00560-2 (color). ISBN 0-388-10560-7 (black and white).

Fundamental skills and rules are demonstrated by novice and expert players, including slow motion views of stroking.

48   BADMINTON FUNDAMENTALS. 16mm. film or 3/4-inch videocassette. Color. Sound. 12 minutes. 1970. Purchase: AIMS. Rental: AIMS (16mm. film only); University of Illinois (16mm. film only); Indiana University (16mm. film only); University of Kansas (16mm. film only).

This film demonstrates basic skills using slow motion and shows court dimensions for singles and doubles. Skilled players discuss when and why the various strokes are employed.

49   BADMINTON IN ONTARIO. Slides with accompanying sound track. Rental: Ontario Badminton Association.

This is a promotional display showing people of all ages playing badminton.

50   THE BASIC STROKES. 1/2-inch videotape. Sound. 30 minutes. Rental: Ontario Badminton Association.

Abdul Shaikh, Thomas Cup player from India, demonstrates and comments on the basic strokes. Some slow motion shots are shown.

51   FUNDAMENTALS OF BADMINTON. 16mm. film. Black and white. Sound. 12 minutes. 1960. Rental: University of Illinois; University of Iowa; Pennsylvania State University. ISBN 0-699-11436-5. LC FiA61-73.

Outstanding left- and right-handed players demonstrate basics in slow motion and regular speed.

52   INTRODUCING BADMINTON. 16mm. film. Color. Sound. 27 minutes. Purchases: Ontario Badminton Association. Rental: Ontario Badminton Association.

Useful for teachers as well as beginners, this film shows how to execute basic strokes and how to use twenty-four players on one court, either working in groups or competing in simple games. Scenes of topflight play in the all England tournament are included.

53   INTRODUCING BADMINTON. 35mm. filmstrip. Color. Silent with captions. Thirty-nine frames. 1966. Rental: National Film Board of Canada.

This is an introduction to the basic skills of the game.

54   INTRODUCTION TO BADMINTON LAWS AND UMPIRING. Sixty-three slides with script. Rental: Ontario Badminton Association.

The basic duties of linespersons, referees, service judges, and umpires are demonstrated.

54A   1973 NATIONAL BADMINTON CHAMPIONSHIPS. 16mm. film. Color. Sound. 20 minutes. Rental: Travelers Film Library.

55   1977 NATIONAL CHAMPIONSHIPS, CANADA. 3/4-inch videocassette or 1/2-inch videocassette. 30 minutes. Purchase: Coaching Association of Canada.

This presents highlights of the Canadian Nationals.

56   1973 CANADIAN OPEN MEN'S SINGLES FINAL. 16mm. film. Color. Sound. Rental: Ontario Badminton Association.

This shows a match between Jamie Paulson and Bruce Rollick.

BOOKS

57   Annarino, Anthony. BADMINTON: INDIVIDUALIZED INSTRUCTIONAL PROGRAM. Englewood Cliffs, N.J.: Prentice Hall, 1973. 98 p. Paperbound. ISBN 0-13-55384-0.

After taking a pre-test to determine present knowledge of the game, students can use this badminton workbook to chart their own progress. The pupil is given a progression of lessons, each with a written part and a skill assignment.

58   BADMINTON. 12th ed. Know the Game Series. Wakefield, Engl.: EP Publishing, 1974. Distributed in the United States by Charles River Books, Boston. 40 p. Photos., dgrms., line dwgs. Paperbound. ISBN 0-7158-0103-1.

A guide to the basics, this book discusses the court and its dimensions, equipment, serving and receiving serves, strokes, and rules. The deep serve is not covered at all.

59   [Bloss], Margaret Varner, and Brown, Virginia. BADMINTON. 3d ed.
       Physical Education Activities Series. Dubuque, Iowa: William C. Brown,
       1975. 88 p. Photos., dgrms., line dwgs., bibliog. Paperbound. ISBN
       0-697-07058-1. LC 74-27898.

       This work gives instruction for the beginning and intermediate
       player and includes sequence photographs illustrating strokes
       and line drawings showing the most common mistakes. Practice
       drills are included for strokes, and there is a chapter on tac-
       tics and strategy for singles and doubles. A bibliography of
       books and films and a rules summary are given. The bounda-
       ries for double services are not explained in the rules sum-
       mary, however.

60   Breen, James. BADMINTON. Chicago: Athletic Institute, 1969. 47 p.
       Photos., dgrms., line dwgs., gloss. Paperbound. ISBN 0-87670-035-0.
       LC 79-10949.

       This is primarily a photographic guide with very little text on
       each page. Topics covered are grip, footwork, and strokes.
       Line drawings illustrate the more common rules.

61   Brown, Edward. THE COMPLETE BOOK OF BADMINTON. Harrisburg,
       Pa.: Stackpole, 1969. 187p. Photos., dgrms., line dwgs.; ISBN 0-571-
       08795-7. LC 72-402087. BADMINTON. Plymouth, Engl.: Latimer Trend,
       1969. Distributed in the United States by Transatlantic Arts, New York.

       This is a thorough instruction book. All the standard items
       are here in great detail--conditioning, strokes, singles and
       doubles tactics, and mental aspects. There is particular em-
       phasis on anticipation and how to read opponents.

62   Brundle, Fred. BADMINTON. 3d ed. Teach Yourself Books. New
       York: David McKay, 1975. 161 p. Photos., dgrms., line dwgs. Paper-
       bound. ISBN 0-679-10351-1.

       This book begins with an imaginary visit to Wembly, England,
       to watch two matches between world class players. Instruc-
       tion includes a section on what a player might expect at her
       or his first tournament. A bit of the history of the game is
       told, and a concluding section discusses badminton in countries
       other than England, where the book was first published (London:
       St. Paul's, 1975).

63   Burris, Barbara, and Olson, Arne. BADMINTON. Basic Concepts and
       Skills of Physical Activities Series. Boston: Allyn and Bacon, 1974.
       69 p. Photos., dgrms., line dwgs. Paperbound. ISBN 0-205-04388-7.
       LC 73-84849.

       Overly academic in tone, each chapter begins with a "concept";
       the learner is guided in developing the motor and cognitive

concepts via "learning experiences"; and a list of "outcomes" concludes. In short, it presents (1) the basic idea, (2) practice to help one achieve it, and (3) a test to see if one has learned it. Detailed instruction with drawings on fundamental and advanced skills is provided.

64   Canadian Badminton Association. REGIONAL COACHES MANUAL: LEVEL II. Ottawa: Canadian Badminton Association, 1976. 78 p. Photos., dgrms., line dwgs., bibliog. Spiral bound.

Coaching manuals are available in Canada at the local, regional, and provincial levels with the degree of difficulty greater at each level. This regional manual was the only one seen by the editor. It covers in thorough detail how the various strokes should be hit, common faults made in each stroke as well as how to analyze and correct them, strategic and tactical points for singles, doubles, and mixed doubles, and conditioning exercises.

65   Crossley, Ken. PROGRESSIVE BADMINTON. London: G. Bell, 1970. Distributed in the United States by Soccer Associates, New Rochelle, N.Y. 1975; ISBN 0-392-00794-0. LC 74-31730. TEACH YOURSELF BADMINTON. Toronto: Coles, 1976. 130 p. Photos., dgrms. Paperbound. ISBN 0-7135-1940-1 (Bell).

English references abound in this one. For example, one should hit the overhead "like a first-class cricketer throwing a ball from the boundary." It has a clear, strong section on tactics. Photographs for the individual shots are not sequence photographs except for a poor series on the short serve.

66   Davidson, Kenneth, and Gustavson, Lealand. WINNING BADMINTON. Rev. printing. New York: Ronald, 1964. 150 p. Photos., dgrms., line dwgs., gloss. ISBN 0-8260-2405-X. LC 64-18464.

This is an immensely detailed instruction book that is particularly strong in the advanced badminton sections on tactics and strategy, for example, "Pros and Cons of Cross-courting." It is divided into three sections: "Elementary," "Advanced," and "Organizing." The latter refers to group instruction in schools, as well as club organization and junior development.

67   Davis, Pat. THE BADMINTON COACH: A MANUAL FOR COACHES, TEACHERS AND PLAYERS. Rev. ed. London: Kaye and Ward, 1976. Distributed in the United States by Soccer Associates, New Rochelle, N.Y. 160 p. Photos., dgrms. ISBN 0-7182-0837-4.

Most chapters of this book are written in what might be termed "detailed outline" form. For example, under the heading "Overhead Backhand Strokes" one finds such subheads as "Basic Use" (for those strokes), "Grip," "Feet," "Backswing," "Forward Swing," "Error," "Correction," and more.

68 _____. BADMINTON COMPLETE. Cranbury, N.J.: A.S. Barnes, 1976. 176 p. Photos., dgrms. ISBN 0-498-01696-X. LC 75-5170.

> Although this is a well-illustrated, well-diagrammed thorough instruction book on all aspects of the game, women readers may find the occasional use of the term "girls" irritating. Also, a book calling itself BADMINTON COMPLETE should include the rules of the game; this does not.

69 _____. HOW TO PLAY BADMINTON. Toronto: Pickwick, 1975. 96 p. Photos., dgrms. Paperbound.

> There are some obscure references in this review of fundamentals. Readers are told when moving on the court to "emulate the Henry Cooper shuffle or Warwick Shute bounce." The labelling of one stroke as "the Swedish swish" may occasion some unintended humor. There is some intended humor, and that plus clear illustrations are strong points.

70 Devlin, J. Frank, and Lardner, Rex. SPORTS ILLUSTRATED BADMINTON. Philadelphia: J.B. Lippincott, 1973. 96 p. Photos., dgrms., dwgs., gloss. ISBN 0-397-00967-4. LC 72-10556.

> The authors briefly outline "how to" points of grips, serves, clears, smashes, drop and net shots, drives, and tactics. All strokes are illustrated with sequence drawings. It concludes with a chapter on suggested practice routines and gives the rules.

71 Downey, Jake. BETTER BADMINTON FOR ALL. London: Pelham Books, 1969. Distributed in the United States by Transatlantic Arts, New York. 224 p. Photos., dgrms. ISBN 0-7207-0228-3. LC 79-40670.

> Part 1 of this three-part book covers the basics of the game from the very beginning through elementary tactics. Part 2 discusses the physical requirements for people playing badminton and gives exercises that will help meet those requirements. Part 3 lays out a ten-lesson plan for teaching the game to beginners plus some tips for teaching intermediates.

72 _____. THE SINGLES GAME. Toronto: Privately published by the author, 1976. Available from the Ontario Badminton Association, 559 Jarvis Street, Toronto, Ontario M4Y 2J1. 62 p. Dgrms.

> The author takes situations in rearcourt, midcourt, and frontcourt and analyzes the possible moves open in each situation that will enable a player to go on the attack.

73 _____. TEACH YOUR CHILD BADMINTON. Toronto: Con Ed Media, 1976. 96 p. Photos., dgrms., dwgs., bibliog. ISBN 0-86019-007-2.

> The author does not explain how to hit various shots, but

rather explains their functions and leaves how to do it up to the child (presumably being taught by an experienced adult). Arranged as a series of lesson plans, the book also has commentary and advice for the parent-teacher.

74   Finston, Irving, and Remsberg, Charles. INSIDE BADMINTON. Inside Sports Series. Chicago: Contemporary Books, 1978. 99 p. Photos., dgrms., dwgs., gloss. ISBN 0-8092-7653-4. LC 78-57467.

Chapters on serving, the other strokes, strategy and tactics in singles and doubles, fitness drills, information on club play-- how to find or organize a club and methods of making tournament draws--and the rules are included in this complete view of instruction. It must be noted that text and accompanying pictures do not always coincide.

75   Gregory, Douglas, and Webb, Gerald. TEACHING BADMINTON. 2d ed. rev. and enl. Bellevue, Wash.: Surrey County, 1973. 110 p. Photos., dgrms. ISBN 0-9501358-0-1.

This is an instruction book for teachers to use in conjunction with any other instruction book. The chapters are divided as if they were instruction sessions for twenty-four lessons and assume there are both beginners and intermediate players in a class.

76   Hashman, Judy, and Jones, C.M. BEGINNING BADMINTON. New York: Arco, 1977. 96 p. Photos., dgrms. ISBN 0-668-04265-6. LC 77-5535.

This book covers the basics from knowing how to throw correctly (particularly important in badminton because of the many overhead shots) through tactics. There is only one paragraph on the smash, the authors evidently believing that their discussion of the overhead clear stroke plus that paragraph is all that is necessary. The text may be a bit advanced for a beginner.

77   Mills, Roger. BADMINTON. EP Sport Series. Wakefield, Engl.: EP Publishing, 1975. Distributed in the United States by Charles River Books, Boston. 113 p. Photos., dgrms. ISBN 0-7158-0595-9. LC 76-379299.

Very complete sequence photographs are the hallmark of this book, not only for strokes but for exercises good for physical fitness for the game. An information glossary gives information for England--for example, names and addresses of associations and publications.

78   Pelton, Barry. BADMINTON. Englewood Cliffs, N.J.: Prentice-Hall, 1971. 82 p. Dgrms., line dwgs., gloss., bibliog. ISBN 0-13-055376-X. LC 78-92377.

This is a text for beginning and intermediate players. The book deals with standard grip and stroke information, as well as the physical and mental qualities of the badminton player. Serves, clears, and drives are the strokes the author considers fundamental. Information on smashes and drop shots is not given until the intermediate section.

79 Poole, James. BADMINTON. 2d ed. Goodyear Physical Activities Series. Pacific Palisades, Calif.: Goodyear, 1973. 115 p. Photos., dgrms., line dwgs., gloss., bibliog. Paperbound. ISBN 0-87620-089-7. LC 72-90982.

Poole emphasizes using forearm rotation rather than wrist snap as the source of power in strokes. In addition to strokes and strategy, there are chapters on conditioning and drills. See also 46.

80 Rogers, Wynn. ADVANCED BADMINTON. Physical Education Activities Series. Dubuque, Iowa: William C. Brown, 1970. 66 p. Photos., dgrms., dwgs. Paperbound. ISBN 0-697-07002-6. LC 70-9438.

A detailed exposition of strategy for the reader who already plays a good basic game, this book provides a few illustrations but is mostly text with a host of specific play situations both offensive and defensive.

81 Rutledge, Abbie, and Friedrich, John. BEGINNING BADMINTON. Rev. ed. Sports Skills Series. Belmont, Calif.: Wadsworth, 1969. 62 p. Dgrms., line dwgs., gloss., bibliog. Paperbound. LC 70-85223.

This is a clear exposition of fundamentals. Side-by-side illustrations of the singles and doubles serving courts are particularly helpful to the tennis player studying badminton, since singles and doubles areas in the two games are different.

82 Sullivan, George. GUIDE TO BADMINTON. New York: Fleet, 1968. 116 p. Photos., dgrms., gloss. ISBN 0-8303-003-1. LC 67-31525.

This book gives fundamentals of strokes and strategy for singles and doubles. A curious mixture of writing styles is presented, with some chapters reading like a children's primer with numerous one-sentence paragraphs, while others are more advanced. Full-page sequence illustrations are given for some of the strokes.

83 Whetnall, Paul, and Whetnall, Sue. BADMINTON. Pelham Pictorial Sports Instruction Series. London: Pelham Books, 1975. Available in North America from the Ontario Badminton Association, 559 Jarvis Street, Toronto, Ontario M4Y 2J1. 64 p. Photos., dgrms. ISBN 0-7207-0867-2.

A strong point in this book of badminton basics are the illustrations. Many half-page photographs and diagrams illustrate grips, strokes, and basic positions in singles and doubles and , how those positions change depending on what the opponent does. Practice and fitness routines are included.

84   Wright, Len. YOUR BOOK OF BADMINTON. Your Book Series. London: Faber and Faber, 1972. Distributed in the United States by Transatlantic Arts, New York. 72 p. Photos., dgrms., bibliog. ISBN 0-571-09890-8.

Offering elementary and intermediate instruction to juvenile readers, this book is written for an English audience without modification for the North American reader. As a consequence one finds, for example, a list of information sources for England only. Grades six and up.

CAMPS

Check the information in the "Camps" section of the introduction to this book (p. xvii) for information connected with the listings below. Canada is a good area for camps. Write to the Canadian Badminton Association (see 35) for information. A list of U.S. camps follows.

85   CONNECTICUT BADMINTON CAMP. c/o Rosemary McGuire, 87 Lancaster Road, Bristol, Conn. 06010.

This is an adult camp and a junior coeducational camp.

86   ILLINOIS BADMINTON CAMP. c/o Bruce Pontow, 2417 Cochran, Blue Island, Ill. 60606.

This is a junior coeducational camp.

87   OREGON BADMINTON CAMP. c/o John Rowley, City Hall, Estacada, Oreg. 97023.

88   PANTHER BADMINTON CAMP. c/o Bob Hussey, Eastern Illinois University, Charleston, Ill. 61920.

This is a girls' camp.

PERIODICALS

89   BADMINTON U.S.A. Formerly BIRD CHATTER. United States Badminton Association, P.O. Box 237, Swartz Creek, Mich. 48473, 1941-- . Irregular.

A brief history has been given on page 18 of this official publication of the United States Badminton Association (see 38).

Badminton

The first issue of the revised periodical contained instruction, tournament results and schedules, feature articles, and the results of a survey on what kinds of articles future issues should contain.

Chapter 3

PADDLEBALL

The name associated with the development of paddleball is Earl Riskey. Watching tennis players hitting practice shots against a handball court wall at the University of Michigan in the early 1930s, Riskey conceived the idea of a game like handball played on handball courts that would include some of the skills of tennis. For a while the new game was a hazard, as sweating palms lost control of the paddle tennis paddle used in the early days and made it a dangerous flying object. Riskey developed a rope loop attached to the paddle that wrapped around the wrist. That loop became the leather thong that is still required in some areas, but is not commonly used on the East Coast.

Currently the sport has suffered somewhat in comparison with racquetball. Principal centers of activity are Michigan and California for the four-wall game, and the East Coast for the single-wall form of play. New York City is a hotbed of one-wall paddleball activity. According to TENNIS magazine (see 31) in its February 1978 issue, paddleball is second only to basketball as a popular playground activity in New York City (p. 108). The two forms of play--one-wall and four-wall--are quite different.

ASSOCIATIONS, FOUNDATIONS, ORGANIZATIONS

90　AMERICAN PADDLEBALL ASSOCIATION.　26 Old Brick Road, New City, N.Y.　10956

> This is an association of one-wall paddleball players whose main purpose is to promote that game via tournaments and clinics. It publishes a newsletter.

91　NATIONAL PADDLEBALL ASSOCIATION.　P.O. Box 712, Flint, Mich. 48501.

> This is the governing body for the four-wall game in the United States. It sponsors the national singles and doubles championships each year, as well as some smaller tournaments. It publishes a newsletter.

92 PADDLEBALL PLAYERS ASSOCIATION. 24-04 Deerfield Road, Far Rockaway, N.Y. 11691.

> Devoted to advancing the cause of one-wall paddleball, this association claims to have produced the first set of professional rules for that game and to have founded the Paddleball Hall of Fame. It publishes a newsletter.

BOOKS

Books covering paddleball and racquetball are listed below.

93 Allsen, Philip, and Witbeck, Alan. RACQUETBALL/PADDLEBALL. Physical Education Activities Series. Dubuque, Iowa: William C. Brown, 1972. 52 p. Photos., dgrms., gloss. Paperbound. ISBN 0-697-07047-6. LC 78-167727.

> After an introductory chapter on the games and equipment, the authors cover each stroke with text and sequence photography. Succeeding chapters discuss kill and passing shots, advanced serving, and play patterns for singles and doubles. Conditioning exercises, drills, and paddleball rules are included.

94 Fleming, A. William, and Bloom, Joel. PADDLEBALL AND RACQUETBALL. Goodyear Physical Activities Series. Pacific Palisades, Calif.: Goodyear, 1973. 97 p. Photos., dgrms., bibliog. Paperbound. ISBN 0-87620-660-7. LC 72-90984.

> The two games are carefully distinguished in this manual with the rules for both in all their various versions--four-, three-, and one-wall. Basic strokes, shots, and strategies in singles and doubles are covered, and the illustrations for the different grips show both right and left hands holding the paddle.

95 Hammer, Howard. PADDLEBALL: HOW TO PLAY THE GAME. New York: Grosset and Dunlap, 1974. 84 p. Photos., dgrms., gloss. Paperbound. ISBN 0-448-01496-3. LC 74-186665.

> Instruction in one-wall paddleball is given. The book reflects the handball origins of the game rather than its relationship to tennis. Hammer recommends switching hands rather than hitting backhands when possible, and he discusses the choke and power grips, which are not found in other books. Sequence photographs for strokes are included.

96 Kozar, Andrew; Grambeau, Rodney; and Riskey, Earl. BEGINNING PADDLEBALL. Sports Skills Series. Belmont, Calif.: Wadsworth, 1967. 58 p. Dgrms., line dwgs., gloss., bibliog. Paperbound. LC 67-25824.

All the basics needed to understand and play the game in all its wall varieties are included. In addition to standard strokes, shots, and tactics information, the book gives performance and written self-tests.

97   Wickstrom, Ralph, and Larson, Charles. RACQUETBALL AND PADDLE-BALL FUNDAMENTALS. Merrill Sports Series. Columbus, Ohio: Charles Merrill, 1972. 84 p. Dgrms., line dwgs. Paperbound. ISBN 0-675-09173-X. LC 78-172488.

The authors cover the basic strokes (illustrated by sequence drawings), rules of all the various wall games, strategy, and drills. Emphasis, though, is on the one-wall game.

PERIODICALS

THE WALLBANGER NEWS. Wallbanger News, P.O. Box 295, Gracie Station, N.Y. 10028, 1978-- . Bimonthly.

For annotation, see 34.

Chapter 4

PLATFORM TENNIS

Platform tennis was invented in 1928. Two names closely associated with its development are Fessenden Blanchard and James Cogswell. These two men plus a group of Scarsdale, New York, businessmen decided to build a raised platform on Cogswell's property on which a variety of games could be played during the New York winter when outdoor tennis was impossible. A chicken-mesh wire screen was installed around the platform to keep stray dogs out and stray balls in. When Cogswell brought along some of the tools of paddle tennis--short paddles and rubber balls--the Scarsdale group found what seemed to be an ideal winter game, particularly after they allowed balls that struck the wire to be played again.

Over fifty years later, platform tennis has grown immensely, and New York City suburbs remain its most popular playground. Canada had its second national championship in 1978 and the International Platform Tennis Association went into its second year. Commercial sponsorship enabled U.S. matches to be seen on television. Platform tennis is the official name, but the game is still referred to informally as "paddle," which has been a source of confusion for the layperson and a source of irritation to those playing paddle tennis.

Through 1979, platform tennis was unique among racket sports in that doubles only was played on a tournament level. In 1980, the American Platform Tennis Association endorsed the singles game for the first time.

ASSOCIATIONS, FOUNDATIONS, ORGANIZATIONS

98 AMERICAN PLATFORM TENNIS ASSOCIATION. 52 Upper Montclair Plaza, Upper Montclair, N.J. 07043.

> This is the governing body for platform tennis in the United States. It promotes the game, sanctions tournaments and officials, and regulates all aspects of play. There are four regional divisions with three of the four representing East Coast states, the main areas where the sport is played.

99   AMERICAN PROFESSIONAL PLATFORM TENNIS ASSOCIATION. 527
East Seventy-second Street, Apt. 2-A, New York, N.Y. 10021.

An association of professional platform tennis instructors, this
group conducts seminars and gives certification tests for would-
be teachers.

100 CANADIAN PLATFORM TENNIS ASSOCIATION. 47 Whitehall Road,
Toronto, Ontario M4W 2C5.

This organization (which did not respond to this editor's correspondence) is presumably the governing body for the game
in Canada, with functions similar to the American Platform
Tennis Association.

AUDIOVISUAL MATERIALS

Only the names or acronyms of distributors are given in the annotations below.
An alphabetical list of distributors' full names with addresses can be found in
the appendix to this book, pp. 205-10.

101 FIFTY YEARS OF PLATFORM TENNIS. Audio-slide presentation. Color
and black and white. Sound. 15 minutes. 1979. Free loan to member
clubs of the American Platform Tennis Association (see 98). Rental:
American Platform Tennis Association.

A history of the game and an explanation of the basics are
given.

102 PADDLE AT FOREST HILLS. 16mm. film. Color. Sound. 20 minutes.
Rental: Richard J. Reilly Jr.

This film shows highlights of men's and women's matches at the
1976 Tribuno World Platform Tennis championships.

103 PLATFORM TENNIS--STROKES AND STRATEGY. 16mm. film. Color.
Sound. 22 minutes. 1977. Free loan: Modern Talking Picture.

Dick Squires narrates the 1977 championships held in New
York. Playing tips as well as game footage are presented.
(Note: film no longer available as of 1980.)

104 PLAY THE SCREENS. 16mm. film. Color. Sound. 12 minutes. 1973.
Free loan: Richard J. Reilly Jr., Inc.

Here is an introduction to the game that includes scenes from
the Tribuno championships.

BOOKS

105 Ballard, Bill, and Hevener, Jim. THE ILLUSTRATED GUIDE TO PLAT-
FORM TENNIS. New York: Mason Charter, 1977. 115 p. Dgrms.,
line dwgs., gloss. ISBN 0-88405-616-3. LC 77-24688.

A breezily written (cartoons, quizzes) and thorough instruction
manual. The authors use a wooden model to depict strokes,
claiming this is clearer than trying to figure out how arm and
shoulder are turning through a sweater. Troubleshooter sections are included to help players correct errors.

106 Callaway, Bob, and Hughes, Michael. PLATFORM TENNIS. Philadelphia: J.B. Lippincott, 1977. 224 p. Photos. ISBN 0-397-01183-0.
LC 77-7775.

The strong points of this instruction book are the sequence
photographs of all strokes, the chapters on playing the forehand and backhand corners, court positioning and teamwork,
and right-handed and left-handed partnerships. Drills and
ideas on how to practice are included.

107 Durrell, Oliver. THE OFFICIAL GUIDE TO PLATFORM TENNIS. Ken-
nebunkport, Maine: Durrell Publications, 1967. 77 p. Photos., dgrms.
An unrevised paperbound version was published in New York: Grossett
and Dunlap, 1971. 79 p. ISBN 0-448-02485-3 (Grossett). LC 67-
31349 (Durrell).

How the game began, how to play it, how to run tournaments,
where to buy equipment, and how to construct one's own court
are all provided. The "how to play" section assumes the
reader knows how to hit strokes, so it concentrates on strategy
only. Tournament records up to the date of publication are
included.

108 Iseman, Jay. PLAY PADDLE! AN INTRODUCTION TO PLATFORM TEN-
NIS. New York: Dutton, 1976. 144 p. Photos., line dwgs., gloss.
Paperbound. ISBN 0-87690-217-4. LC 76-7078.

This is a clear exposition of basic and advanced techniques.
Line drawings and sequence photographs illustrate instruction
points, and the chapters include advice on screen shots,
strategy, court etiquette, and a brief history of the game.

109 Russell, Doug, and Chu, Ernest. CONTEMPORARY PLATFORM TENNIS.
Chicago: Contemporary Books, 1978. 101 p. Photos., dgrms., line
dwgs., dwgs., gloss. ISBN 0-8092-7553-8. LC 77-91171.

An elementary version of the authors' WINNING PLATFORM
TENNIS, this work concentrates on the basics of ground strokes,
volleys, overheads, serves, and screen play, with a final chapter giving first pointers on tactics.

110 _____. WINNING PLATFORM TENNIS. Chicago: Contemporary
Books, 1977. 250 p. Photos., dgrms., line dwgs., gloss. ISBN 0-8092-
7931-2. LC 77-75848.

> This is a detailed instruction book with some additional features
> provided: for example, a chapter for tennis players to help
> them adjust to the platform game, a proposal for a singles
> game, and a method of measuring how points are won and lost
> in top-level play. It gives the official rules as of the date
> of publication.

111 Squires, Dick. HOW TO PLAY PLATFORM TENNIS. 4th rev. ed. New
York: McGraw-Hill, 1977. 134 p. Photos., dgrms., line dwgs. Paperbound. ISBN 0-07-060530-0. LC 77-6820.

> This begins with a brief history and then covers the standard
> strokes, screen play, tactics, and mixed doubles topics. Three
> chapters are written by other authorities discussing medical
> problems connected with the game, as well as implementing a
> platform tennis program and a proposed singles game.

112 _____, ed. THE COMPLETE BOOK OF PLATFORM TENNIS. Boston:
Houghton Mifflin, 1974. 202 p. Photos., dgrms. ISBN 0-395-19445-8.
LC 74-13313.

> This is a compilation of articles by leading figures in the game
> on such topics as strokes, screen play, conducting a clinic,
> and more. There is no chapter on the backhand, and there
> is some repetition--a men's doubles chapter followed by a
> women's doubles chapter, followed by two chapters on mixed
> doubles, all making many of the same points.

113 Sullivan, George. PADDLE: THE BEGINNER'S GUIDE TO PLATFORM
TENNIS. New York: Coward, McCann and Geoghegan, 1975. 223 p.
Photos., dgrms., gloss., bibliog. ISBN 0-698-10693-8. LC 75-10478.

> This is a complete guide to the game, with rules, instruction,
> sequence photographs, court construction information, places
> to play in the United States, and more.

COURT CONSTRUCTION

In addition to the books by Durrell (see 107) and Sullivan (see 113) annotated
above, chapters on building platform tennis courts can be found in the books
by MacLean (see 12) and Neal (see 848).

PERIODICALS

PADDLE WORLD. Circle Publications. (see 28)

114 PLATFORM TENNIS. American Platform Tennis Association, 52 Upper
     Montclair Plaza, Upper Montclair, N.J. 07043, 1979-- . Quarterly.

> This is the official publication of the association, which also
> publishes a newsletter in alternate months. The standard an-
> notation (see p. xvii) applies.

Chapter 5

RACQUETBALL

Racquetball writers have diverged in their accounts of the origins of the game. John Sobeck, a tennis and squash professional at the Greenwich, Connecticut, YMCA, invented it, says one.[1] Joe Sobeck, a Bridgeport, Connecticut, executive, invented it in 1949, says another.[2] Joe Sobeck did it in 1950, says a third.[3] Those wanting details from Sobeck himself are referred to the sources given in footnotes four and five.

Racquetball is developing into a very popular sport. Jeffrey Bairstow has pointed out that racquetball has attributes that lead to success in other professional sports. "It's very fast-moving, the scoring is simple, most of the top players are a little weird and actual violence does erupt from time to time on the court."[6] The United States Racquetball Association provides impressive statistics. In 1975, there were 1.4 million players and 5 million balls were sold; in 1977, there were 5.5 million players and 14 million balls were sold. Racquetball publicists and enthusiasts predict that, although tennis was the sport of the 1970s, racquetball will be the sport of the 1980s, and by the end of that decade will surpass tennis in numbers of participants.

1. Carll Tucker, "Slam! Crash! Racquetball!" NEW YORK TIMES MAGAZINE, 28 November 1976, pp. 63, 65.
2. Terry Fancher, THE HISTORY OF RACQUETBALL (Skokie, Ill.: United States Racquetball Association, n.d., p. 5.
3. Norman MacLean, HOW TO PLAY PLATFORM TENNIS RACQUETBALL & PADDLEBALL (New York: Drake, 1977), p. 39.
4. Joe Pisani, "The Man Who Invented Racquetball," RACQUETBALL ILLUSTRATED, February 1979, pp. 20-24.
5. Tom Carlson, "In the Beginning . . . ," RACQUETBALL, January-February 1979, pp. 15-17. Sobeck felt that paddleball could be improved by using a strung racket rather than the comparatively heavy paddle. He designed the first racket, wrote ball specifications, and publicized the game.
6. Jeffrey Bairstow, "Racquetball," TENNIS, September 1976, p. 104.

ASSOCIATIONS, FOUNDATIONS, ORGANIZATIONS

115 AMERICAN AMATEUR RACQUETBALL ASSOCIATION. 5545 Murray Avenue, Memphis, Tenn. 38117.

Formerly known as the International Racquetball Association, this group promotes racquetball, encourages it to be a sport governed by and for the players, conducts tournaments, and is concerned for the amateur game. It has affiliate associations in most states.

116 AMERICAN PROFESSIONAL RACQUETBALL ASSOCIATION. 730 Pine Street, Deerfield, Ill. 60015.

An organization for professional teachers, this group conducts clinics and gives certification tests for teaching competency.

117 ASSOCIATION OF RACQUETBALL PROFESSIONALS. 640 Solona Circle, No. 18, Solona Beach, Calif. 92075.

The purpose is to " . . . protect all racquetball players' mutual interests, promote the drafting of just and reasonable rules governing players and sponsors, improve playing conditions, and maintain ethical standards to govern the conduct of members."

118 CANADIAN RACQUETBALL ASSOCIATION. 333 River Road, Vanier, Ontario K1L 8B9.

This is the governing body for the game in Canada. It promotes clinics and other educational programs, runs tournaments, provides prizes in competitions, and sends worthy members of the association to competitions.

119 NATIONAL COURT CLUBS ASSOCIATION. 666 Dundee Road, Northbrook, Ill. 60062.

This is an association of court club owners that offers information about costs and construction of building and operating a racquetball club, as well as the opportunity to purchase property and casualty insurance at group rates. The association runs an annual racquetball convention in conjunction with the racquetball industry trade show.

119A NATIONAL RACQUETBALL CLINICS, INC. 5567 Kearney Villa Road, San Diego, Calif. 92123.

This organization provides professional racquetball players for clinics and exhibitions.

120 NATIONAL RACQUETBALL CLUB. 4101 Dempster Street, Skokie, Ill. 60076.

This is the governing body for professional racquetball. It

organizes the professional tour, arranges for prize money and television coverage.

121 NATIONAL RACQUET SPORTS ASSOCIATION. 3430 Sunset Avenue, Wanamassa, N.J. 07712.

An organization providing insurance against injuries or loss of equipment in racquetball, this group gives discounts to members on such items as car rentals, tours, and subscriptions to RACQUETBALL ILLUSTRATED (see 169).

122 UNITED STATES RACQUETBALL ASSOCIATION. 4101 Dempster Street, Skokie, Ill. 60076.

This group competes with the American Amateur Racquetball Association (see 115) to be the governing body for amateur racquetball in the United States. It sponsors tournaments on the state, regional, and national levels and has affiliates in all fifty states.

123 WOMEN'S PROFESSIONAL RACQUETBALL ASSOCIATION. c/o Dan Seaton, 3727 Centennial Circle, Las Vegas, Nev. 89120.

This group began in 1979 as an association representing the interests of women touring professional players and with the aim of establishing a separate tour for women.

AUDIOVISUAL MATERIALS

Only the names or acronyms of distributors are given in the annotations below. An alphabetical list of distributors' full names with addresses can be found in the appendix (pp. 205-10).

124 FUN AND FUNDAMENTALS OF RACQUETBALL. 16mm. film. Black and white. Sound. 20 minutes. Purchase: Sports Films and Talents. Rental: Sports Films and Talents.

Fundamental techniques of the game are shown by Bud Muehleisen with action sequences of men and women players.

125 INSTRUCTIONAL AID TO RACQUETBALL. 16mm. film. Color. Sound. 15 minutes. 1974. Rental: Washington State University. ISBN 0-699-14961-4.

Steve Keeley demonstrates how to play.

126 NATIONAL PRO-AM RACQUETBALL. 3/4-inch videocassette. Color. Sound. 60 minutes. 1977. Purchase: Public Television Library. Rental: Public Television Library.

Highlights of a tournament in Westminster, California, are shown with Davey Bledsoe, Charlie Brumfield, Marty Hogan, Shannon Wright, and others.

127 1977 U.S.R.A. NATIONAL RACQUETBALL CHAMPIONSHIP. 1/2- or 3/4-inch videocassette. Color. Sound. 10 minutes or 30 minutes. 1978. Purchase: Atlas Health Club.

The ten-minute tape shows "scenes promoting the 1977 Nationals." The thirty-minute tape covers highlights of the men's and women's finals and the men's quarter and semifinals. Selected shots are shown in slow motion.

127A OFF THE WALL. 16mm. film. Color. Sound. 15 minutes. 1979. Rental: AMF Head.

128 RACQUETBALL. Three 16mm. films, super 8mm. or videocassettes. Color. Sound. Purchase: Champions on Film.

Contents: (1) INTRODUCTION--the warm-up, grips, and strokes. (2) SERVING. (3) BASIC SHOTS--the pass, kill, and Z-ball, and more.

129 RACQUETBALL: MOVING FAST. 16mm. film. Color. Sound. 15 minutes. 1978. Purchase and Rental: BFA Educational Media. LC 78-701685.

Instructors Mark Morrow and Joy Koppel demonstrate execution of strokes and serves, with diagrams of the latter to show the intended effects. Instruction is interspersed with scenes showing game points.

130 RACQUETBALL LESSONS MADE EASY. Two audio cassettes with 40-page booklet. 60 minutes each. Purchase: Service Press.

The cassettes are divided into six twenty-minute lessons covering such topics as equipment, the shots, strokes, and strategy. The lessons and booklet are by Steve Keeley.

131 RACQUETBALL SERIES. Four 16mm. films or super 8mm. cassettes. Color. Sound. 10 minutes each. 1979. Purchase: Athletic Institute.

These films were done in cooperation with the United States Racquetball Association (see 122). Slow motion and stop action capture the technique of four professionals--Terry Fancher, Janell Marriott, Steve Strandemo, and Kathy Williams. Contents: (1) FUNDAMENTALS OF RACQUETBALL. (2) RACQUETBALL SHOTS. (3) RACQUETBALL SERVES AND SERVE RETURNS. (4) STRATEGY FOR SINGLES, DOUBLES, CUTTHROAT.

132 ROLLOUT. 16 mm. film or super 8mm. cassette. Color. Sound. 5 minutes. 1975. Purchase: AMF Voit. Rental: AMF Voit. LC 75-700479.

This shows a group of "average people" (actually four profes-
sionals--Steve Keeley, Steve Serot, Steve Strandemo, and
Charlie Brumfield) getting together to play a game and encourage others to play. An amusing account of the making
of the film can be found in the chapter "I Are a Star" in
Keeley's book IT'S A RACQUET (see 138).

132A WINNING RACQUETBALL. Six 1/2- or 3/4-inch videocassettes. Color.
Sound. 30 minutes each. Purchase: KCOE Television Foundation.

Contents: (1) WHERE TO BEGIN. (2) FOREHAND AND
BACKHAND. (3) SERVICE AND SERVICE RETURN. (4)
SHOT SELECTION AND TECHNIQUE. (5) MORE SELEC-
TION AND TECHNIQUE. (6) PUTTING IT ALL TOGETHER.

BOOKS

132B Boccaccio, Tony. RACQUETBALL BASICS. Englewood Cliffs, N.J.:
Prentice Hall, 1979. 48 p. Photos., dgrms., dwgs. ISBN 0-13-129585-
3. LC 79-15234.

Intended for younger readers, this volume covers such fundamentals as clothing and equipment, strokes, and simple strategy.
The single paragraph on the history of the game is inadequate,
and the text is marred throughout by the use of "volley" for
"rally." Photographs by Paul Jacobs show people playing the
game, and cartoon-like drawings by Bill Gow support the instruction. Grades four and up.

133 Brumfield, Charles, and Bairstow, Jeffrey. OFF THE WALL: CHAMPION-
SHIP RACQUETBALL FOR THE ARDENT AMATEUR. New York: Dial,
1978. 173 p. Photos., dgrms. ISBN 0-8037-7276-6. LC 78-8031.

Strokes, shots, and strategy on offense and defense are presented in clear text and diagrams. Sequence photographs of
Brumfield, a national champion, demonstrate the strokes.
Doubles, conditioning, and selection of equipment are discussed, and there are a few paragraphs on racquetball injuries.

133A CHAMPIONSHIP RACQUETBALL BY THE EXPERTS. Edited by John Rez-
nik and James Peterson. West Point Sports, Fitness Series. West Point,
N.Y.: Leisure Press, 1978. 192 p. Photos., dgrms. Paperbound.
ISBN 0-918438-03-9.

This is a compilation of undated articles that originally appeared in RACQUETBALL magazine (see 166). Many were
probably written in the early 1970s. The authors include big
names in the field--Charlie Brumfield, Steve Keeley, Bud
Muehleisen--and topics covered in addition to the standard
instruction include how to teach the game and conducting a
clinic or tournament.

133B Dowell, Linus, and Grice, William. RACQUETBALL. Boston: American Press, 1979. 126 p. Photos., dgrms., gloss., bibliog.

Standard instruction is given with inadequate sequence photographs. A stroke the authors labeled the forehand and backhand "jab" was not described in other instruction books. A strong point is a section on skill evaluation with detailed information on tests and how to score them.

133C Fichter, George. RACQUETBALL. New York: Franklin Watts, 1979. 64 p. Photos., dgrms., dwgs., gloss., bibliog. ISBN 0-531-04078-X. LC 79-11876.

A lot of good information is packed into this book designed for younger readers. Brief information is given on all the racket sports before concentrating on shots, strokes, and brief strategy information for racquetball. There is an insufficient number of illustrative drawings showing the strokes. Grades five and up.

134 Fink, Jack. SO YOU'RE NEW TO RACQUETBALL. Alameda, Calif.: Privately published by the author, 1976. Available from Fink at 2137 Otis Drive, Alameda, Calif. 94501. 19 p. Dwgs., bibliog. Paperbound.

This is a pamphlet presenting in clear, informal style what the beginner needs to know--summarized rules, physical preparation for the game, strokes and strategy in brief.

135 Garfinkel, Charles. RACQUETBALL THE EASY WAY. New York: Atheneum, 1978. 148 p. Photos., dgrms. Paperbound. ISBN 0-689-10916-4. LC 78-53835.

This is a full text on the game by the inventor of the "Garfinkel serve," one of the advanced strokes. Chapters on the strokes have sequence photographs, and shots, tactics, and doubles are each given a chapter.

136 Hogan, Marty; Brumfield, Charles; and Shay, Arthur. MARTY HOGAN'S POWER RACQUETBALL. Chicago: Contemporary Books, 1979. 135 p. Photos. ISBN 0-8092-7577-5. LC 78-12498.

Photographs and text show and discuss the way Hogan, U.S. champion for several years, hits the ball--no grip change between forehand and backhand, hitting off the back rather than the front foot, swinging in an arc, and keeping the head down through the stroke. Strategy, conditioning, and psyching are other topics covered in this thorough text.

137 Keeley, Steve. THE COMPLETE BOOK OF RACQUETBALL. Chicago: Follett, 1976. 288 p. Photos., dgrms., gloss. Paperbound. ISBN 0-

695-80651-3. LC 75-37355.

This book lives up to its title. Everything anyone would want to know from history through complete rules is here in exhaustive detail. The chapters begin with a summary in outline form of the points that will be covered.

138 _____. IT'S A RACQUET! Haslett, Mich.: Service Press, 1978. 193 p. Dwgs. Paperbound. ISBN 0-931824-02-8. LC 78-55336.

Keeley describes fellow competitors in a flamboyant style, parodies the Biblical account of creation as applied to racquetball, and fashions other whimsies about himself and the game.

139 Kramer, Jack. BEGINNER'S RACQUETBALL. Mountain View, Calif.: World, 1979. 129 p. Photos., dgrms., line dwgs., gloss., bibliog. Paperbound. ISBN 0-89037-160-1. LC 78-64387.

Kramer supplies a text for the beginner. The author, who is not the famous tennis player of the same name, emphasizes the recreational aspects of the game and gives detailed standard instruction. One omission was noted: neither text nor photographs of the backhand indicate the correct point where the racket should meet the ball.

140 Lawrence, A. Paul. FUNDAMENTALS OF RACQUETBALL. San Diego, Calif.: Ektelon, 1973. 22 p. Photos., dgrms. Paperbound.

Sequence photographs of the basic strokes and diagrams for the shots, along with brief tips on defensive play and match play, are given in this pamphlet.

141 Leve, Chuck. INSIDE RACQUETBALL. Inside Sports Series. Chicago: Regnery, 1973. 87 p. Photos., dgrms., gloss. ISBN 0-8092-8899-0.

This book begins with a chapter on equipment, continues with grip and ground strokes, serve and serve return, and concludes with sections on advanced play. Shots of top players in action are shown with commentary.

142 Lubarsky, Steve; Delson, Rod; and Scagnetti, Jack. RACQUETBALL MADE EASY. North Hollywood, Calif.: Wilshire, 1978. 127 p. Photos., dgrms., gloss. Paperbound. ISBN 0-87980-361-4. LC 78-62761.

Brief but thorough chapters on choosing equipment, shots, strokes, defensive play, doubles, strategy, and drills are presented. There are no sequence photographs, and pictures are not always placed well in relation to the text.

142A McShirley, Susan. RACQUETBALL, WHERE TO PLAY U.S.A.: A COMPLETE DIRECTORY OF RACQUETBALL FACILITIES. Los Angeles: S.R.M. Press, 1979. 344 p. Dwgs. Paperbound.

This directory of racquetball courts in the United States includes the amenities each place offers (child care, swimming pool, restaurant, and more), whether other racket sports can be played there, and the charge cards that are accepted. Brief quotations from such eminent philosophers as Ralph Waldo Emerson and Charlie Brumfield are scattered through the text.

143 Mjehovich, Michael. RACQUETBALL STEP BY STEP. San Jose, Calif.: Privately published by the author, 1977. Available from Mjehovich at 1155 Weyburn Lane, San Jose, Calif. 95129. 33 p. Photos., dgrms., gloss. Paperbound.

This is an analysis of the fundamentals of the game in a progressive order--grip, strokes, shots, court positioning--aimed at instruction for beginners and review for intermediates and above. Most chapters include how to practice and how to overcome problems.

143A Moore, Alan; Scott, Thomas; and Harlan, William. RACQUETBALL FOR ALL. Dubuque, Iowa: Kendall Hunt, 1979. 112 p. Photos., dgrms., dwgs., gloss., bibliog. Spiral bound. ISBN 0-8403-2033-7.

This is not so much an instructional manual as it is a handbook of information not found in such detail in other books on the game. For example, there are thorough descriptions of cutthroat (three-person) racquetball as well as the one- and three-wall forms of the game, a long chapter on proper warming up, and tests to determine one's knowledge of the sport.

144 National Association for Girls and Women in Sport. NAGWS GUIDE: TEAM HANDBALL, RACQUETBALL, ORIENTEERING. Washington, D.C.: American Alliance for Health, Physical Education and Recreation, 1976-- . Biannual. Dgrms., gloss., bibliog. Paperbound.

A collection of racquetball articles by different authors, primarily instructional in nature and written for women, is included.

145 Reznik, John. RACQUETBALL. New York: Sterling, 1979. 192 p. Photos., dgrms., gloss. ISBN 0-8069-4138-3. LC 78-66320.

This is a clear and thorough text on the game. There is an outstanding section on methods of analyzing play.

146 Reznik, John; Matthews, David; and Peterson, James. RACQUETBALL FOR MEN AND WOMEN. Champaign, Ill.: Stipes, 1972. 84 p. Photos., dgrms., gloss. Paperbound.

The text begins with a discussion of equipment and rules, and covers the standard grips, strokes, shots, strategy, and drills. The same analysis method as in the previous book (see 145) is here, but in less detail.

147 Rich, Jim. FUNDAMENTALS OF RACQUETBALL. 2d ed. Dubuque, Iowa: Kendall Hunt, 1977. 53 p. Photos., dgrms., gloss. Paperbound. ISBN 0-8403-1214-8.

Only twenty-four of the fifty-three pages are instructional in this book. The remaining pages consist of a glossary and the rules. The instruction is in very short chapters on groundstrokes, serve and return of serve, the basic shots, and one page of playing hints.

148 Sauser, Jean, and Shay, Arthur. INSIDE RACQUETBALL FOR WOMEN. Inside Sports Series. Chicago: Contemporary Books, 1977. 107 p. Photos., gloss. ISBN 0-8092-7821-9. LC 77-75846.

The authors contend that different teaching methods for the different sexes are necessary, and that women generally err by dance stepping, since for many of them dance is the main physical movement they know. It is primarily a picture book showing common errors and how to correct them.

148A _____. RACQUETBALL STRATEGY. Chicago: Contemporary Books, 1979. 87 p. Photos., dgrms., gloss. ISBN 0-8092-7366-7. LC 78-73676.

This is a book for the intermediate player; it offers a series of specific playing situations in singles and doubles followed by the correct strategy for them. At times the advice is obvious--"Situation: Your partner on the right is too close to the wall . . . Strategy: Encourage your partner away from the wall" (p. 74)--but more often it is worthwhile.

149 _____. TEACHING YOUR CHILD RACQUETBALL. Chicago: Contemporary Books, 1978. 68 p. Photos., dgrms., bibliog. ISBN 0-8092-7588-0. LC 77-23709.

The authors given ten lessons on how to give ten lessons to a beginning junior player. Emphasis is placed on keeping the vocabulary simple, ending each lesson with a play period, and reinforcing what was learned in the previous lesson.

150 Scott, Eugene. RACQUETBALL: THE CULT. New York: Doubleday, 1979. 115 p. Photos., dgrms. Paperbound. ISBN 0-385-13006-6. LC 77-75883.

The author goes beyond the instruction of other books on the game and offers reflections on its past and future, as well as verbal portraits of many of its leading players. He repeats some of the same information; for example, the chapter entitled "Mecca" and the introduction say the same things about San Diego as the national headquarters for the game.

151 Shay, Arthur, and Fancher, Terry. 40 COMMON ERRORS IN RACQUET-BALL AND HOW TO CORRECT THEM. Chicago: Contemporary Books, 1978. 108 p. Photos., dgrms. ISBN 0-8092-7704-2. LC 77-23707.

Text and large photographs on the left-hand side of the page show the error; text and photograph on the right show the correction. There is a unusual index with entries under terms such as "not using your head," "head, failure to use," "using your head, mistake of not."

152 Shay, Arthur, and Leve, Chuck. WINNING RACQUETBALL. Chicago: Regnery, 1976. 164 p. Photos., dgrms., line dwgs. ISBN 0-8092-8086-8. LC 75-32992.

This is an instruction book for intermediate and advanced players on why one loses and what one can do about it. The basics are reviewed, and then topics such as the importance of the center court position, the kill and spin, and how to use the rules to one's best advantage are covered.

153 Sheftel, Chuck, and Shay, Arthur. CONTEMPORARY RACQUETBALL. Chicago: Contemporary Books, 1978. 90 p. Photos., dwgs. ISBN 0-8092-7547-3. LC 77-91179.

A syllabus for eight one-hour lessons as they might be given to a beginning player, this book is useful, therefore, for teachers as well as players. The authors use "volley" when "rally" is meant throughout.

154 Spear, Victor. HOW TO WIN AT RACQUETBALL. Rockford, Ill.: Win Publishing, 1976. 75 p. Dgrms. Paperbound.

Spear says that the guiding principle should be either to end the point in one's favor with every shot one hits or at least to put the opponent in the worst possible position to do the same. Correct shots to accomplish that aim in all situations are given here. The author also feels that the center court control concept is not always valid.

155 _____. SPORTS ILLUSTRATED RACQUETBALL. Philadelphia: J.B. Lippincott, 1979. 176 p. Photos., dgrms., gloss. ISBN 0-397-01306-X. LC 78-27348.

This is an alive, informed, and dogmatic book on how racquetball should be played. Spear is a doctor, and he expresses strong opinions on diet and conditioning.

156 Stafford, Randy. RACQUETBALL: THE SPORT FOR EVERYONE. Memphis: S.C. Toof, 1975. 80 p. Photos., dgrms., gloss. Paperbound.

This book covers all the standard points from grips through strategy. Sequence photographs for most strokes and diagrams for shot paths are shown, as well as a thorough section on practicing those shots.

157 Strandemo, Steve, and Bruns, Bill. THE RACQUETBALL BOOK. New York: Pocket Books, 1977. 207 p. Photos., dgrms., gloss. Paperbound. ISBN 0-671-81712-4.

Clear photographs are the hallmark of this book for the intermediate who wants to improve. The guiding principle is the center court theory; the player who controls the area from just behind the back service line to about nine feet from the back wall and within two or three feet of both side walls, will win.

158 Verner, Bill, and Skowrup, Drew. RACQUETBALL. Palo Alto, Calif.: Mayfield, 1977. 113 p. Photos., dgrms., line dwgs., gloss., bibliog. Paperbound. ISBN 0-87484-426-6. LC 77-089923.

This is a thorough guide to all elements of the game. There are strong sections on doubles and on refereeing. Rules are included.

159 Vockell, Ed, and Campbell, Ottis. DEVELOPING RACQUETBALL SKILLS. Niles, Ill.: Hewitt Printing, 1975. 111 p. Dgrms., gloss. Paperbound.

This is a book describing methods for developing skills useful in racquetball--identifying the skill, systematically practicing it, and getting feedback on progress. It concludes with a section of specific situations and asks the reader what shots would work best in each situation and why.

160 Weckstein, Joyce. RACQUETBALL "FOR WOMEN." Royal Oak, Mich.: Lincoln Press, 1975. 50 p. Photos., dgrms. Paperbound. LC 75-39292.

This book covers the essentials of history, strokes, and shots. The final chapter reads as if it were written by one who has discovered the true faith--racquetball worship--and wishes to convert all females to it.

CAMPS

Check the information in the "Camps" section of the introduction to this book (pp. xvii) for information connected with the listings below.

161 THE ASPEN ATHLETIC CLUB PRO CAMP. 720 East Hyman Avenue, Aspen, Colo. 81611.

This is an adult camp.

162   ATLAS HEALTH CLUB RACQUETBALL CAMP. 901 Hotel Circle South, P.O. Box 80097, San Diego, Calif. 92138.

      This is an adult camp.

163   DAVEY BLEDSOE RACQUETBALL RANCH. Storm Meadows Athletic Club, Steamboat Springs, Colo. 80477.

      This is an adult camp.

164   STEVE STRANDEMO RACQUETBALL CAMP. Seven Springs Mountain Resort, Champion, Pa. 15622.

      This is an adult camp.

PERIODICALS

Some of the titles annotated in the "Periodicals" section of chapter 1 of this book cover racquetball.

165   NATIONAL RACQUETBALL. United States Racquetball Association, 4101 Dempster Street, Skokie, Ill. 60076, 1973-- . Monthly.

      This is the official publication of the United States Racquetball Association (see 122). The standard annotation (see p. xvii) applies. Each issue contains a "Women in Racquetball" section.

166   RACQUETBALL. American Amateur Racquetball Association, 5545 Murray Avenue, Memphis, Tenn. 38117, 1972-- . Bimonthly.

      This is the official publication of the American Amateur Racquetball Association (see 115). The standard annotation applies (see p. xvii).

167   RACQUETBALL CANADA. Canadian Racquetball Association, 333 River Road, Vanier City, Ontario K1L 8B9, 1975-- . Irregular.

      This is the official publication of the Canadian Racquetball Association (see 118). The standard annotation applies (see p. xvii).

168   RACQUETBALL HANDBALL NEWS. Scott and Associates, 1510 Fayette Street, El Cajon, Calif. 92020, 1976-- . Monthly.

      This is a newspaper format publication with the standard annotation (see p. xvii).

169   RACQUETBALL ILLUSTRATED. CFW Enterprises, 7011 Sunset Boulevard, Hollywood, Calif. 90028, 1978-- . Monthly.

This is the newest of the racquetball periodicals. Illustrations are featured, and there is occasional fiction in addition to the materials in the standard annotation (see p. xvii).

Chapter 6

SQUASH RACQUETS

Squash racquets descended from racquets, a game covered briefly in this book in chapter 9, "Other Games." One of the places where racquets developed was Harrow, the English public school, located in Middlesex, London. The game was popular there, but there was only one court. In order to accommodate the many boys interested in playing racquets, a similar game was invented that did not require as large a playing area. Since the hard racquets ball might have caused injuries in the more confined space, a softer ball was introduced that sounded and felt rather squashy in comparison, hence squash racquets. Readers interested in longer accounts of racquets, squash racquets, and squash tennis (also covered here in chapter 9) are referred to Dick Squire's book THE OTHER RACQUET SPORTS (see 17) or to two out-of-print volumes not annotated in this book: Allison Danzig's THE RACQUET GAME (New York: Macmillan, 1930) or John R. Tunis's SPORT FOR THE FUN OF IT (New York: A.S. Barnes, 1940).

Today there are two games of squash racquets: the North American game played in most of Canada, Mexico, and the United States; and the international game (sometimes called the English game) played everywhere else.[1] In the international game the ball is softer, the racquet lighter, the court wider, and the scoring different. The result is a primarily defensive game of position play requiring great stamina. The North American game is faster and does not last as long. The famous differentiation is that the international game is one ". . . in which two gentlemen chase a small black ball around a court, and the American game is the one where the small black ball chases the two gen-

---

1. The introduction of the 70 + ball to the United States and its adoption by the United States Squash Racquets Association (see 175) for all official tournaments, added a new element to the situation. The ball was originally used for summer play (hence the name--seventy degrees plus) and is softer than the North American ball but harder than the international ball. The obvious hope was to make a compromise ball, but as of the time this was written the two games are still separate, although the 70+ ball has largely replaced the original harder ball.

tlemen."[2] Supporters of the North American game are fond of comparing it with other sports in terms such as ". . . forty-five minutes of squash provides exercise equivalent to two hours of lawn tennis or some thirty years of watching 'The Wide World of Sports.'"[3] Such comparisons have a built-in appeal for the man or woman who wants a good workout in a short time. Squash racquets has rarely been seen on American television, but if future court expansion includes glass enclosed courts (squash pioneered in having one wall of glass, but racquetball has extended and multiplied the idea) that barrier to future growth may also fall.

ASSOCIATIONS, FOUNDATIONS, ORGANIZATIONS

170   CANADIAN PROFESSIONAL SQUASH ASSOCIATION. c/o John Frittenburg, Regency Racquets Club, 25 Kings Cross Road, Bramalea, Ontario L6T 3V5.

> This is an association for professional players in Canada that offers clinics, runs tournaments, and serves as a placement and information center for professionals or amateurs wishing to become professionals.

171   CANADIAN SQUASH RACQUETS ASSOCIATION. 333 River Road, Vanier, Ontario K1L 8B9.

> Although this organization did not respond to this editor's correspondence, presumably its function is similar to the U.S. association (see 175) as the governing body for the amateur game in Canada.

172   NATIONAL INTERCOLLEGIATE SQUASH RACQUETS ASSOCIATION. c/o Edward Serues, Athletics Department, Amherst College, Amherst, Mass. 01002.

> This is an association dedicated to the encouragement of squash via the promotion of intercollegiate matches.

173   NATIONAL SQUASH RACQUETS EDUCATIONAL FOUNDATION. 10 Bainbridge Road, West Hartford, Conn. 06119.

> This foundation was originally established as a method for tax deductible support for various projects connected with the game. It still continues as a recipient for gifts that a donor might prefer to have administered by an independent body.

---

2. Richard Hawkey in his NEWER ANGLES ON SQUASH (see 191) quotes this definition on pp. 17-18.
3. George Rutler, INTRODUCING SQUASH RACQUETS (see 198), p. 2.

174 SQUASHCON. 625 Cassatt Road, Berwyn, Pa. 19312.

> This is a commercial corporation that constructs and operates squash playing facilities and sponsors tournaments and exhibitions.

175 UNITED STATES SQUASH RACQUETS ASSOCIATION. 211 Ford Road, Bala Cynwyd, Pa. 19004.

> As the U.S. governing body for the game, it runs the national tournaments, assigns rankings, reviews the rules, sets refereeing standards, and promotes the sport.

176 WORLD PROFESSIONAL SQUASH ASSOCIATION. c/o Clive Caldwell, 123 Queen Street West, Toronto, Ontario M5H 2M9.

> An organization acting on behalf of playing and teaching professionals, it organizes tournament circuits and acts as a bargaining agent for players, disseminates information on group instruction methods, and is concerned with standards for equipment and for teaching competence.

AUDIOVISUAL MATERIALS

Only the names or acronyms of distributors are given in the annotations below. An alphabetical list of distributors' full names with addresses can be found in the appendix (pp. 205-10).

177 CHAMPIONSHIP SQUASH. 16mm. film. Color. Sound. 14 minutes. Purchase: United States Squash Racquets Association. Rental: United States Squash Racquets Association.

> Sharif Khan and Vic Niederhoffer are shown in an exhibition match, with commentary. There are some slow motion shots.

178 SQUASH. Three 16mm. films or super 8mm. films. Color. Sound. 10 minutes each. 1979. Purchase and Rental: United States Squash Racquets Association.

> Contents: (1) GRIP/FOREHAND/BACKHAND. (2) SERVES/ RETURNS/VOLLEYS. (3) BASIC SHOTS AND TACTICS.

179 SQUASH, EVERYONE'S RACQUET. 16mm. film. Color. Sound. 13 minutes. Purchase and Rental: United States Squash Racquets Association.

> This film gives instruction in the basic fundamentals of the game and shows a few minutes of a game between Sharif Khan and Victor Niederhoffer illustrating points made in the introduction.

180 SQUASH RACQUETS. Four 16mm. films. Color. Sound. Purchase: Coaching Association of Canada.

>Contents: (1) INTRODUCTION TO THE GAME. (2) BASIC SHOTS. (3) ATTACKING AND DEFENSIVE SHOTS. (4) MATCH PLAY.

BOOKS

181 Barnaby, Jack. SQUASH RACQUETS IN BRIEF. Center Harbor, N.H.: Privately published by the author, 1961. Available from Barnaby at Bean Road, RD 1, Center Harbor, N.H. 03226. 19 p. Photos., dgrms. Paperbound.

>This pamphlet is packed with information. The treatment is primarily in terms of strategy with strokes discussed in relation to tactics. Barnaby is one of the few authors who recommend shifting the grip between forehand and backhand.

182 _____. WINNING SQUASH RACQUETS. Boston: Allyn and Bacon, 1979. 286 p. Photos., dgrms. ISBN 0-205-06175-3. LC 78-25730.

>This is an instruction manual for players, teachers, and spectators by the long-time Harvard coach. Personal reminiscences are frequently used to make instructional points, and such topics as psychology, the differences between men's and women's tactics, gamesmanship, great players of past and present, and more are discussed with wisdom and good humor, in addition to detailed coverage of such standard topics as strokes, shots, and tactics.

183 [Bloss], Margaret Varner, and Bramall, Norman. SQUASH RACQUETS. Physical Education Activities Series. Dubuque, Iowa: William C. Brown, 1967. 70 p. Photos., dgrms., gloss., bibliog. Paperbound. ISBN 0-697-07027-1. LC 66-21271.

>This is a text for college physical education classes that can also be used by the club player. It covers the strokes with sequence photography, conditioning exercises and footwork drills, strategy for singles and doubles, and squash etiquette.

184 Chapman, Claire. WINNING SQUASH. Toronto: Coles, 1976. 89 p. Photos., dgrms. Paperbound.

>Intended for the squash instructor, this book contains pointers on both individual and group coaching. It has chapters on errors (how to spot and correct them), and lesson plans for group instruction. The book was first published in England under the title TEACHING SQUASH (London: G. Bell, 1976). When Coles republished it, they left out the bibliography--an unfortunate omission, since the text refers to it on several occasions.

185 Constable, Betty; Peck, Norman; and White, Dan. SQUASH BASICS FOR MEN AND WOMEN. New York: Hawthorn, 1979. 100 p. Photos., dgrms., gloss. Paperbound. ISBN 0-8015-7039-5. LC 78-61579.

> This is just what the title indicates: the basics of the game from preparation to hit through match play. The first two authors teach the game at Princeton University. Chapters on how to practice, conditioning, and common injuries are included, and the rules are given.

186 Francis, Austin. SMART SQUASH: USING YOUR HEAD TO WIN. Philadelphia: J.B. Lippincott, 1977. 192 p. Dgrms., dwgs., ISBN 0-397-01238-1. LC 77-22011.

> Seven leading North American men and women squash players are quoted profusely--Francis is almost as much an editor as he is an author--on topics such as developing one's own style, pre-match preparation, match play, doubles, gamesmanship, and more. This is a book for intermediate and advanced players.

187 Giles, Jack. SQUASH RACQUETS. Rev. ed. London: Kaye and Ward, 1972. Distributed in the United States by Sportshelf, New Rochelle, N.Y. 96 p. Photos., dgrms., line dwgs. ISBN 0-7812-0905-2. LC 73-179463.

> This gives information on strokes, shots, and strategy used in the international game, as well as sections on errors and their correction, refereeing, and coaching.

188 Goddard, Adrian. SQUASH! THE NEW PLAYER, THE NEW GAME. New York: St. Martin's, 1979. 184 p. Photos., dgrms. ISBN 0-312-75432-9. LC 78-19585.

> The "new game" of the title is squash played with the 70 + ball. The sequence photographs are placed in the upper right hand corners so one can flip them to illustrate strokes. There is a useful list of places in the United States to play the game as of 1977.

189 Hawkey, Richard. BEGINNER'S GUIDE TO SQUASH. London: Pelham Books, 1973. Distributed in the United States by Transatlantic Arts, New York. 143 p. Photos., dgrms. ISBN 0-7207-0682-3. LC 73-179463.

> The four books by Hawkey (see also 190, 191, 192) are all on the international game; he is the man in charge of the examination of coaches in England. This book takes the beginner from the basics of court, equipment, and rules to the time when match play instruction is necessary.

190 _____. IMPROVING YOUR SQUASH. London: Faber and Faber, 1967. Distributed in the United States by Transatlantic Arts, New York, in 1972. 126 p. Photos., dgrms. Paperbound. ISBN 0-571-09949-1. LC 73-152687.

The author repeats information from his BEGINNER'S GUIDE TO SQUASH and in the chapter on tactics builds on the foundation laid in the other book.

191 _____. NEWER ANGLES ON SQUASH. London: Faber and Faber, 1973. Distributed in the United States by Transatlantic Arts, New York. 143 p. Dgrms. ISBN 0-571-10259-X. LC 73-166917.

A revision of the author's out-of-print book NEW ANGLES ON SQUASH (1962), this book reflects a lifetime of think- ing and writing about the sport. It is a thorough text not only on the game but also on coaching, refereeing, and tech- nical aspects of court design.

192 _____. STARTING SQUASH. Toronto: Coles, 1975. 78 p. Photos., dgrms. Paperbound.

The method of presenting material here is different from the author's BEGINNER'S GUIDE TO SQUASH; it is not as com- plete in its information, but it is clearer and beginners may find it easier to use.

193 Khan, Hashim, and Randall, Richard. SQUASH RACQUETS: THE KHAN GAME. Detroit: Wayne State University Press, 1967. 160 p. Photos., dgrms. ISBN 0-8143-1469-4. LC 68-12250.

Here is squash instruction from the greatest of them all. Khan, who never learned to speak or write textbook English, does it almost like a talking book with a broken but clear style. Descriptions of his life and the importance of his suc- cess to the Pakistan government are given as well as instruc- tion.

194 McKay, Heather, and Batten, Jack. HEATHER McKAY'S COMPLETE BOOK OF SQUASH. New York: Ballentine, 1979. 143 p. Photos., dgrms., gloss. ISBN 0-345-28271-X. LC 78-27080.

This was originally published in McKay's new home country of Canada (Toronto: Jonathan James, 1977). It begins with an overall view of squash, pointing out the differences between the international and North American games. The clear in- struction is geared to the latter and is standard--the strokes and shots, basic tactics, drills and conditioning. The glos- sary is incomplete, which might be a disadvantage to the beginner; "boast" is used on p. 30 but not defined in the glossary or in the text until p. 77. There are brief sequence photographs of McKay hitting most of the shots.

195 Molloy, Al, Jr. CONTEMPORARY SQUASH. Chicago: Contemporary Books, 1978. 136 p. Photos., dgrms., dwgs., gloss. ISBN 0-8092-7551-1. LC 78-1003.

The author's WINNING SQUASH is aimed at the intermediate player while this one is for the beginner. Even so the two books show many similarities; the sections entitled "Watching the Ball" are almost word for word the same. The topics are covered in the same order--history, equipment selection, basic techniques, and so forth--but the other book has more to it.

196 _____. WINNING SQUASH. Chicago: Contemporary Books, 1978. 178 p. Photos., dgrms., line dwgs., gloss. ISBN 0-8092-7661-5. LC 77-91163.

Molloy says in his preface that this is a "summary of the history, pleasures, and techniques of the game." Written for the intermediate player, Molloy discusses and illustrates the differences in stroking technique that the 70+ ball requires. It also contains one of the most detailed discussions of the doubles game of all the instruction books presented here.

197 Rowland, Jim. SQUASH BASICS. Sports Basics Books. New York: Two Continents, Methuen, 1975. 99 p. Photos., dgrms., gloss. Paperbound. ISBN 0-8467-0121-9. LC 75-27115.

A guide to the game as played in Canada (both international and North American games) and the United States, this one covers all the basics from grip through strategy. It includes diagrams and illustrations, but many of the latter are simply photographs of players in action rather than directly relating to the text.

198 Rutler, George. INTRODUCING SQUASH RACQUETS: A GUIDE FOR BEGINNERS. Philadelphia: Dorrance, 1978. 72 p. Dgrms., line dwgs., gloss. Paperbound. ISBN 0-8059-2492-2.

This is a very clear exposition of groundstrokes, serves and the simpler shots for the beginner.

199 Satterthwaite, Frank. THE THREE-WALL NICK AND OTHER ANGLES: A SQUASH AUTOBIOGRAPHY. New York: Holt, Rinehart and Winston, 1979. 284 p. Dgrms., gloss. ISBN 0-03-016666-7. LC 78-14173.

Instruction and autobiography are mixed with comments and reflections on the game by one of its leading players. There are verbal portraits of some of the current professionals, such as the Khans, Vic Niederhoffer, and Heather McKay.

200   Skillman, John. SQUASH RACQUETS. 2d ed. New York: Ronald, 1964. 86 p. Photos., dgrms. ISBN 0-8260-8255-6. LC 64-11826.

This is a long established work (the first edition appeared in 1937) by a former Yale coach. It covers all the basics, and what is called strategy and tactics in more modern books is listed by Skillman as "My Theory of the Game of Squash Rackets."

201   Sports Illustrated. SPORTS ILLUSTRATED SQUASH. Rev. ed. Philadelphia: J.B. Lippincott, 1971. 96 p. Photos., dgrms., dwgs., gloss. ISBN 0-397-00837-6. LC 70-161579.

(Bibliographic note: As of the date of publication, this is the only Sports Illustrated instruction book for which the Library of Congress used "Sports Illustrated" as the main entry. In all other instances--Devlin for badminton (see 70), Spear for racquetball (see 155), Miles for table tennis (see 234), Talbert for tennis (see 702)--the main entry was under the author's name. To add to the confusion, the name of one of the two authors of this book was spelled incorrectly on the "Contents" page. The two authors are Al Molloy, Jr., and Rex Lardner; Molloy's name is spelled "Malloy.")

All the fundamentals needed to play the game are here. Diagrammed instruction for each shot, black and white line drawings for the various strokes, and practice tips are included.

202   SQUASH RACQUETS. New ed. Know the Game Series. Wakefield, Engl.: EP Publishing, 1974. Distributed in the United States by Charles River Books, Boston. 47 p. Photos., dgrms. Paperbound. ISBN 0-7158-0217-8.

This pamphlet presents information on how to play the international game (singles only). Stroke information does not differentiate between the forehand and backhand. Numerous full-page illustrations are included.

203   Swift, Tony. SQUASH RACQUETS. Wakefield, Engl.: EP Publishing, 1974. Distributed in the United States by Charles River Books, Boston. 119 p. Photos., dgrms. ISBN 0-7158-0854-3-3. LC 75-313863; PLAY SQUASH. Toronto: Coles, 1975. 120 p. Paperbound.

A wealth of illustrations on the international game is the distinguishing feature of this review of basic and advanced shots. There is a section on match play and tactics.

204   Torbet, Laura, and McLaggan, Doug. SQUASH: HOW TO PLAY, HOW TO WIN. New York: Doubleday, 1978. 207 p. Photos., dgrms., gloss., bibliog. Paperbound. ISBN 0-385-12556-9. LC 77-76284.

Instructional points are made and then commented upon by some of the top players of the 1970s--Geoff Hunt, Sharif Khan,

Gretchen Spruance, and twelve others. These players do
disagree with each other on some points. The instruction is
quite detailed with sequence photographs.

205 Truby, John, Jr. THE SCIENCE AND STRATEGY OF SQUASH. New
York: Charles Scribner's Sons, 1975. 260 p. Photos., dgrms., bibliog.
ISBN 0-684-14260-0. LC 75-6818.

This is a thorough, detailed explanation of the theoretical
and practical aspects of squash. It is divided into three main
sections: "Mobility" (controlling the T, anticipation), "Shot-
making" (the swing and the interrelationship of power, control,
and deception), and "Tactics and Strategy." Photographs are
numerous and show correct and incorrect methods.

206 United States Squash Racquets Association. OFFICIAL YEARBOOK. 211
Ford Road, Bala Cynwyd, Pa. 19004, 1925-- . Annual.

This is a review of the preceding year, including reports from
the association and its regional affiliates, historical information, tournament results, national rankings, reports from such
associations as the Canadian, the intercollegiate, and so forth.

207 Wood, Peter. THE BOOK OF SQUASH. Sports and Leisure Series.
New York: Van Nostrand Reinhold, 1972. 127 p. Photos., dgrms.,
gloss. ISBN 0-442-29545-6. LC 78-149268.

Beginning with a description of an actual match, this book
covers basics (conditioning, equipment, grip); shots; strokes;
tactics (basic and advanced); rules and their interpretation;
and world squash. There is a long chapter on the Khans and
their effect on the game. There are illustrations, but only a
few of them relate to the text on the page on which they are
placed.

CAMPS

Check the information in the "Camps" section of the introduction to this book
(p. xvii) for information connected with the listings below.

208 ALPHA SQUASH CLINIC. P.O. Box 129, Wellesley Hills, Mass. 02181.

This is an adult camp and junior coeducational camp.

209 NEW ENGLAND SQUASH CAMP. 831 North Twenty-sixth Street, Philadelphia, Pa. 19130.

This is an adult camp and junior coeducational camp.

210   OHIO SQUASH CAMP.   17638 Walnut Trail, Chagrin Falls, Ohio 44022.

This is an adult camp and junior coeducational camp.

211   PHILADELPHIA SQUASH RACQUETS ASSOCIATION AND SQUASHCON SQUASH CAMP.   625 Cassatt Road, Berwyn, Pa. 19512.

This is an adult camp and junior coeducational camp.

PERIODICALS

Some of the titles annotated in the "Periodicals" section of chapter 1 of this book cover squash (see pp. 11-12).

212   SQUASH NEWS.   Squash News.   1199 Park Avenue, New York, N.Y. 10028.   1978-- .   Monthly.

This newspaper-format magazine can be subscribed to independently or received as a benefit of membership in several squash clubs and associations.   In addition to the standard annotation material (see p. xvii) it frequently runs a medical column, reviews new books, and publishes fiction.

Chapter 7

TABLE TENNIS

Table tennis originated in the second half of the nineteenth century in England. As is often the case, the early period was one of little standardization; a British pamphlet describes the early games played by undergraduate students who used books in place of a net in some areas, a string in others, bats made of cardboard or wood, balls of rubber or cork, tables of different widths and lengths, and alternate means of scoring and varying other rules in different areas of the country.[1] In the 1890s, James Gibb returned to England from a U.S. trip bringing with him some toy celluloid balls that gave off the sounds of "ping" and "pong" when they were struck with hollow vellum bats. That name was registered throughout the world by a toymaker friend of Gibb's, John Jacques, who sold it to Parker Brothers in the United States. Standardization did not occur until the formation of what was first called a ping pong association after World War I. Legal restrictions due to the trade name registration made a change necessary, and the International Table Tennis Foundation became the official body in 1926.

Tennis magazine (see 31) estimates that there are thirty-five million players in the United States. The same issue refers to the game as the second most popular world sport after soccer,[2] and sport it is everywhere but the United States with full-time athletes undergoing special training. The breech of the China wall by a group of U.S. table tennis players in April 1971 put the sport on the front pages for a short time, but in the United States, even with an estimated ten thousand tournament class players, it is still regarded as more of a basement game than a serious athletic activity. The establishment of a permanent executive director and headquarters for the United States Table Tennis Association (see 215) was the first necessary step to change that image.

---

1. International Table Tennis Federation, INTERNATIONAL TABLE TENNIS-- THE FIRST FIFTY YEARS (East Sussex, Engl.: 1977), p. 2.
2. "Table Tennis," TENNIS, February 1978, p. 106.

ASSOCIATIONS, FOUNDATIONS, ORGANIZATIONS

213 CANADIAN TABLE TENNIS ASSOCIATION. 333 River Road, Vanier, Ontario K1L 8B9.

This governing body for the game in Canada has the usual functions--sanctioning tournaments, as well as producing and distributing pamphlets, books, and films and providing general promotion of the game. It publishes an informal bulletin with news and results.

214 NATIONAL JUNIOR TABLE TENNIS FOUNDATION. 31 Huntington Bay Road, Huntington, N.Y. 11743.

The principal purposes of this group are to coordinate school and youth educational programs for the game, and to provide help, via publications and direct advice, on how to set up such programs, as well as on how to coach.

215 UNITED STATES TABLE TENNIS ASSOCIATION. P.O. Box J, Bridgeton, Mo. 63044.

This is the U.S. governing body for the game. It sanctions tournaments, publishes booklets, reviews the rules, and establishes standards for equipment. There are local clubs and leagues that are affiliates in many cities. A complete list of such organizations arranged by state can be found in TABLE TENNIS TOPICS (see 251) July, August 1979, on p. 31, and that magazine will update the information from time to time.

AUDIOVISUAL MATERIALS

Only the names or acronyms of distributors are given in the annotations below. An alphabetical list of distributors' full names with addresses can be found in the appendix to this book, pp. 205-10.

The Canadian Table Tennis Association (see 213) has a list of films available. That list simply gives the title and format (i.e., .16mm., super 8) with no indication of length, sound or silent, color or black and white, or content. It is suggested that those interested write directly to the association. The material is available on free loan in Canada only, and in most cases the title will give some indication of the content. No listings for these films and tapes are given below.

The United States Table Tennis Association (see 215) is in the process of transferring the 16mm. films in its collection to videocassette format. The titles were not available as of the date of publication of this book and are, therefore, not listed below. Those interested should either write to the association or to the chairperson of its film committee, Mr. C.F. Liu, 1603 South Highland Avenue, Arlington Heights, Ill. 60005.

Listings for individual materials that are available follow.

216 BASIC STROKES. Thirty-eight 35mm. slides. Color. Purchase: Coaching Association of Canada.

These slides illustrate the basic strokes covered in the COACHING MANUAL, LEVEL 1 of the Canadian Table Tennis Association (see 213). They are demonstrated by Zlatko Cordas.

217 CANADIAN OPEN, QUEBEC 1975. Eighteen 16mm. films or 1/2- or 3/4-inch videocassettes. Black and white. Silent. Purchase: Coaching Association of Canada.

This is a series of films of individual men's singles, men's doubles, and women's singles matches that may either be purchased singly or as three sets.

218 CLINIC, AGONQUIN COLLEGE 1974. Thirteen 16mm. films and film loops (endless or open reel) or 1/2- or 3/4-inch videocassettes. Color. Silent. Purchase: Coaching Association of Canada.

Canadian players Violetta Nesukaitis and Earl Gaetano demonstrate basic shots in a series of some films, some loops, that may either be purchased singly or as one set.

219 INTERNATIONAL PARAPLEGIC GAMES: TABLE TENNIS. 3/4-inch videocassette. Silent. 30 minutes. Purchase: Coaching Association of Canada.

This shows part of the men's finals held at Stoke, Great Britain, in 1975.

220 PING-PONG. 16mm. film or videocassette. Color. Sound. 14 minutes. Rental: University of California (16mm. film only); National Film Board of Canada.

This film shows competitions between teams of young Canadians and Chinese that took place in China in 1973 with highlights of play, as well as some sightseeing with the Canadians. It is a film without commentary.

221 TABLE TENNIS. 16mm. film. Black and white. Sound. 9 minutes. 1936. Rental: University of Illinois. ISBN 0-699-28666-2.

This is a demonstration by experts of some basic shots--push, forehand and backhand drives, serve, spin and how to counter it--and footwork. As a 1936 item, it is by now considerably dated.

BOOKS

222   Barna, Victor. YOUR BOOK OF TABLE TENNIS. Your Book Series.
       London: Faber and Faber, 1971. Distributed in the United States by
       Transatlantic Arts, New York. 77 p. Photos., dgrms., line dwgs.
       ISBN 0-571-09345-0. LC 78-578976.

       This is instruction primarily addressed to young adult players,
       but adults can benefit. Choosing a bat, strokes, the expedite
       rule, fitness, doubles, and temperament are all covered.

223   Barnes, Chester. ADVANCED TABLE TENNIS TECHNIQUES: HOW THE
       WORLD'S TOP PLAYERS WIN. New York: Arco, 1977. 112 p. Pho-
       tos., dgrms., line dwgs. ISBN 0-668-04233-8. LC 76-52386.

       This is the game as it is played at the highest levels, which
       do not include women's play; Barnes makes his feelings most
       explicit that women still play the defensive game of twenty
       years ago. Such topics as the necessary training top players
       must go through, and how today's great names hit the strokes
       are included.

224   _____. MODERN TABLE TENNIS TACTICS. Cranbury, N.J.: A.S.
       Barnes, 1973. 127 p. Photos., dgrms. ISBN 0-498-01387-1. LC 73-
       3761.

       About one half of this book is instruction, concentrating on
       strokes and tactics. The rest is commentary by the author
       on his past table tennis history, other good players, and the
       Chinese table tennis team's tour of England. The book was
       originally published in that country (London: Pelham, 1972),
       quotes prices in British pounds, tells where to obtain instruc-
       tion in England, and so forth.

225   _____. TABLE TENNIS. Pictorial Sports Instruction Series. New York:
       Barrons, 1977. 60 p. Photos. ISBN 0-8120-0720-4. LC 76-375344.

       Text and illustrations on serve, return of serve, attack and
       counter attack, the loop and when to use it, setting up the
       forehand smash, and more are given. A discussion of modern
       match play and of the game played in the United States (the
       book was originally published in London [Pelham Books,
       1975]) is included.

226   [Bloss], Margaret Varner, and Harrison, J. Rufford. TABLE TENNIS.
       Physical Education Activities Series. Dubuque, Iowa: William C. Brown,
       1967. 72 p. Photos., dgrms., gloss., bibliog. Paperbound. ISBN 0-
       697-07029-8. LC 67-21322.

       A fundamental point of this instruction book is to begin with
       the backhand. Beginners, say the authors, should start learn-

ing with a backhand serve and make returns with a backhand block, progress to a backhand drive, and only then learn the forehand. Sequence photographs are shown for the strokes.

227 Boggan, Tim. WINNING TABLE TENNIS. Chicago: Regnery, 1976. 197 p. Photos., line dwgs. ISBN 0-8092-8155-4. LC 75-32967.

This is a combination of a life story, discussion of strokes and how the author hits them, and an instruction manual on the game as played in the 1970s. A detailed comparison of various bat surfaces, basic and advanced strokes and play, strategy, and verbal and photographic portraits of some leading players are presented along with a section on how to stay fit. The rules are given.

228 Carr, Jack. ADVANCED TABLE TENNIS. Cranbury, N.J.: A.S. Barnes, 1969. 122 p. Photos., line dwgs., bibliog. ISBN 0-498-06857-9. LC 68-27244. Rev. ed. New York: Cornerstone, 1972. 128 p. Photos., line dwgs. Paperbound.

The instruction in both editions is identical; the revised edition did not include the bibliography but added a chapter on the Chinese team's tour of the United States and a brief history of the game. The assumption is that the basics are known, so concentration is on attack and defense tactics and preparation for tournament play. A lengthy appendix includes sections by different authors on topics such as nutrition, how to teach the game, and more.

229 Carrington, Jack. TEACH YOURSELF TABLE TENNIS. Toronto: Coles, 1976. 127 p. Photos., dgrms., line dwgs. Paperbound.

This is a most unusual instruction book. Much of the text is in the form of a dialogue among characters--student, coach, teacher, and SUPERMAN (spelled in caps but not Clark Kent, it represents a super player)--in which advice is given to players of various levels of experience--the learner, the improver, the advancer, the match player.

230 Cowan, Glenn. THE BOOK OF TABLE TENNIS--HOW TO PLAY THE GAME. New York: Grosset and Dunlap, 1972. 77 p. Photos. ISBN 0-448-01493-9. LC 70-18664.

A unique feature of this instruction book is that by reversing photographs all shots are shown being hit by a left hander as well as a right hander. Sequence photographs are included, but only three per stroke, which makes for incompleteness, particularly on such shots as the forehand lob. There is only one page on strategy.

231 Danner, Fred. NATIONAL SCHOOL TABLE TENNIS GUIDE WITH OF-
FICIAL RULES. Huntington, N.Y.: National Junior Table Tennis Foundation, 1976. 123 p. Photos., dwgs., bibliog. Paperbound.

This is written as a guide to persons who wish to know how
to coach and how to organize a table tennis program in a
school. The chapter on tactics is particularly strong; it is
also marred by a large number of typographical and grammati-
cal errors. The umpire's test for United States Table Tennis
Association (see 215) officials is included in the text.

232 Leach, Johnny. TABLE TENNIS FOR THE 'SEVENTIES. Cranbury, N.J.:
A.S. Barnes, 1971. 160 p. Photos. ISBN 0-498-07968-6. LC 79-
156953. TABLE TENNIS MADE EASY. North Hollywood, Calif.:
Wilshire, 1974. Paperbound.

Chapters on playing the western style grip, the penholder
grip and how to play against it, tactics in singles and doubles,
equipment, conditioning and umpiring are given. Clear stroke
photographs and others showing the sequence of play during
doubles points are provided.

233 Miles, Dick. THE GAME OF TABLE TENNIS. Philadelphia: J.B.
Lippincott, 1968. 141 p. Dwgs. ISBN 0-397-00878-3. LC 67-24010.

Clear drawings to illustrate strokes, pointers on practice, and
strategies to use against different types of opponents (the
blocker, the basher, etc.) are highlights. Doubles is not
covered, and only one paragraph is devoted to the loop.
For a detailed exposition by Miles on how to hit the loop,
see "Put Down by a Top Spin," SPORTS ILLUSTRATED, 8
March 1976, pp. 50-51.

234 _____. SPORTS ILLUSTRATED TABLE TENNIS. Philadelphia: J.B.
Lippincott, 1974. 95 p. Photos. ISBN 0-397-01024-9. LC 74-5513.

The fundamentals of the game are presented in a clear style.
The book's purpose is to make the average player a winner
against casual opponents: for example, those encountered in
a shipboard tournament. The push, drive, and chop are shown
with demonstration pictures of Miles. There is nothing on tactics;
the point is that mastery of the basic shots is enough to do well.

235 Philip, David, and Cohen, Joel. TABLE TENNIS. New York: Atheneum, 1975. 213 p. Photos., dgrms., dwgs., gloss. ISBN 0-689-10684-
X. LC 75-13565.

This is a lengthy exposition of all aspects of the game. For
example, there is a whole chapter on stance and footwork.
Philip uses his own experiences to illustrate points. A useful
summary and outline is included indicating where to contact
the ball, bat angle, backswing, stroking action, and follow
through for all strokes.

236 Reisman, Marty. THE MONEY PLAYER: THE CONFESSIONS OF AMERICA'S GREATEST TABLE TENNIS CHAMPION AND HUSTLER. New York: William Morrow, 1974. 241 p. Photos. ISBN 0-688-00273-0. LC 74-6197.

This story, although fascinating, is not a pretty one. The author has hustled, cheated, stolen, and smuggled, sometimes to stay alive, other times because he enjoyed it. Great names from the past of world table tennis are portrayed by the man who beat them and was beaten by them, and who traveled the world to do it.

237 Rudulph, Bob. STARTING AND OPERATING A TABLE TENNIS CLUB. Bridgeton, Mo.: United States Tables Tennis Association, 1972. 56 p. Dgrms., bibliog. Paperbound.

This is a how-to-do-it guide from the first step--calling a meeting of table tennis enthusiasts--through all the succeeding ones. It discusses writing a constitution, financing, intraclub and interclub activities, club facilities, lighting arrangements, and how to hold onto old members and obtain new ones.

238 Sklorz, Martin. TABLE TENNIS. EP Sport Series. Wakefield, Engl.: EP Publishing, 1971. Distributed in the United States by Charles River Books, Boston. 118 p. Photos., dgrms., dwgs. ISBN 0-7158-0582-7.

This is a detailed text with sequence photographs of all shots plus information on training and conditioning and practice exercises on and off the table. Doubles is given short shrift. The text does not read smoothly.

239 Sullivan, George. BETTER TABLE TENNIS FOR BOYS AND GIRLS. New York: Dodd, Mead, 1972. 64 p. Photos., dgrms., gloss. ISBN 0-396-06643-7. LC 72-3154.

Written with Sullivan's usual clarity, this instruction book explains the shots from push to lob with the more basic ones illustrated with sequence photographs. (The chop sequence shows more sidespin than is necessary). There are sections on doubles and on dealing with various opponents--the hitter, the blocker, and so forth. Grades five and up.

240 TABLE TENNIS. 8th ed. Know the Game Series. Wakefield, Engl.: EP Publishing, 1974. Distributed in the United States by Charles River Books, Boston. 36 p. Dgrms., dwgs. Paperbound. ISBN 0-8277-4862-0.

The essentials of the game are provided in brief. Equipment, groundstrokes, serve and return of serve, attacking and defensive play, and practice drills are included. Drawn figures illustrate points made.

241 Thonan, Larry. A GUIDE TO THE EXPERIENCE OF PLAYING TABLE
TENNIS. Nashville: Privately published by the author, 1979. Avail-
able from Thonan at 370 Wallace Road, Nashville, Tenn. 37211. 28 p.
Paperbound.

> This is a detailed analysis of the various strokes in modern
> table tennis, what they do, and what can be done against
> them. The book has text only and is for the upper inter-
> mediate and above player who knows the basics and needs
> a good theoretical foundation for what to practice to go
> higher. A small section of tactical and strategic information
> on how to play various types of opponents is also included.

242 United States Table Tennis Association. HANDBOOK. 4th rev. ed.
Bridgeton, Mo.: 1976. Var. pag. Paperbound.

> This gives basic information about the association--its consti-
> tution, bylaws, how players are ranked, international team
> selection, tournament information, and duties of umpires and
> referees.

242A _____ . TABLE TENNIS ANNUAL. Bridgeton, Mo.: 1979-- . Photos.

> A review of the previous year in table tennis, including
> national rankings, summaries of regional activities, text about
> and photographs of leading players and association officers,
> feature articles, and a list of affiliate clubs of the associa-
> tion.

243 Wasserman, Si. TABLE TENNIS. Athletic Institute Series. New York:
Sterling Publishing, 1971. 96 p. Photos. ISBN 0-8069-4328-9. LC
63-11592.

> This is primarily an account of fundamental strokes and basic
> tactics with many pictures for the young audience at which
> it is aimed. It is out of date since the loop shot and the
> expedite rule are not mentioned. Grades six and up.

CAMPS

Check the information in the "Camps" section of the introduction to this book
(pp. xvii), for information connected with the listings below. Except for the
camp in item 247, none of the camps indicated whether it was for adult and/
or junior age levels in its literature or advertisements. Presumably all ages
are accepted.

244 ATTILA MALEK TRAINING CAMP. Chicago Table Tennis Club, 2200
West Lawrence Avenue, Chicago, Ill. 60625.

245 D.J. LEE COACHING CLINICS. P.O. Box 11457, Columbus, Ohio 43211.

246 MIKE BUSH COACHING CLINIC. 48 Hardy Road, Levittown, Pa. 19056.

247 NATIONAL GIRLS TABLE TENNIS CAMP. c/o Yvonne Kronlage, 5134 Durham Road W., Columbia, Md. 21044.

248 ONTARIO TABLE TENNIS FEDERATION CAMP. 1415 Jarry Street East, Montreal, Quebec M4Y 2J1.

249 SEEMILLER TABLE TENNIS CAMP. 119 Ravilla Avenue, Pittsburgh, Pa. 15210.

250 TABLE TENNIS ENTERPRISES, LTD. P.O. Box 81, Rockville Centre, N.Y. 11571.

PERIODICALS

251 TABLE TENNIS TOPICS. United States Table Tennis Association, 12 Lake Avenue, Merrick, N.Y. 11566, 1933-- . Bimonthly.

> This lively newspaper-format magazine is the official publication of the United States Table Tennis Association (see item 215). The standard annotation applies (see p. xvii).

Chapter 8

TENNIS

The story of the "invention" of this game by Major Walter Clopton Wingfield at Nantclwyd in Wales has been told and retold, often by Wingfield himself. Wingfield printed the first rules and called the game, "Sphairistike, or Lawn Tennis"; the patent he took out in February 1874 was for a new court, not a new game. For a thorough discussion of this, see chapter 18 of Robert Henderson's fine book BALL, BAT AND BISHOP (New York: Rockport, 1947. Reprint. Detroit: Gale Research Co., 1974).

By the end of the 1970s tennis was an enormous sport and industry, with its own trade shows, warring organizations, television scandals, and astronomical salaries paid to top players. (Jimmy Connors earned more money than any athlete except Muhammad Ali in 1977.)[1] In terms of public participation, tennis is the big game. Only tennis has an instructional comic strip ("Stan Smith's Tennis Clinic"), and only tennis has "Dial a Tennis Tip" (212) 989-9223. The other racket games compare themselves with it, and truthfully say they are easier to learn, but in spite of that, the number of tennis associations, books, camps, films, and so forth exceed the totals of all the other sports in this guide put together.

ASSOCIATIONS, FOUNDATIONS, ORGANIZATIONS

252 AMERICAN MEDICAL TENNIS ASSOCIATION. P.O. Box 183, Alton, III. 52002.

> Although this organization did not respond to this editor's correspondence, it presumably conducts tournaments for physicians and their families.

253 AMERICAN TENNIS ASSOCIATION. c/o Dr. Eugene Houston, 474 Riverside Drive, New York, N.Y. 10027.

---

1. "Money in Sports: Part 2. For the Athlete How Much is Too Much?" SPORTS ILLUSTRATED, 24 July 1978, p. 42.

Founded in 1916, this is the oldest Afro-American sports organization in the United States. Black people were excluded from official tennis then, and the association was formed from local clubs to provide tournaments for black athletes to fight discrimination. Those purposes still exist, and the association, a federation of direct member clubs as well as state and regional associations, runs about fifty tournaments and helps develop junior players. A useful article to read in this connection is "Black Tennis in America," by Cheryl Davis, TENNIS magazine (see 31) December 1974, pp. 24-30.

254 ASSOCIATION FOR THE TENNIS INDUSTRY. 15720 Ventura Boulevard, Encino, Calif. 91436.

This is an association of retailers, manufacturers, and others (for example, teaching pros who have a shop) in the business end of tennis. Membership allows discounts on room rates at buying shows, faster shipments of merchandise, and other business-related benefits.

255 ASSOCIATION OF TENNIS PROFESSIONALS. 319 Country Club Road, Garland, Tex. 75040.

An association of male professional players and teachers, this group sponsors tournaments, publishes a conduct code, computer ranks its members, and offers those members benefits similar to those of a trade union. A history of the association can be found in Rich Koster's book THE TENNIS BUBBLE (see 453). It publishes a weekly newsletter.

255A FEDERATION OF TENNIS UMPIRES ASSOCIATION. c/o George Parker, P.O. Box 176, Princeton, Mass. 01541.

This organization was formed to act as a resource center for all aspects of umpiring--consistency in standards, information on financial aspects, and relationships between tournaments and officials.

256 HANDI-RACKET TENNIS. c/o Jan MacLeod, 197 High Rock Street, Needham, Mass. 02192.

This is an association that provides professional instruction for handicapped children.

257 INTERCOLLEGIATE TENNIS COACHES ASSOCIATION. c/o David Benjamin, Department of Athletics, Princeton University, Princeton, N.J. 08540.

This association of coaches in colleges and universities did not respond to this editor's correspondence. According to the ENCYCLOPEDIA OF ASSOCIATIONS (Detroit: Gale Research

Co., 1961-- . Annual), it "Seeks to teach the spirit of fair play and sportsmanship in the game . . ."

258 INTERNATIONAL OPEN TENNIS FEDERATION. c/o Harz Sports, 2132 South Forty-third Street, Omaha, Nebr. 68105.

The federation runs tournaments allowing the spaghetti (double strung) tennis rackets to be used. (Such rackets can not be used in any International Tennis Federation tournaments.) For additional information see the NEW YORK TIMES, 15 January 1979, sec. C, p. 2. For details on the racket, see TENNIS USA Magazine, December 1977, pp. 28-31, "Unraveling the Spaghetti Racket" by Alexander McNab.

259 INTERNATIONAL TENNIS ENTHUSIASTS ASSOCIATION. 338 Sierra Avenue, Moorpark, Calif. 93021.

This is an association formed as a means of getting the world-wide tennis-playing public together. It publishes a newsletter that includes such features as names and addresses of persons interested in exchanging tennis holidays and gripes about the game from the average player's point of view.

260 INTERNATIONAL TENNIS HALL OF FAME. 194 Bellevue Avenue, Newport, R.I. 02840.

This is an institution that focuses on players, memorabilia, books, and films dealing with tennis and court tennis. For articles dealing with and commenting on the past history of the hall, see TENNIS magazine (see 31) July 1976, pp. 29-34, and WORLD TENNIS (see 876) September 1976, pp. 48-51.

260A ITALO-AMERICAN TENNIS FOUNDATION. 700 Horton Drive, Silver Spring, Md. 20902.

An organization that runs summer tours to Italy for players of Italian descent under twenty one years. Matches are played against nationally ranked Italian junior players.

261 LOVE-5. c/o Ted Nordahl, Suite 2001, 919 North Michigan Avenue, Chicago, Ill. 60611.

This is an association of persons whose jobs require travel-- primarily hotel executives, exposition managers, and the like. Its purpose is to provide travelers with tennis partners.

262 MAJOR WINGFIELD CLUB. c/o Melvin Bergman, 3444 Bentley Boulevard, Toledo, Ohio 43606.

This is a social organization of members of long service to the United States Tennis Association (see 284) who have contributed much to the game at the national level. Membership

starts at age sixty and is by invitation only. Branches are
being formed in England and France.

263 MAUREEN CONNOLLY BRINKER TENNIS FOUNDATION. 5419 Wateka
Drive, Dallas Tex. 75209.

Founded by and named after a great tennis player, the foundation's primary aim is the promotion of tennis, particularly
at the junior level. It sponsors tournaments, clinics, and
other programs for boys and girls.

264 MEN'S INTERNATIONAL PROFESSIONAL TENNIS COUNCIL. c/o Association of Tennis Professionals, 319 Country Club Road, Garland, Tex.
75040.

This nine-person council consists of three player representatives, three tournament directors representatives, and three
International Tennis Federation (the worldwide governing body
for the sport) representatives who govern the Volvo Grand
Prix tennis circuit.

265 NATIONAL JUNIOR TENNIS LEAGUE. 500 East Sixty-second Street,
New York, N.Y. 10021.

An association aimed at assisting communities in developing
a broadly based participation program for youths in tennis,
it hopes that such participation will create a lifelong interest
in the game. At the time of publication of this book, over
one hundred cities had league chapters.

266 NATIONAL PUBLIC PARKS TENNIS ASSOCIATION. 155 West Washington Boulevard, Los Angeles, Calif. 90015.

This is an association of public recreation agencies and other
organizations in the United States whose objectives are to promote public tennis programs in their communities. It conducts
adult and junior tournaments for parks players.

267 NATIONAL SENIOR WOMEN'S TENNIS ASSOCIATION. 112 Park Avenue South, Winter Park, Fla. 32789.

This group conducts tournaments and publishes a newsletter for
women players over thirty-five years of age.

268 NATIONAL TENNIS ASSOCIATION. Formerly the NATIONAL INDOOR
TENNIS ASSOCIATION. P.O. Box 11097, Chicago, Ill. 60611.

This is an association of owners of indoor and outdoor commercial clubs as well as firms that make products for such
clubs. An annual convention and a newsletter serve to ex-
change ideas and information and set quality standards.

269 NATIONAL TENNIS FOUNDATION. 194 Bellevue Avenue, Newport, R.I. 02840.

> This association's purpose is to encourage and develop tennis interest, particularly on the junior and amateur levels. It conducts the national fast serve tournament and co-sponsors a tennis rating system (see pp. 185–86). In 1977 it merged with the International Tennis Hall of Fame (see 260).

270 NORTH AMERICAN INDIAN TENNIS ASSOCIATION. Haskell Indian Junior College, Lawrence, Kans. 66044.

> This organization did not respond to this editor's correspondence. According to TENNIS magazine (see 31) May 1978, pp. 20–21, it encourages Indian participation in the game and conducts the American Indian tennis championships.

271 NORTH AMERICAN TENNIS TOURNAMENT DIRECTORS ASSOCIATION. 536 Moredon Road, Huntington Valley, Pa. 19006.

> This group is a liaison organization for tournament directors to share knowledge and ideas on operation and promotion.

272 PEPSI-COLA MOBILE TENNIS. Pepsi-Cola Co., Purchase, N.Y. 10577.

> This program did not respond to this editor's correspondence, but apparently is one whose purpose is to bring introductory level tennis to youths in economically disadvantaged areas. Free instruction and equipment are given.

273 PETER BURWASH INTERNATIONAL LIMITED. 1909 Ala Wai Boulevard, Suite 1507, Honolulu, Hawaii 96815.

> This is an organization of traveling tennis professionals who take clinics to any part of the world. All professionals are trained in the Burwash instructional system, which encompasses not only a teaching method but also such practical aspects as accounting and racket stringing.

274 PROFESSIONAL TENNIS REGISTRY--USA. 1629 K Street N.W., Washington, D.C. 20006.

> This is an organization that tests and certifies tennis teachers via a three-part examination that includes a written section, a skill demonstration section, and a demonstration of teaching ability. Members are required to attend an annual refresher course.

275 PRO TENNIS REFEREES ASSOCIATION. 46-B Crestwood Drive, Huntington Station, N.Y. 11746.

> This is an organization providing referees, umpires, and lines-

persons for professional tennis tournaments throughout the United States. Members are selected based on scouting reports and ratings submitted by evaluators.

276   RICK ELLSTEIN TENNIS INSTITUTE AND RESEARCH CENTER. Box 1, Roslyn, N.Y. 11576.

This institute offers courses in techniques for teaching tennis.

277   SUPER SENIOR TENNIS. P.O. Box 5165, Charlottesville, Va. 22903.

This is an organization designed to give tournament competition to men in six age categories--fifty-five through fifty-nine; sixty through sixty-four; sixty-five through sixty-nine; seventy through seventy-five; seventy-five through eighty; and eighty and over. A newsletter giving tournament dates and results is sent to members.

278   TENNIS & CINEMA PRODUCTIONS INTERNATIONAL. P.O. Box 117, Jamaica, N.Y. 11431.

This is an association that both sponsors tournaments and does video analysis of an individual player's game for a fee.

279   TENNIS CANADA. 333 River Road, Vanier, Ontario K1L 8B9.

This is the governing body for amateur and professional tennis in Canada. It is a federation of provincial and regional tennis associations that coordinates and sanctions tournaments, encourages public participation and the development of younger players in the game, and works to upgrade coaching skills.

280   TENNIS FOUNDATION OF NORTH AMERICA. 200 Castlewood Road, North Palm Beach, Fla. 33408.

This is an organization of manufacturers of tennis equipment and clothing whose purpose is to encourage the growth of the game with particular emphasis on relieving the shortage of playing facilities--more courts and better use of existing courts via illumination.

281   TENNIS GRAND MASTERS, INCORPORATED. Williamsburg Court, 7710 Shawnee Run Road, Cincinnati, Ohio 45243.

This organization provides a tournament circuit for players of forty-five or over who won a major national or world championship and who may "still be able to play tennis at a level that would be interesting to the public."

282 UNITED STATES PROFESSIONAL CELEBRITY TENNIS ASSOCIATION.
12953 Marlboro Street, Los Angeles, Calif. 90049.

This organization helps sponsors charities that wish to put on
a professional celebrity event by providing and guaranteeing
the appearance of tennis and show business stars.

283 UNITED STATES PROFESSIONAL TENNIS ASSOCIATION. 1620 Gulf of
Mexico Drive, Colony Beach and Tennis Resort, Longboat Key, Fla. 33548.

This is an association whose purposes are to "raise the standards of teaching tennis as a profession (and) to increase interest and awareness in the sport." Active members must derive
a major portion of their income from teaching; associate members are those who have some full-time connection with tennis
in an executive, administrative, or commercial capacity. The
association runs a teaching academy, certifies teachers via
playing, teaching, and written examinations. It runs national
and divisional tournaments for members.

284 UNITED STATES TENNIS ASSOCIATION. 51 East Forty-second Street,
New York, N.Y. 10017.

The United States National Lawn Tennis Association was organized in 1881. In 1920 the name was changed to United
States Lawn Tennis Association and in 1975 to United States
Tennis Association. The association's purpose, in its own
words, is "to develop tennis as a means of healthful recreation and physical fitness and maintain high standards of ama-
teurism, fair play and sportsmanship." In pursuit of that aim
it engages in a multitude of activities, only some of which
are highlighted here. It compiles local, regional, and national rankings; sanctions thousands of tennis tournaments;
runs a development program to assist those interested in setting
up local tennis programs; runs an Education and Research Center (at 729 Alexander Road, Princeton, N.J. 08540) that answers questions from anyone on any aspect of the game, sells
private publishers' books about tennis and has an extensive
publication program of its own, maintains a film library and
makes those films available to interested parties; conducts
teacher training workshops; and has seventeen sectional offices
and an enormous number of committees.

285 UNITED STATES TENNIS COURT AND TRACK BUILDERS ASSOCIATION.
1800 Pickwick Avenue, Glenview, Ill. 60056.

This association publishes guide specifications for all types of
courts and running tracks. Members are builders, engineers,
manufacturers, and architects in Canada and the United States.
Other areas of concern are maintenance and repair, fencing,
lighting, and safety.

286 UNITED STATES TENNIS WRITERS ASSOCIATION. c/o Barry Lorge, Sports Department, Washington Post, 1150 Fifteenth Street, N.W., Washington, D.C. 20071.

This association serves as a voice for persons who write about the game and concerns itself with such matters as press facilities at tournaments.

287 VAN DER MEER TENNIS UNIVERSITY. 2150 Franklin Street, Oakland, Calif. 94612.

This is a ten-day program that offers both administrative and on-court expertise to anyone interested in teaching the game. The program is given at different locations each year.

288 VIC BRADEN TENNIS COLLEGE. Coto de Caza, 22000 Plano Trabuco Canyon Road, Trabuco Canyon, Calif. 92678.

This is primarily a tennis camp for both average players and those wishing to be teachers. It is listed here because research activities in tennis are carried on at the college. No answers were received from the college to questions asking for details on that aspect of the operation.

289 WOMEN IN TENNIS. 9945 Young Drive, Beverly Hills, Calif. 90212.

This is the most active division of Women In Sports, Inc., which supplements the tournament careers of professional women in sports by providing and locating such opportunities as exhibitions, clinics, and appearances, and provides business and personal management services.

290 WOMEN'S TENNIS ASSOCIATION. 1604 Union Street, San Francisco, Calif. 94123.

This is an organization working for better prize money, better playing conditions, and more opportunities for women in professional tennis. It publishes a newsletter and hopes to give women players a unified voice in working toward further development of the game.

291 WORLD CHAMPIONSHIP TENNIS. 1990 First National Bank Building, Dallas, Tex. 75202.

WCT promotes a series of men's professional tournaments that cumulatively amount to the richest circuit in the world. There are three component parts: the Caesars Palace Challenge Cup, the World Series of Tennis, and the Tournament of Champions. For a history of WCT see the book by Rich Koster, THE TENNIS BUBBLE (see 453).

292 WORLD TEAM TENNIS. c/o Freeman/McCue, 18007 Skypark Circle, Irvine, Calif. 92714.

This league was a blend begun in 1973 of what had been an individual sport with a team concept. The teams represented different U.S. cities, and a format of three doubles and two singles competitions was used, with victory based on cumulative games won. No matches have been scheduled in recent years, but there is still a faint hope that the concept can be revived. For details on past years consult Hoffman (see 448) and Koster (see 453).

293 WORLD TRIPLES TENNIS ASSOCIATION. Texarkana Racquet Club, One Courtside Lane, Texarkana, Tex. 75503.

Membership includes those persons who have participated in the annual triples (three persons on a side) tournament held at the Texarkana Racquet Club.

AUDIOVISUAL MATERIALS

Only the names or acronyms of distributors are given in the annotations below. An alphabetical list of distributors' full names with addresses can be found in the appendix, pp. 205-10.

A few books on tennis are available for the handicapped on phono-records and that has been indicated in the annotations for them. The authors are Ashe (see 429), Budge (see 436), Jacobs (see 508), King (see 452), McPhee (see 845), and Riggs (see 464).

Those who believe that feature films that include tennis scenes began with STRANGERS ON A TRAIN (1951, director Alfred Hitchcock) and ended with PLAYERS (1979, director Anthony Harvey) are referred to the article in TENNIS magazine (see 31) by Richard Szathmary in the June 1975 issue, "Why Does Hollywood Make Such Lousy Tennis Movies?" The author forgot TEA AND SYMPATHY,[1] but his article is a fine survey of what has been done.

To keep up to date on new films the best single source is the United States Tennis Association's Education and Research Center, 729 Alexander Road, Princeton, New Jersey 08540. They annually publish and sell a new list (including worthwhile older films). The International Tennis Hall of Fame (see 260) keeps many older films in its library.

---

[1]. He also forgot HOT RACKETS (date undetermined, director Robert McCallum), probably deliberately. In the interest of research the editor recently viewed this film. Its running time was about one hour and thirty-five minutes, five minutes of which were devoted to badly played tennis.

294 ADVANCED TENNIS. 16mm. film. Black and white. Sound. 11 minutes. 1946. Rental: University of Illinois; University of Tennessee.

Bill Tilden explains and demonstrates fundamental strokes.

295 ADVANTAGE BORG. 16mm. film. Color. Sound. 26 minutes. 1977. Rental: University of Colorado; University of Kansas; Kent State University; Oklahoma State University; Pennsylvania State University.

The career and personality of the Swedish champion are featured.

296 ADVANTAGE UNITED STATES. 16mm. film or 3/4- or 1/2-inch videocassette. Color. Sound. 24 minutes. 1979. Purchase: McManus/Wilson. Rental: USTA.

This film tells the story of the United States Davis Cup quest in 1978, showing victories over South Africa, Chile, and Sweden, as well as the final round defeat of Great Britain.

297 AETNA WORLD CUP 1976 HIGHLIGHTS. 16mm. film or videocassette. Color. Sound. 29 minutes. Free loan: Aetna.

This shows the Hartford, Connecticut, tournament in which the United States won over Australia for the first time since 1971.

298 ALTHEA GIBSON. Audio cassette with thirty-five student-response booklets. 20 minutes. Purchase: Imperial International Learning Corporation.

This is a biography of Gibson. Grades four to eight.

299 AND THEN THERE WAS ONE. 16mm. film or 3/4- or 1/2-inch videocassette. Color. Sound. 26 minutes. 1977. Purchase and Rental: Film Comm; Sportlite.

Jimmy Connors defeats Dick Stockton to win the World Championship of Tennis finals, Dallas 1977. Highlights of earlier matches are shown.

300 APPROACH TO TENNIS. 16mm. film. Color or black and white. Sound. 14 minutes. 1967. Also available in French and Spanish. Purchase: Association; Macmillan. Rental: Association; South Florida University; University of Wisconsin at Madison. ISBN 0-699-01458-1. LC 75-703840.

Arthur Ashe, Gene Scott, and others demonstrate techniques of single play at the West Side Tennis Club in Forest Hills. Scenes from the U.S. championships are included.

301 ARTHUR CLAIMS THE GOLD. 16mm. film or 3/4- or 1/2-inch video-cassette. Color. Sound. 27 minutes. 1975. Purchase: Film

Comm (16mm. film only); Sportlite (16mm. film only). Rental: Film Comm (16mm. film only); Sportlite (16mm. film only).

Arthur Ashe defeats Bjorn Borg to win the World Championship of Tennis finals, Dallas 1975. Highlights of earlier matches are shown.

302 AT 2 P.M. PRECISELY. 16mm. film. Color. Sound. 52 minutes. 1971. Free loan: USTA. LC 72-700222.

John Newcombe defeats Stan Smith to win Wimbledon, 1971. Highlights of earlier men's and women's matches are shown.

303 BASIC TENNIS SKILLS IN ACTION. 35mm. captioned filmstrip. Color. Sound (cassette). 45 frames. 6 minutes. Purchase: Eye Gate.

This covers the fundamentals of the game. Grades seven to twelve.

304 BASIC TENNIS STROKES. 16mm. film. Black and white. Sound. 10 minutes. 1956. Rental: Washington State University. ISBN 0-699-02410-2.

Frank Beeman, coach at Michigan State University, demonstrates proper footwork, body movements, grips, and the forehand, backhand, serve, volley, lob, and smash.

305 BEGINNING TENNIS. 16mm. film. Color and black and white. 14 minutes. 1960. Rental: Idaho State University; University of Illinois; University of Minnesota; Pennsylvania State University. ISBN 0-699-02798-5. LC FiA61-74.

The film shows an instructor teaching tennis to beginning and advanced students. It includes an analysis of the basic strokes and playing situations using those strokes.

306 BILLIE JEAN KING. 16mm. film or videocassette. Color. Sound. 22 minutes. 1972. Purchase: Paramount Communications. Rental: University of Arizona; University of Michigan; Paramount Communications; Pennsylvania State University; Southern Illinois University; University of Wisconsin at La Crosse.

King is shown in action against Chris Evert and in profile in short interview sequences.

307 BILLIE JEAN KING: THE MATCH OF THE CENTURY. 35mm. filmstrip. Color. Sound (cassette or phonograph record). 48 frames. 9 minutes. 1976. Purchase: SVE.

King's win over Bobby Riggs is presented in a filmstrip designed to motivate pupils to seek more information via books and magazines. Grades four to nine.

308 BILLIE JEAN KING'S TENNIS FOR EVERYONE. Thirteen 16mm. films. Color. Sound. 10 minutes each. 1975. Purchase: Association; Kent State University (films 9 and 12 only); Macmillan. Rental: Association; Macmillan. LC 76-701252.

King demonstrates to and teaches pupils from ages twelve to fifty. Contents: (1) THE SERVE. (2) THE FOREHAND. (3) THE BACKHAND. (4) THE VOLLEY. (5) STRATEGY IN SINGLES PLAY. (6) DOUBLES IS A PARTNERSHIP. (7) SPECIAL SHOTS. (8) SOME GOOD PRACTICE DRILLS. (9) DO'S AND DONT'S--QUESTIONS AND ANSWERS. (10) DON'T PRACTICE YOUR MISTAKES. (11) MORE ON SERVES. (12) BILLIE JEAN: A STUDY IN MOTION. (13) GETTING IN SHAPE.

309 BILL TILDEN'S TENNIS FOR BEGINNERS. 16mm. film. Black and white. Sound. 11 minutes. Rental: Indiana University. ISBN 0-699 03150-8. See also film number 387.

Tilden explains proper grips and hitting for groundstrokes.

309A BJORN BORG: THE PLAYER. 16mm. film. Color. Sound. 20 minutes. 1979. Rental: USTA.

310 BRINGING HOME THE PRIZE. 16mm. film. Color. Sound. 27 minutes. 1973. Free loan: USTA.

The 1973 Kemper International Tennis Tournament is shown with Roger Taylor vs. Arthur Ashe for the title.

311 CHALLENGE. 16mm. film. Color. Sound. 26 minutes. 1970. Purchase and Rental: Sportlite; Sports Investors, Inc.; Tennis Films International. LC 71-705984.

Arthur Ashe and Stan Smith win the Davis Cup against Ilie Nastase and Ion Tiriac.

312 CHAMPIONSHIP TENNIS. 16mm. film. Color. Sound. 20 minutes. Purchase and Rental: Tennis Films International.

Strategy in singles and doubles is demonstrated by Don Gale and Butch Krikorian.

313 CHAMPIONSHIP TENNIS. 16mm. film. Black and white. Sound. 52 minutes. 1966. University of Iowa. ISBN 0-699-04730-7.

Don Budge and Bill Leonard comment on international tournament play.

314 CHRIS EVERT--TENNIS. 35mm. captioned filmstrip. Color. Sound (cassette). Purchase: Eye Gate.

This is one of a series of Eye Gate filmstrips on modern sports figures. Basic facts are given about Evert's career.

315 DALLAS '78. 16mm. film or 3/4- or 1/2-inch videocassette. Color. Sound. 27 minutes. 1978. Purchase and Rental: Film Comm; Sportlite.

Vitas Gerulaitis defeats Eddie Dibbs to win the World Championship of Tennis finals, Dallas 1978. Highlights of earlier matches are shown.

316 DAVIS CUP IMPRESSIONS. 16mm. film. Color. Sound. 28 minutes. 1974. Free loan: Local Bell Telephone business office in some areas. LC 74-702630.

The highlights of the 1973 finals between Australia and the United States are shown.

317 DUEL IN THE DESERT. 16mm. film. Color. Sound. 27 minutes. 1976. Free loan: USTA.

Highlights of matches in the 1976 American Airlines Tennis Games in Mission Hills, California, are shown, culminating in Jimmy Connors's win over Roscoe Tanner.

318 ELEMENTARY TENNIS INSTRUCTION. 16mm. film. Color. Sound. 15 minutes. Rental: USTA. LC 73-700400.

Dennis Van der Meer demonstrates tennis skills for young beginners using the graduated length method (hand to paddle to racket). Grades one to six.

319 FAST ACTION SUPERTHINK. Module containing 6 sound cassettes, 12 duplicating masters and a teacher's guide. Purchase: Troll.

Althea Gibson, Arthur Ashe, and Billie Jean King are three of six sports stars presented in a unit designed to help students develop their critical listening and thinking skills. Grades four to six.

320 FIRST GAME, FIRST SET. 16mm. film. Color. Sound. 20 minutes. 1974. Purchase: Trans World International. Rental: USTA.

Pictures of many past great players are shown in this history beginning with court tennis and going through the origins of lawn tennis to the modern game.

321 FOREHAND AND BACKHAND. 16mm. film. Color. Sound. 15 minutes. Also available in French and Spanish. Purchase and Rental: Association (English only); Macmillan. LC 72-701570.

Coach Marty Shaw teaches the two strokes, including practice patterns and drills.

322 FOREST HILLS TENNIS. 3/4-inch videocassette. Color. Sound. 20 minutes. Purchase: Video Tape Network.

> Essentials of the forehand, backhand, volley, and serve are shown.

323 FUNDAMENTALS OF TENNIS. 16mm. film. Black and white. Sound. 20 minutes. 1952. Rental: University of Arizona; University of Colorado; Connecticut University; University of Iowa; University of Minnesota; Northern Illinois University; Pennsylvania State University; Utah State University; Washington State University. ISBN 0-699-11461-6. LC Fia55-553.

> Using slow motion, Don Budge demonstrates the strokes.

324 GATERS FEVER '78. 16mm. film or 3/4- or 1/2-inch videocassette. Color. Sound. 18 minutes. 1978. Purchase: McManus/Wilson.

> Members of the World Team Tennis Golden Gaters team are shown in matches against other league opponents.

325 GO FOR A WINNER. 16mm. film. Color. Sound. 37 minutes. 1976. Purchase and Rental: AMF Head.

> Vic Braden presents an informative and humorous approach to doubles strategy, particularly mixed doubles.

325A THE GREAT ENGLISH GARDEN PARTY. 16mm. film. Color. Sound. 52 minutes. 1979. Purchase: Trans World International.

326 THE GREATEST TENNIS MATCH OF ALL TIME. 16mm. film or 3/4- or 1/2-inch videocassette. Color. Sound. 26 minutes. 1972. Purchase and Rental: Film Comm; Sportlite. See also 624.

> Ken Rosewall defeats Rod Laver to win the World Championship of Tennis finals, Dallas 1972. Highlights of earlier matches are shown.

327 GREAT MOMENTS IN THE HISTORY OF TENNIS. 16mm. film. Black and white. Sound. 40 minutes. 1968. Free loan: USTA. LC FiA67950.

> A compilation of old movie clips of such great players as Bill Tilden, Suzanne Lenglen, Don Budge, Jack Kramer, Pancho Gonzales, Althea Gibson, and Billie Jean King.

328 A GUIDE TO TENNIS. 16mm. film. Color. Sound. 22 minutes. 1971. Purchase: Brentwood; Sportlite. Rental: Brentwood; University of Minnesota; Sportlite; University of Wisconsin at Madison. ISBN 0-699-12536-7.

> This is an introduction to the game in which teenage players demonstrate fundamental strokes, ball control and strategy.

329 HACKERS AND HEROES. 16mm. film. Color. Sound. 28 minutes.
Free loan: Association (only to the six New England states).

Tennis professionals at Longwood play in the U.S. Professional
Tennis Championships. Arthur Ashe and Jimmy Connors comment on the pro game in the 1970s. Bud Collins narrates.

330 HELEN WILLS MOODY. 16mm. film. Black and white. Sound. 15
minutes. Purchase: Star.

Produced from historical footage of the Fox Movietone News
Library, this is the story of "Miss Poker Face," the women's
champion at age seventeen.

331 HOW TO'S OF TENNIS. 16mm. film. Black and white. Sound. 25
minutes. 1964. Purchase and Rental: 9200 Film Center.

Top professionals demonstrate fundamentals of the game.

332 INNER TENNIS. Six 3/4-inch videocassettes. Color. Sound. 60 minutes each. 1976. Purchase and Rental: Inner Game Resources.

Instructor Tim Gallwey explains the term he made famous
(see 597 and 598). Contents: (1) FEAR. (2) HABITS. (3)
BASICS. (4) CONCENTRATION. (5) AWARENESS. (6)
COMPETITION.

333 IN PURSUIT OF NUMBER ONE. 16mm. film or 3/4- or 1/2-inch videocassette. Color. Sound. 25 minutes. 1977. Purchase: Sports Films
and Talents (film only); Sports World Cinema (videocassette only). Rental:
Sports Films and Talents (film only).

This shows highlights of the 1977 National Indoor Professional
Championships in the Philadelphia Spectrum. Dick Stockton
defeated Jimmy Connors in the finals, and there are scenes
of many of the top professionals--Bjorn Borg, Rod Laver, Ken
Rosewall. Bud Collins narrates.

334 INSTRUCTIONAL TENNIS FEATURING ILIE NASTASE. Four 16mm. films.
Color. Sound. 1975. Purchase: Sterling.

Contents: (1) BACKHAND. 13 minutes. LC 76-701873.
(2) FOREHAND. 12 minutes. LC 76-701874. (3) SERVE
AND VOLLEY. 13 minutes. LC 76-701876. (4) STRATEGY
SHOTS. 10 minutes. LC 76-701877.

335 INTRODUCTION TO TENNIS. 16mm. film. Color. Sound. 14 minutes. 1968. Rental: University of Arizona; University of Illinois; Uni-
versity of Iowa; University of Nebraska at Lincoln; South Carolina Uni-
versity; Syracuse University; University of Texas. ISBN 0-699-15200-3.
LC 71-711640.

This film shows tennis to be a fine lifetime sport and follows professional Bill Lufler on a typical working day.

336 INTROSKILL TENNIS. Two super 8mm. cartridges (Kodak or technicolor). Silent with subtitles and a commentary booklet. 4 minutes each. 1975. Purchase: Champions on Film.

Here are introductory skills and basic shots as they might be taught in a clinic. Contents: (1) BASIC GROUND STROKES. (2) SERVE AND VOLLEY.

337 I WANT TO BE A TENNIS PLAYER. 35mm. filmstrip. Color. Sound (cassette or phonograph record). 30 frames. Purchase: Educational Enrichment Materials.

This is based on the book of the same title by Eugene Baker (see 726). Grades kindergarten to three.

338 JAMES MASON AT WIMBLEDON. 16mm. film. Color. Sound. 52 minutes. 1976. Free loan: Rolex. Purchase: Trans World International.

Mason shares his impressions and acts as narrator of highlights of the 1976 Wimbledon championships. In addition to special coverage of the men's and women's singles finals, the film focuses on such backstage matters as heat, pressure, and crowds.

339 JOHN NEWCOMBE. 16mm. film or videocassette. Color. Sound. 22 minutes. 1972. Purchase: Paramount Communications. Rental: University of Arizona (16mm. film only); University of Illinois (16mm. film only); University of Michigan (16mm. film only); Paramount Communications; Pennsylvania State University; University of Wisconsin at La Crosse. ISBN 0-699-15813-3. LC 73-701967.

This film shows Newcombe practicing for and then losing a match in a World Championship of Tennis tournament. Some glimpses of his personal life are shown.

340 KEMPER INTERNATIONAL DESERT CLASSIC. 16mm. film. Color. Sound. 25 minutes. 1974. Free loan: USTA.

James Franciscus narrates the action at this 1974 tournament, featuring such names as Arthur Ashe, Marty Riessen, Rod Laver, and Roscoe Tanner. The celebrity doubles with Bill Cosby is also covered.

341 KILLER INSTINCT. 16mm. film or 3/4- or 1/2-inch videocassette. Color. Sound. 30 minutes. 1977. Purchase and Rental: Sports World Cinema.

Highlights of the 1977 American Airlines games are shown with Brian Gottfried defeating Guillermo Vilas in the finals. Some instruction is also given.

342 LEARNING TO READ TENNIS. 16mm. film. Color. Sound. 10 minutes. 1972. Purchase: Tennis Films International.

Angela Buxton demonstrates how to anticipate what your opponent's next shot will be.

343 LET'S START WITH THE FOREHAND. 16mm. film. Color. Sound. 23 minutes. 1973. Purchase: Golden Door. Rental: University of California; Golden Door; Pennsylvania State University.

Instructor Allie Ritzenberg demonstrates fundamentals--grip, stance, weight balance, and the strokes. Slow motion and stop action are used.

344 LOVE TENNIS. Ten 3/4- or 1/2-inch videocassettes. Color. Sound. 30 minutes each. Purchase and Rental: Maryland Center for Public Broadcasting; Public Television Library.

Instructors Dan Candy and Lew Gerrard give basic instruction on strokes and strategy. Segments from the 1971 U.S. indoor tournament in Salisbury, Maryland, feature such players as Clark Graebner, Cliff Richey, and Ilie Nastase.

345 MARGARET COURT'S TENNIS FILM SERIES. Two 16mm. films. Color. Sound. 25 minutes each. 1972. Purchase: Scholastic Coach. Rental: USTA.

The films stress both individual and group instruction methods. The first covers basic strokes, spins, approach and passing shots, and physical fitness. The second deals with advanced strokes, practicing, footwork, and conditioning.

346 MARTY RIESSEN. 16mm. film or videocassette. Color. Sound. 22 minutes. 1972. Purchase: Paramount Communications. Rental (in all cases 16mm. film only): University of Arizona; University of Illinois; University of Michigan; Paramount Communications; Pennsylvania State University. LC 74-702688.

Riessen loses a tough match to Tom Gorman. He describes how he handles the pressures of a pro tour.

347 NASTY. 16mm. film. Color. Sound. 15 minutes. 1977. Purchase: Carousel Films. The film is one of two in a double program that must be purchased together. The second film is titled, HOW TO LIVE TO BE 100.

This was originally produced for CBS's "60 Minutes." Ilie Nastase is interviewed, and other top players are asked to give their impressions of him.

348 THE NEW ERA. 16mm. film or 3/4- or 1/2-inch videocassette. Color. Sound. 27 minutes. 1973. Purchase and Rental: Film Comm; Sportlite.

Stan Smith defeats Arthur Ashe to win the World Championship of Tennis finals, Dallas 1973. Highlights of earlier matches are shown. It is narrated by Charlton Heston.

349 ON TENNIS SERIES. Three 16mm. films or 3/4- or 1/2-inch videocassettes. Color and black and white. Sound. 15 minutes each. 1969. Purchase: Films, Inc. Rental (in all cases 16mm. film only): Films, Inc.; Indiana University (parts 1 and 2 only); Iowa State University.

These films feature Vic Braden, Billie Jean King, and Eric Van Dillen. Contents: (1) BASIC SERVE AND ADVANCED SERVES. ISBN 0-699-21437-8. LC 77-700933. (2) GROUNDSTROKES: FOREHAND AND BACKHAND. ISBN 0-699-21436-X. LC 70-700934. (3) VOLLEY, LOB, AND OVERHEAD. ISBN 0-699-21438-6. LC 74-700935.

350 PANCHO. 16mm. film. Color. Sound. 26 minutes. 1971. Rental: Ivy.

This film offers a portrait of Pancho Gonzales: who he is and what he thinks about life as well as tennis.

351 PLAYING BETTER TENNIS. 16mm. film or super 8mm. cartridge (Kodak, Fairchild, Supermatic, or Technicolor). Color. Sound. 25 minutes. 1976. Purchase and Rental: Sports Films and Talents. Available as one film or in segments.

Rosie Casals, Wendy Overton, Dennis Ralston, and Marty Riessen illustrate how to hit the groundstrokes, serve, volley, lob, and smash. Doubles strategy is also discussed.

352 PLAY IT STRAIGHT. 16mm. film or 3/4- or 1/2-inch videocassette. Color. Sound. 30 minutes. 1978. Purchase and Rental: Johnson-Nyquist.

Vic Braden, using a question and answer format, illustrates some aspects of Nick Powel's "THE CODE" (see 803). These are the unwritten rules of tennis etiquette.

353 PORTRAIT OF A CHAMPION--TENNIS. 16mm. film. Color. Sound. 12 minutes. 1976. Free loan: Converse.

Mark Wheaton, 1975 Minnesota state high school champion, describes and illustrates the methods he uses to stay fit. He focuses on the attitude and dedication that resulted in his success.

354 PRACTICE WITH THE PROS. 16mm. film. Color. Sound. 28 minutes. 1976. Free loan: Converse.

Vic Braden illustrates teaching tips with demonstrations by Tom Gorman, Brian Gottfried, Jim McManus, Charles Pasarell, Ismail el Shafei, Harold Solomon, and Roscoe Tanner.

355 PRIDE IN PERFORMANCE. 16mm. film. Color. Sound. 13 minutes. 1977. Purchase and Rental: Vantage.

> This is a film on motivation using examples from tennis competition with such players as Arthur Ashe, Bjorn Borg, Jimmy Connors, Ilie Nastase, Raul Ramirez, and Roscoe Tanner.

356 THE PROS. 16mm. film or super 8mm. cartridge. Color. Sound. 25 minutes. 1972. Purchase and Rental: Sports Investors.

> With many slow motion shots set to a rock music background, this documentary shows both triumphant and tragic moments at the 1972 United States Open, particularly Arthur Ashe in defeat and Ilie Nastase in victory.

357 REVOLUTION IN CHURCH ROAD. 16mm. film or 3/4- or 1/2-inch videocassette. Color. Sound. 52 minutes. 1974. Purchase: Trans World International. Purchase and Rental: Sports World Cinema.

> Here are scenes of Wimbledon in 1974 when Jimmy Connors demolished Ken Rosewall and Chris Evert won her first championship.

357A ROBERT F. KENNEDY PRO-CELEBRITY TENNIS TOURNAMENT. 16mm. film or 3/4- or 1/2-inch videocassette. Color. Sound. 8 minutes. 1979. Purchase: McManus/Wilson.

358 ROY EMERSON TALKING TENNIS. Two audio cassette tapes. 40 minutes per side. Purchase: Sales and Marketing Associates.

> Emerson presents his ideas about the critical elements involved in basic strokes. He also discusses the attitudes that helped him enjoy the game while competing at the top level.

359 THE SERVICE. 16mm. film. Color, and black and white. Sound. 14 minutes. Purchase: Sportlite; Tennis Films International. Rental: Sportlite.

> Gary Thorne, Syracuse University coach, covers basic and advanced serves.

359A SEVEN DAYS IN MAY. 16mm. film. Color. Sound. 26 minutes. 1979. Purchase and Rental: Film Comm; Sportlite.

360 SHOOTOUT AT HIGH NOON. 16mm. or 3/4- or 1/2-inch videocassette. Color. Sound. 26 minutes. 1971. Purchase and Rental: Film Comm; Sportlite.

> Ken Rosewall defeats Rod Laver in the World Championship of Tennis finals, Dallas 1971. Highlights of earlier matches are shown.

361 65,000 MILES TO DALLAS. 16mm. film or 3/4- or 1/2-inch videocassette. Color. Sound. 25 minutes. 1974. Purchase (in all cases 16mm. film only);

Film Comm; Sportlite. Rental: (16mm. film only); Sportlite (16mm. film only); Sports World Cinema.

John Newcombe defeats Bjorn Borg in the World Championship of Tennis finals, Dallas 1974. Highlights of earlier matches are shown. It is narrated by Charlton Heston.

362 STROKES. 16mm. film. Color. Sound. 13 minutes. Purchase and Rental: Brentwood; Sportlite.

The film highlights Myron McNamara with teenagers in mixed doubles. Stop action demonstrates the basics from grip through groundstrokes.

363 TECHNIQUE OF TENNIS. 16mm. film. Black and white. Sound. 9 minutes. 1959. Rental: University of Illinois. ISBN 0-699-28965-3.

Lloyd Budge shows correct grips, how to hit groundstrokes and serves, and how to play the net. Some slow motion shots are shown.

364 TENNIS. 16mm. film or seven 8mm. film cartridges. Color. Silent. 11 minutes. 1967. Purchase: Scope.

Elain Mason, founder of the graduated length method of instruction, is the demonstrator. Contents of the cartridges: (1) GRIP AND FOREHAND; (2) GRIP AND BACKHAND; (3) VOLLEY PROGRESSIONS; (4) SERVE PROGRESSIONS; (5) FOOTWORK--RUNNING APPROACH; (6) FOOTWORK--STEP AWAY PATTERN; (7) SELF-DROP.

365 TENNIS. Six 8mm. captioned film loops (Kodak or Technicolor). Color. Silent. 3 1/2 minutes each. 1969. Purchase: Champions on Film.

This is a series by Chet Murphy using slow motion freeze frames. Contents: (1) FOREHAND GROUNDSTROKES. LC 71-700673; (2) BACKHAND GROUNDSTROKES. LC 74-700671; (3) THE SERVE. LC 79-700675; (4) VOLLEYS AND HALF-VOLLEYS. LC 72-700676; (5) LOBS AND SMASHES. LC 75-700674; and (6) FOOTWORK. LC 78-700672.

366 TENNIS. Four super 8mm. film loops. Color. Silent. 4 minutes each. 1969. Purchase: Association.

Bill Lufler is the consultant. Contents: (1) FOREHAND; (2) BACKHAND; (3) SERVE AND SMASH; (4) COURT POSITION AND VOLLEY.

367 TENNIS. Sixteen super 8mm. film loop cartridges. Color. Silent. 3 1/2 minutes each. 1970. Purchase: AAHPERD; Athletic Institute; A.W. Peller; Mason; SVE.

Dave Snyder is the consultant. Two sets are available. Number 1: men's tennis. Contents: (1) FOREHAND STROKE. LC 75-71187; (2) FOREHAND VARIATIONS. LC 79-71188; (3) BACKHAND STROKE. LC 72-71189; (4) BACKHAND VARIATIONS. LC 77-71190; (5) VOLLEY. LC 70-71191; (6) BASIC SERVE. LC 74-71192; (7) FLAT SERVE, AMERICAN TWIST SERVE. LC 78-71193; (8) OVERHEAD. LC 71-71194. Number 2: women's tennis. Contents: (1) FOREHAND STROKE. LC 75-71179; (2) FOREHAND VARIATIONS. LC 70-71180; (3) BACKHAND STROKE. LC 73-71181; (4) BACKHAND VARIATIONS. LC 77-71182; (5) VOLLEY. LC 70-71183; (6) BASIC SERVE. LC 74-71184; (7) FLAT SERVE, AMERICAN TWIST SRRVE. LC 78-71185; and (8) OVERHEAD. LC 71-71186.

368 TENNIS. Two 16mm. films, super 8mm. films, or videocassettes. 7 and 6 minutes. 1976. Purchase: Champions on Film.

Chet Murphy shows basic to advanced techniques, with some slow motion. Contents: (1) BACKHAND, FOREHAND, SERVES, and (2) VOLLEYS, LOBS, SMASHES, FOOTWORK.

369 TENNIS. 16mm. film (sound), super 8mm. film (silent), or 3/4- or 1/2-inch videocassettes (sound). Color. 20 minutes. 1976. Purchase: Forest Hills Productions (film only); Video Tape Network (videocassetess only).

United States Professional Tennis Association pro Chris Busa demonstrates the forehand, backhand, volley, and serve. The film utilizes slow motion and freeze frames.

370 TENNIS. Four 16mm. films or super 8mm. cassettes, loop films. Purchase: AAHPERD; Athletic Institute; A.W. Peller (8mm. loop only); Mason. Rental: USTA.

Dick Gould and Tom Chivington demonstrate how to do tennis group instruction. Contents: (1) FOREHAND AND BACKHAND STROKE FUNDAMENTALS. 23 minutes. LC 76-701215; (2) APPLYING FOREHAND AND BACKHAND STROKES. 20 minutes. LC 76-701216; (3) THE SERVE. 20 minutes. LC 76-701217; (4) NET PLAY. 21 minutes. LC 76-701218.

371 TENNIS. This package one comes in four separate formats as follows: 1. Seven super 8mm. films. Color. Silent with printed script. 50 feet each. Purchase: Cloud 9; Sportlite (either individually or as a set).

Jack Roach demonstrates and explains strokes and strategy, using slow motion and freeze action to emphasize key points. Contents: (1) FOREHAND; (2) BACKHAND; (3) VOLLEY; (4) SERVE; (5) LOB, OVERHEAD; (6) SINGLES STRATEGY; (7) RETURN OF SERVE.

2. 16mm. film. Color. Sound. 12 minutes. Rental: Cloud 9.

See (1) through (4) in contents above.

3. Three 8mm. cartridges. Color. Sound. Purchase: Cloud 9 (either individually or as a set).

    Contents: (1) FOREHAND AND BACKHAND. 6 minutes; (2) VOLLEY AND SERVE. 6 minutes; (3) LOB, OVERHEAD. 3 minutes.

4. 8mm. cartridge. Color. Silent. 6 minutes. Purchase: Cloud 9.

    Contents: SINGLES STRATEGY AND RETURN OF SERVE.

371A TENNIS, AMERICAN STYLE. 16mm. film or 3/4- or 1/2-inch video-cassette. Color. Sound. 24 minutes. 1979. Purchase: McManus/Wilson. Rental: USTA.

372 TENNIS: BASIC SKILLS EXPLAINED. Six 35mm. filmstrips. Color. Sound (cassette). 10–12 minutes each. 49–60 frames each. Purchase: A.W. Peller; Bergwall; Educational Audio Visual, Inc. LC 76-730721.

    This package contains a basic instructional program using clear closeup photographs. Contents: (1) THE FOREHAND DRIVE; (2) THE BACKHAND; (3) THE SERVE; (4) THE VOLLEY; (5) THE OVERHEAD SMASH; (6) PROGRESSION; ONE SUCCESSFUL METHOD OF INSTRUCTION.

373 TENNIS: BASIC TACTICS FOR DOUBLES. 16mm. film. Color. Sound. 13 minutes. 1968. Purchase: BFA. Rental: University of Arizona; BFA; University of Illinois; University of Iowa; Kent State University; University of Nebraska at Lincoln; Oklahoma State University; Pennsylvania State University; Syracuse University; University of Texas; University of Wyoming. ISBN 0-699-29085-6. LC 78-7111118.

    This film describes doubles as a game of quick reflexes, power, touch, team strategy, and action. It points out basic tactics and shows how knowledgeable teamwork can defeat two players who may be individually superior. The narration is by Efrem Zimbalist.

374 TENNIS: BASIC TACTICS FOR SINGLES. 16mm. film. Color. Sound. 13 minutes. 1968. Purchase: BFA. Rental: University of Arizona; BFA; University of Illinois; University of Iowa; Kent State University; University of Nebraska at Lincoln; Oklahoma State University; Pennsylvania State University; Syracuse University; University of Texas; University of Wyoming. ISBN 0-699-29086-4. LC 71-7111119.

    This film presents pointers basic to a well thought-out singles game--where to serve, when to come to the net, how to take advantage of an opponent's weakness. The narration is by Efrem Zimbalist.

375 TENNIS: ELEMENTARY FUNDAMENTALS. 16mm. film. Color. Sound. 11 minutes. 1965. Rental: University of Illinois; South Florida Univer-

sity; Washington State University. ISBN 0-699-29087-2. LC FiA66-1189.

This presents, in slow motion with stop frame action, Darlene Hard, Karen Sussman, and Torey Fretz as they demonstrate elementary fundamentals of the game. See also 378.

376 TENNIS--EVERYBODY'S GAME. 16mm. film. Color. Sound. 28 minutes. 1973. Free loan: Association Films.

Butch Buchholz takes the viewer on a helicopter ride across the United States to see the game being played in a variety of locations and to discuss its history. He demonstrates basic strokes and footwork.

377 TENNIS: HOW TO PLAY THE GAME. Five 35mm. filmstrips. Color. Sound (cassette). 14 minutes each. About 98 frames each. Purchase: Encyclopedia Britannica.

Wes Tenney teaches and demonstrates the basics. A teacher's guide is included with each unit. Contents: (1) THE FUNDAMENTALS; (2) THE GROUNDSTROKES; (3) THE SERVE AND OVERHEAD; (4) SUPPLEMENTARY STROKES; (5) STRATEGY AND TACTICS.

378 TENNIS: INTERMEDIATE AND ADVANCED FUNDAMENTALS. 16mm. film. Color, and black and white. Sound. 11 minutes. 1965. Rental: University of Illinois; South Florida University (black and white version only). ISBN 0-699-29091-0. LC FiA66-119.

Darlene Hard, Karen Sussman, and Torey Fretz demonstrate intermediate and advanced fundamentals with slow motion and freeze frame. A sequel to film 375.

379 TENNIS: THE SPORT OF A LIFETIME. 16mm. film. Color. Sound. 28 minutes. 1960. Rental: University of Arizona. LC FiA68-3076.

This film shows how a class at North Hollywood High School was organized to learn tennis via such aids as stroke developers, painted footprints, and utilizing court space effectively.

380 TENNIS ACES. Two 3/4- or 1/2-inch videocassettes. Color. Sound. 30 minutes each. Purchase: Video Tape Network.

Julie Heldman and John Alexander instruct Bud Collins. The first videocassette covers groundstrokes, the serve and return, equipment advice, conditioning, and how to play doubles. The second covers serve variations, the volley, lob, smash, and drop shot.

381 TENNIS ANYONE. Six 3/4-inch videocassettes or 1/2-inch open reel videocassettes. Color. Sound. 10 minutes each. Purchase and Rental: Time-Life.

Dennis Van der Meer teaches basics in a manner designed both for beginners and as a refresher for advanced players. Contents: (1) INTRODUCTION; (2) THE SERVE; (3) THE FORE-

HAND; (4) THE BACKHAND; (5) SPECIALTY STROKES; (6)
STRATEGY AND TACTICS.

382 TENNIS BALLS. 16mm. film or 3/4- or 1/2-inch videocassette. Color.
Sound. 4 minutes. Purchase and Rental: Films, Inc.

Jonathan Winters, Woody Allen, and JoAnne Worley ask
children how tennis balls are made. The actual process is
depicted. Grades one to six.

383 TENNIS BASICS BY DENNIS RALSTON. Four 16mm. films or 3/4- or 1/2-
inch videocassettes. Color. Sound. 8-10 minutes each. 1976. Purchase:
Churchill. Rental: Churchill; University of Illinois; University of Iowa; Kent
State University (films 3 and 4 only); University of Kansas (film 1 only).

Ralston discusses and players demonstrate the basics in a con-
trolled situation. Viewers are asked to practice with the
demonstration in order to instill kinesthetic learning. Contents: (1) THE FOREHAND. ISBN 0-699-10810-1; (2) THE
BACKHAND. ISBN 0-699-02161-8; (3) THE SERVE. ISBN
0-699-26232-1; (4) THE VOLLEY. ISBN 0-699-31221-3.

384 TENNIS CLASS ORGANIZATION. 16mm. film. Color. Sound. 15
minutes. 1961. Free loan: USTA.

Paul Xanthos demonstrates how to teach large classes.

385 TENNIS EVERYONE! 16mm. film. Color. Sound. 15 minutes. 1968.
Free loan: Coca-Cola. LC 70-702608.

Using stop action frames and slow motion, Dennis Ralston shows
how to hit the serve, forehand, backhand, lob, and smash.

386. TENNIS EVERYONE! 16mm. film. Color. Sound. 26 minutes. 1974.
Free loan: West Glen. Purchase and Rental: Sportlite.

John Newcombe is the guide on an excursion into modern tennis as practiced by young and old, amateur and professional,
in tennis clubs, camps, and tournaments across the United
States. Included are shots of such players as Jimmy Connors,
Arthur Ashe, Billie Jean King, Bjorn Borg, and Ken Rosewall.

387 TENNIS FOR BEGINNERS. 16mm. film. Black and white. Sound. 9
minutes. 1947. Rental: University of Illinois; University of Tennessee.
ISBN 0-699-29088-0. See also film number 309.

Bill Tilden demonstrates grips, footwork, groundstrokes, and serve to
a young boy and then plays a game with him. Grades four to twelve.

387A TENNIS FOR BEGINNERS. 16mm. film. Black and white. Sound. 16
minutes. 1959. Rental: University of Arizona. LC FiA59-749.

388   TENNIS FUNDAMENTALS. 16mm. film or super 8mm. film, or ten
technicolor loops or tape cassette and illustrated book. Color. Sound
or titled for the 8mm. 30 minutes. 1970. Purchase and Rental: Tennis
Films International. LC 72-702953.

The Welby Van Horn balance system of teaching tennis is explained in detail for groundstrokes and serve. Common errors
are shown. Some slow motion and freeze frames are used.

389   TENNIS GRIPS AND STROKES. 16mm. film. Color. Sound. 11 minutes. 1966. Purchase: BFA. Rental: University of Arizona; BFA;
Boston University; University of Connecticut; University of Illinois; Indiana University; Kent State University; University of Minnesota; Northern
Illinois University; Oklahoma State University; Syracuse University; University of Wisconsin at Madison; University of Wyoming. ISBN 0-699-
29089-9. LC FiA67-1438.

Top amateur tennis players demonstrate fundamentals of grips
and strokes. Slow motion, freeze frame, and identification
titles are used to clarify concepts presented.

390   TENNIS LESSON. 16mm. film. Black and white. Sound. 8 minutes.
Purchase: Phoenix. Rental: Phoenix; Welling.

This is a comedy short about a woman who prepares for what
the audience assumes will be a tennis game. Instead she
sets up a machine that battles her by returning all her strokes.

391   THE TENNIS MATCH. 16mm. film or 3/4- or 1/2-inch videocassette. Color.
Sound. 15 minutes. 1978. Purchase and Rental: Phoenix. LC 78-701801.

This is a film making fun of the fierceness that many players
bring to their weekly games. Prematch aggravations, sarcas-
tic comments, coaching the other players in a doubles match
are all shown, with the camera darting back and forth almost
like a tennis ball.

392   TENNIS MOTHERS. 16mm. film. Color. Sound. 14 minutes. 1976.
Purchase: Carousel. Rental: Carousel; Michigan University; USTA.

Not only mother but father puts pressure on a twelve-year-old
Staten Island girl to be a champion. This was originally
shown on CBS's "60 Minutes" program.

393   TENNIS RACQUET. 16mm. film. Color. Sound. 7 minutes. 1977.
Purchase and Rental: Walt Disney.

This is a very animated cartoon with the character Goofy
playing tennis despite such distractions as a gardener planting
grass seeds and mowing the court.

394   TENNIS SHOES. 16mm. film or 3/4- or 1/2-inch videocassette. Color.
Sound. 5 minutes. Purchase and Rental: Films, Inc.

This film shows how tennis shoes are made. Grades one to six.

395 TENNIS TACTICS. 16mm. film. Black and white. Sound. 10 minutes. 1937. Rental: University of Illinois. ISBN 0-699-29092-9.

Fred Perry shows basic tactics, as well as teaching techniques, with extensive use of slow motion.

396 TENNIS TECHNIQUE. 16mm. film. Color. Sound. 9 minutes. 1947. Rental: University of Illinois.

This film illustrates groundstrokes, serve, and volley and how to teach those strokes to groups. Pauline Betz Addie is shown in action.

397 TENNIS THE NASTY WAY. Four 16mm. or 3/4- or 1/2-inch videocassettes. Color. Sound. 14 minutes each. 1977. Purchase: AIMS. Rental: AIMS; Kent State University.

Ilie Nastase demonstrates tennis basics. CONTENTS: (1) THE FOREHAND; (2) THE BACKHAND; (3) THE SERVE AND VOLLEY; (4) STRATEGY SHOTS.

398 TENNIS TOURNAMENT DAY. 35mm. filmstrip. Color. Sound (cassette tape). 41 frames. 1973. Accompanied by a teacher's guide and answer sheet. Purchase: Colonial Films.

The experiences and emotions of a boy entering his first tournament are explored. Grade three.

398A TENNIS TO WIN. Six 3/4-inch videocassettes. Color. Sound. 30 minutes each. Purchase: Trans World International.

399 TENNIS WITH KEN ROSEWALL. 16mm. film. Color. Sound. 25 minutes. 1972. Rental: USTA.

Rosewall shows how he hits all the strokes.

400 TIPS FOR TENNIS. Three 16mm. films. Color. Sound. 11 minutes each. 1976. Free loan: Coca-Cola.

Dennis Ralston and Arthur Ashe are the demonstrators. Contents: (1) GROUNDSTROKES. Includes grips, footwork, and hitting strokes on the run; (2) NET PLAY; (3) THE SERVE.

401 TIPS FROM TENNIS TOPS. 16mm. film. Black and white. Sound. 30 minutes. 1960. Rental: University of Arizona.

Slow motion photography shows professional players demonstrating methods of improving one's game.

402 Entry deleted.

403 TOURNAMENT. 16mm. film or super 8mm. cartridge. Color. Sound. 27 minutes. 1972. Purchase: Sports Investors, Inc. Rental: University of Illinois; Sports Investors. ISBN 0-699-29849-0. LC 72-702440.

Chris Evert, Pancho Gonzales, Billie Jean King, and Stan Smith are among the competitors in the 1971 U.S. Open.

404 TRAIN FOR WIMBLEDON. Three 16mm. films. Black and white. Sound. 21 minutes each. 1967. Purchase: Tennis Films International.

Some of the famous players of the 1960s demonstrate the fundamental shots, which are then tied in with the same players hitting those shots shot in actual competition at the tournament at Wimbledon. Contents: (1) SERVICE AND OVERHEAD; (2) GROUNDSTROKES; (3) VOLLEY.

405 UNITED STATES CHALLENGES AUSTRALIA. 16mm. film. Black and white. Sound. 20 minutes. 1954. Rental: University of Michigan; Washington State University. ISBN 0-699-30599-3.

Vic Seixas and Tony Trabert regain the Davis Cup for the United States from Australia, 1954.

405A UNITED STATES OPEN CLAY COURT TENNIS CHAMPIONSHIPS. 16mm. film or 3/4- or 1/2-inch videocassette. Color. Sound. 25 minutes. 1979. Purchase: Stan Malless, P.O.Box 26035, Indianapolis, Ind. 46226. Rental: USTA.

406 U.S. OPEN 1975. 16mm. film or 3/4- or 1/2-inch videocassette. Color. Sound. 20 minutes. 1954. Purchase and Rental: Sports World Cinema.

The Manolo Orantes come-from-behind victory over Guillermo Vilas in the semifinals, and his win over Jimmy Connors in the finals are shown. Chris Evert defeats Evonne Goolagong in the women's finals.

407 U.S. OPEN 1976. 16mm. film or 3/4- or 1/2-inch videocassette. Color. Sound. 30 minutes. 1976. Purchase: Sports World Cinema. Rental: Sports World Cinema; USTA.

Highlights of the matches are shown in which Jimmy Connors defeats Bjorn Borg in the men's final and Chris Evert wins over Evonne Goolagong in the women's.

408 U.S. OPEN 1977: FAREWELL, FOREST HILLS. 16mm. film. Color. Sound. 25 minutes. 1977. Free loan: West Glen. Purchase: Sports World Cinema. Rental: Sports World Cinema.

This film shows Guillermo Vilas over Jimmy Connors and Chris Evert over Wendy Turnbull. Also, Mike Fishbach demonstrates the spaghetti racket, and Tracy Austin plays her first Open.

409 U.S. OPEN 1978. 16mm. film. Color. Sound. 24 minutes. 1978. Purchase and Rental: Sports World Cinema.

Jimmy Connors defeats a thumb-injured Bjorn Borg and Pam
Shriver wins hearts while losing to Chris Evert in the first
tournament held in the National Tennis Center in Flushing
Meadow, N.Y. Highlights of other matches are shown.

409A U.S. OPEN 1979. 16mm. film. Color. Sound. 30 minutes. 1979.
Purchase: Fisher/Feld. Rental: USTA.

410 USTINOV AT WIMBLEDON. 16mm. film or videocassette. Color. Sound.
52 minutes. 1975. Free loan: Rolex Watch (16mm. film only); USTA. Purchase: Trans World International. Purchase and Rental: Sports World Cinema
(videocassette only).

Peter Ustinov narrates the 1975 championships. Highlights of many
matches are shown with details on the finals--Arthur Ashe over
Jimmy Connors and Billie Jean King over Evonne Goologong.

411 VAN DER MEER CLINIC AT FOREST HILLS. 16mm. film. Color. Sound.
14 minutes. 1976. Purchase: Chevron.

Leading tennis teacher Dennis Van der Meer takes a humorous
look at the average player's game and then shows how that player
might improve.

412 VIC BRADEN TENNIS TRAINING FILMS. Fourteen 16mm. films or super
8mm. film cartridges or 3/4- or 1/2-inch videocassettes. Color. Sound.
3-5 minutes each. Purchase: Johnson-Nyquist.

Tennis teacher Braden demonstrates fundamentals. Contents: (1)
FOREHAND DRIVE; (2) BACKHAND DRIVE; (3) HALF VOLLEY;
(4) APPROACH SHOTS; (5) FOREHAND VOLLEY; (6) BACKHAND
VOLLEY; (7) BASIC SERVE; (8) OVERHEAD; (9) ADVANCED SERVE;
(10) THE LOB; (11) BALL ROTATION; (12) FOOTWORK; (13)
SINGLES STRATEGY; (14) DOUBLES STRATEGY.

413 VOLVO INTERNATIONAL TENNIS TOURNAMENT. 16mm. film or 3/4- or
1/2-inch videocassette. Color. Sound. 20 minutes. Free loan: USTA.

A description of what went on behind, as well as on the
scenes, at the 1977 tournament. John Alexander defeated
Manolo Orantes in the finals, and there is also footage of
such players as Arthur Ashe, Jimmy Connors, Eddie Dibbs,
Brian Gottfried, Raul Ramirez, and Harold Solomon.

414 THE WAY TO WIMBLEDON. Three 16mm. films or 3/4- or 1/2-inch
videocassettes. Black and white. Sound. 2-25 minutes each. Purchase:
Coaching Association of Canada.

414A WE SHALL RETURN. 16mm. film or 3/4- or 1/2-inch videocassette.
Color. Sound. 24 minutes. Purchase: McManus/Wilson.

415 WHAT YOU SHOULD KNOW ABOUT TENNIS. 16mm. film. Color.
Sound. 30 minutes. 1976. Free loan: USTA. Purchase and Rental:
Sports films and Talents.

Tips are given by Rod Laver on warming up and getting in shape,
choosing proper equipment, the effect of different court surfaces,
and obtaining help from a pro. Scenes of top players are shown.

416 WHO'S FOR TENNIS. 16mm. film. Color. Sound. 7 minutes. 1969.
Rental: Australian Information Service. LC 77-709230.

Almost everyone's for tennis in Australia according to this
brief glimpse of the game there.

417 WIMBLEDON 1977. 16mm. film. Color. Sound. 52 minutes. 1977.
Free loan: Rolex Watch. Purchase: Trans World International.

The championships are shown in the year Ginny fizzed; Virginia
Wade defeats Betty Stove and Bjorn Borg wins over Jimmy Connors.

418 WIMBLEDON 1978. 16mm. film. Color. Sound. 52 minutes. 1978.
Free loan: Rolex Watch. Purchase: Trans World International.

418A WIMBLEDON 1979. 16mm. film. Color. Sound. 52 minutes. 1979. Free
loan: Rolex Watch. Purchase: Trans World International.

419 THE WINNING SERVE. 16mm. film. Color. Sound. 15 minutes. 1974.
Purchase: Golden Door.

Allie Ritzenberg explains and demonstrates the flat, slice,
and twist serves.

420 WINNING TENNIS. Module containing a 35mm. filmstrip, cassette, ten
books, and activity cards in a self-contained slipcase box. Purchase: Mason;
Troll.

This is a skill kit designed to encourage students to read. It
is part of the "Be a Winner" series. Grades four to eight.

421 WOMEN'S TENNIS. Seven super 8mm. cartridges (Kodak or Technicolor).
Color. Silent. 3 1/2 matches each. 1975. Purchase (either singly or as
a set): Champions on Film.

Women players demonstrate the basic strokes using slow motion.
Contents: (1) FOREHAND STROKES; (2) ONE-HANDED BACK-
HAND; (3) TWO-HANDED BACKHAND; (4) THE SERVE; (5)
VOLLEYS AND HALF-VOLLEYS; (6) LOBS AND SMASHES;
(7) FOOTWORK.

WORLD CHAMPIONSHIP OF TENNIS. Each year the WCT holds its tournament finals in Dallas, and the highlights are put on film. See the following
titles in this listing:

AND THEN THERE WAS ONE (see 299).
ARTHUR CLAIMS THE GOLD (see 301).
DALLAS '78 (see 315).
THE GREATEST TENNIS MATCH OF ALL TIME (see 326).
THE NEW ERA (see 348).
SEVEN DAYS IN MAY (see 359A)
SHOOTOUT AT HIGH NOON (see 360).
65,000 MILES TO DALLAS (see 361).
THE YOUNGEST CHAMPION (see 423).

422 Entry deleted.

423 THE YOUNGEST CHAMPION. 16mm. film or 3/4- or 1/2-inch videocassette. Color. Sound. 26 minutes. 1976. Purchase: Film Comm;
Sportlite. Rental: Film Comm; Sportlite.

Bjorn Borg defeats Guillermo Vilas in the World Championship of Tennis finals, Dallas 1976. Highlights of
earlier matches are shown.

424 YOU'RE PLAYING AT WIMBLEDON. 16mm. film or 3/4- or 1/2-inch
videocassette. Color. Sound. 27 minutes. 1974. Purchase: Sports
World Cinema. Rental: Sports World Cinema; USTA.

Jack Kramer discusses similarities and differences in styles and
mental attitudes between the great and the second-rate player.

425 YOUR TURN ON COURT. Two 16mm. films or 8mm. films (reel to reel
or cartridge). Color. Sound. 1976. Free loan: USTA. Purchase:
Lord and King. Rental: University of Nebraska at Lincoln.

Ken Stuart, United States Professional Tennis Association profes-
sional, demonstrates fundamental strokes. Contents: (1) THE
SERVE AND VOLLEY. 16 minutes. ISBN 0-699-33066-1; (2)
THE GROUND STROKES. 22 minutes. ISBN 0-699-33065-3.

426 YOU'VE COME A LONG WAY, BABY. 16mm. film or super 8mm. cartridge.
Color. Sound. 26 minutes. 1974. Purchase and Rental: Sports Investors, Inc.

This is a history of women's tennis, primarily shown as played
at Forest Hills. In addition to styles of play, it also shows
the evolution of tennis wear. Margaret Court, Chris Evert,
Evonne Goolagong, and Billie Jean King are featured.

BOOKS

The books cited below have been grouped into the following sections: "Autobiography, Biography and History"; "Fiction" (including juvenile fiction); "Instruction";
"Juvenile" (including juvenile biography); "Reference"; and "Miscellaneous." Some
books fit under more than one category, and for such titles cross references are shown.
There are no annotations for fiction.

Autobiography, Biography, History

427 Alexander, George. LAWN TENNIS: ITS FOUNDERS AND EARLY
DAYS. Lynn, Mass.: H.O. Zimman, 1974. 127 p. Photos., dgrms.,
dwgs., bibliog. LC 74-195103.

A well-written, well-researched account of the origins of the
game that includes reprints of articles from THE FIELD (London,
1853--), the English periodical in which early descriptions
of tennis were published; Walter Wingfield's first book of
rules; and a thorough discussion of the question of who first
brought tennis to the United States.

428 Anderson, Dave. THE RETURN OF A CHAMPION: PANCHO GON-
ZALES' GOLDEN YEAR 1964. Englewood Cliffs, N.J.: Prentice-Hall,
1973. 123 p. Photos. ISBN 0-13-778605-0. LC 73-6614.

The life story of Gonzales is told with special concentration
on one tournament in 1964 when, at age thirty-six and sup-
posedly "over the hill," he defeated Rod Laver, Lew Hoad,
and Ken Rosewall successively. Brief biographies of those
three opponents are also included. The book is flawed by
some text misprints and incorrectly labeled photographs.

429 Ashe, Arthur, and DeFord, Frank. ARTHUR ASHE: PORTRAIT IN MO-
TION. Boston: Houghton Mifflin, 1975. 272 p. Photos. ISBN 0-395-
20429-1. LC 74-34465. This book is also available to blind and other
physically handicapped readers through a national network of libraries.
To obtain the name and address of the closest one, write to National
Library Service, Division for the Blind and Physically Handicapped,
Library of Congress, Washington, D.C. 20542.

"In motion" is correct. This diary, going from Wimbledon
1973 to Wimbledon 1974, shows the harried life of a typical
tennis professional as he goes from tournaments to exhibitions
to commercial appearances to clinics. Portraits of fellow
players (including a particularly perceptive chapter on the
Australians) and Ashe's views on social issues from blacks to
birth control are included.

430 Ashe, Arthur, and Gewecke, Clifford. ADVANTAGE ASHE. New York:
Coward McGann, 1967. 192 p. Photos. LC 67-24532.

This is the Ashe story until two years before open tennis. The
early years' prejudices and his feelings about those prejudices,
the rise to the top ranks, what he thinks about during a match
(not always the next shot), and estimates of many of his court
contemporaries are included.

431   Audette, Larry. BJORN BORG. New York: Quick Fox, 1979. 106 p.
      Paperbound. Photos. ISBN 0-8526-3931-X. LC 78-68485.

      The Borg story through his third consecutive Wimbledon victory
      in 1978 is told primarily in chronological order with a final
      chapter discussing how he hits the various shots. Many of the
      photographs are spread across two pages, which makes full
      viewing difficult.

432   Bell, Marty. CARNIVAL AT FOREST HILLS: ANATOMY OF A TENNIS
      TOURNAMENT. New York: Random House, 1975. 193 p. Photos.
      ISBN 0-394-49595-0. LC 74-29602.

      Bell compares the U.S. Open championship in 1974 to a car-
      nival with its crowds, color, excitement, commercialism, and
      hucksterism. There are many descriptions of matches and per-
      sonalities, and the descriptions are not always flattering.

433   Bodo, Peter. INSIDE TENNIS: A SEASON ON THE PRO TOUR. New
      York: Delacorte, 1979. 288 p. Photos. ISBN 0-440-04297-6. LC
      79-17398.

      The author, with photographer June Harrison, covers a tennis
      season from the Italian championships in the spring through the
      U.S. Open in late summer of 1978. The portrait combines a
      description of the physical setting of the various tournaments,
      interviews with and characterizations of the men and women
      players, and comments on the various matches and the game
      itself.

434   Borg, Bjorn. THE BJORN BORG STORY. Translated from the Swedish
      by Joan Tate. Chicago: Regnery, 1975. 96 p. Photos. ISBN 0-8092-
      8184-8. LC 75-321039.

      This is the life of the champion through 1974. How he be-
      came interested in tennis, descriptions of matches won and
      lost, his effect on British teenage girls, and baby to adult
      pictures are all included. Inconsistencies a professional writer
      might have caught are here: "I never give up on a match,"
      is followed one paragraph later by "Naturally there are also
      matches which I more or less gave away."

435   Bortstein, Larry. GREAT TENNIS PLAYERS. New York: Grosset and
      Dunlap, 1974. 148 p. Paperbound. ISBN 0-448-05731-X.

      Biographies of four leading women are presented--Margaret
      Court, Chris Evert, Evonne Goolagong, and Billie Jean King.
      Controversy is absent from these pages; the biographies are
      descriptive not evaluative.

436 Budge, Don. DON BUDGE: A TENNIS MEMOIR. New York: Viking, 1969. 184 p. Photos. ISBN 0-670-27838-6. LC 69-15661. The book is also available to blind and other physically handicapped readers through a national network of libraries. To obtain the name and address of the closest one, write to the National Library Service, Division for the Blind and Physically Handicapped, Library of Congress, Washington, D.C. 20542.

Beginning with his account of the famous Cramm match in 1937, Budge tells his life story from his Oakland beginnings through competition in the senior championships at the first open Wimbledon in 1968. Also included are instruction tips and comments on fellow competitors. The most interesting is on page 148 where he writes that Tilden cannot be ". . . rated anywhere near the top in any listing of best players. . . ."

437 Burke, Jim. THE WORLD OF JIMMY CONNORS. New York: Nordon Publications, 1976. 217 p. Photos. Paperbound.

A breezy biography of Connors and of some of those who inhabit his world, this book includes a chapter on Chris Evert and stories of "bad boys" of tennis like Ilie Nastase. Many of Connors's matches even in minor tournaments are summarized, the years with Bill Riordan are discussed, and the story goes through his loss to Manolo Orantes at Forest Hills in 1975.

438 Clerici, Gianni. THE ULTIMATE TENNIS BOOK. Translated from the Italian by Richard Wiezell. Chicago: Follett, 1975. 335 p. Photos., dwgs. ISBN 0-695-80559-2. LC 75-18748.

"Ultimate" is indeed the word for this supreme example of coffee table art. Photographs, drawings, reproductions of paintings, and text follow the history of tennis and its predecessors from the Greeks to Ilie Nastase (with a final one-page chapter on Jimmy Connors added by American editors to the English-language version).

439 Court, Margaret, and McGann, George. COURT ON COURT: A LIFE IN TENNIS. New York: Dodd Mead, 1975. 211 p. Photos. ISBN 0-396-07207-0. LC 75-17650.

This is the life story of Court, whom her coauthor calls "the best woman player of them all." It covers her life through the "Mother's Day Massacre" with Bobby Riggs, and she makes comments about players she likes and does not like, with Billie Jean King in first place in the latter category.

440 Danzig, Allison, and Schwed, Peter. THE FIRESIDE BOOK OF TENNIS. New York: Simon and Schuster, 1972. 1043 p. Photos., dwgs. ISBN 0-671-21128-5. LC 70-165538.

Three sections mark this compilation of tennis articles: (1)

leading players and events in tennis history; (2) descriptions
of great matches from 1877 to 1971; and (3) selections from
various instruction books. Well-known tennis authors are
represented plus some surprises--James Thurber and Peter Ustinov. Selections represent what might be called "the Danzig
era" in tennis; impeccable players in impeccable whites playing a noble game. The only discussion of "shamateurism" in
this sizeable volume is buried in the article on Roy Emerson,
and that term does not appear in the index.

441 Davidson, Owen, and Jones, C.M. GREAT WOMEN TENNIS PLAYERS.
The Great Ones Series. London: Pelham Books, 1971. Distributed in
the United States by Transatlantic Arts, New York. 142 p. Photos.
ISBN 0-7207-0460-X. LC 72-176149.

Career information is given on past and present well-known
names from Lambert-Chambers through King, with accounts
of great matches played. The frequency of one-sentence
paragraphs sometimes gives this book the appearance of a
child's primer.

442 _____. LAWN TENNIS: THE GREAT ONES. The Great Ones Series.
London: Pelham Books, 1970. Distributed in the United States by Transatlantic Arts, New York. 160 p. Photos. ISBN 0-7207-0380-8. LC
70-509027.

These are brief portraits of leading players from Bill Tilden
to Rod Laver. There is much repetition, perhaps unavoidable
in dealing with so many overlapping lives, but it seems at
times that chapters were written with no regard for what was
said earlier. British spelling and vocabulary reflect the book's
original publication in that country.

443 DeFord, Frank. BIG BILL TILDEN: THE TRIUMPHS AND THE TRAGEDY.
New York: Simon and Schuster, 1976. 286 p. Photos. ISBN 0-671-
22254-6. LC 75-45011.

This is an account of the life of "the greatest athlete of the
first half of the century." (Tilden received more than twice
the votes of any rival for that title in a poll of sportswriters
in 1950). The great matches, the homosexuality, the curious
contradictions that went to make up William Tatem Tilden are
all here. The book is written in two parts, the public career
and the personal life, with a certain amount of overlapping.

444 Evans, Richard. NASTY: ILIE NASTASE VS. TENNIS. New York:
Stein and Day, 1979. 242 p. Photos. ISBN 0-8128-2540-3. LC 78-
588815.

This is a biography and in-depth portrait of tennis's "Terrible
Tempered Mr. Bang." The twin aspects of the Nastase per-

sonality--"lovable, charming and generous; temperamental, arrogant and obscene"--are illustrated and explored, along with descriptions of fellow players and others in this talented player's orbit.

445   Gibson, Althea, and Fitzgerald, Ed. I ALWAYS WANTED TO BE SOME-BODY. New York: Harper, 1958. 176 p. Photos. LC 58-12447.

This is Gibson's life story from her days as a Harlem truant through the winning of her second Wimbledon title in 1958. The title sums up the story--a natural athlete who overcame poverty and hardships via a burning ambition to "be some-body" and who, with the help of a few friends at the right times, made it to the top.

446   Goolagong, Evonne, and Collins, Bud. EVONNE! ON THE MOVE. New York: Dutton, 1975. 190 p. Photos. ISBN 0-525-10115-2. LC 74-3245.

"Though the voice much of the time is clearly Collins'--es-pecially in the political explanations, match analyses and background anecdotes--the spirit and sentiment are Evonne's." That quote from Linda Timms's review (WORLD TENNIS, September 1975, p. 16) accurately sums up this book on the career of the Australian tennis player from growing up through her brief World Team Tennis career.

447   Grimsley, Will. TENNIS: ITS HISTORY, PEOPLE AND EVENTS. STYLES OF THE GREATS BY JULIUS HELDMAN. Englewood Cliff, N.J.: Prentice-Hall, 1971. 380 p. Photos. ISBN 0-13-90337-7. LC 76-144006.

From prehistory to wars between the tennis groups, this book tells it all--the great names, matches, tournaments are here--and Grimsley is not afraid to express an opinion. Heldman analyzes how some leading players from Tilden to Ashe hit the ball and played the game.

448   Hoffman, Gregg. THE ART OF WORLD TEAM TENNIS. San Francisco: San Francisco Book Co., 1977. 138 p. Photos. ISBN 0-913374-65-2. LC 77-70223.

Beginning with the background of the various warring tennis organizations through 1974 (when World Team Tennis made its first appearance), this book tells the story of that organiza-tion through rose-colored glasses. A discussion of the innova-tions in scoring, format, officiating, and the multi-hued court itself is followed by individual team histories, record statistics, and some instructional tips by leading players.

449 Jacobs, Helen. GALLERY OF CHAMPIONS. New York: A.S. Barnes, 1949. Reprint. Freeport, N.Y.: Books for Libraries Press, 1970. 224 p. Photos. ISBN 0-8369-8043-3. LC 71-136648.

> Fifteen players who won the American, English, or French championships and who played against the author in the 1920s through 1940s are ranked and some of their matches described. The "feud" between Helen Wills and Helen Jacobs is covered.

450 Janoff, Murray. TENNIS REVOLUTION. Originally published as the August 1974 issue of SPORTSCENE. New York: Stadia Sports Publishing, 1974. 159 p. Photos. Paperbound. LC 74-193270.

> This is an informal, poorly proofread account of what was happening in the tennis world as of 1974. The boom, wars between the various organizations, the "women's lob" movement, and the Van Alen Simplified Scoring System are all given a quick review.

451 Jones, Ann. A GAME TO LOVE. London: Stanley Paul, 1971. Distributed in the United States by Sportshelf, New Rochelle, N.Y. 180 p. Photos. ISBN 0-09-105170-X. LC 72-181221.

> Originally published in the author's home country, England, this is "our Ann's" story of her life--the early table tennis triumphs, the switch to tennis, the many wins and losses leading up to winning Wimbledon in 1969.

452 King, Billie Jean, and Chapin, Kim. BILLIE JEAN. New York: Harper and Row, 1974. 208 p. Photos. ISBN 0-06-012392-3. LC 73-4099. The book is also available to blind and other physically handicapped readers through a national network of libraries. To obtain the name and address of the closest one, write to the National Library Service, Division for the Blind and Physically Handicapped, Library of Congress, Washington, D.C. 20542.

> The life story of King until the beginning of World Team Tennis is presented, interspersed with comments on other players, details of the "shamateurism" under which players lived before open tennis, reflections on women's liberation, the Riggs spectacular, and more. Told in an informal manner, the book reflects the author's style.

453 Koster, Rich. THE TENNIS BUBBLE: BIG-MONEY TENNIS; HOW IT GREW AND WHERE IT'S GOING. New York: Quadrangle, 1976. 209 p. Photos. ISBN 0-8129-0646-2. LC 76-9710.

> These are detailed portraits of and lengthy quotes from the people who represent the various warring factions that marked the great growth of tennis in the late 1960s and early 1970s. This confusing story is made as clear as possibly by Koster who gives his own opinion in the final chapter.

454 Kramer, Jack, and DeFord, Frank. THE GAME: MY 40 YEARS IN TENNIS. New York: G.P. Putnam's Sons, 1979. 318 p. Photos. ISBN 0-399-12336-9. LC 78-31299.

Kramer, who may well have made more people angry at him than anyone else in tennis, tells his side of the story in this account of his life and his views. It is the most complete account we have of the era of under-the-table payments and of the professional tours before the advent of open tennis in 1968. Strong opinions are presented on today's versus yester-day's great players, women's tennis, and much more.

455 Laney, Al. COVERING THE COURT: A 50 YEAR LOVE AFFAIR WITH THE GAME OF TENNIS. New York: Simon and Schuster, 1968. 285 p. LC 68-19944.

This is a memoir by a tennis reporter who covered the game from Maurice McLoughlin in 1914 to the first open tournament in 1968. The concentration is on the Lenglen, Tilden, Muske-teers era, and there are many descriptions of great matches in that time. The term musketeers refers to Rene Lacoste, Henri Cochet, Jean Borotra, and Jacques Brugnon (four musketeers rather than three, but the first three were the mainstays) who combined to allow France to take the Davis Cup away from Tilden and the United States in the late twenties, and to give that country a preeminence in the tennis world that it never had before and has never had since. Reflections on the professional game and why it did not have the clout of the amateur conclude this warm, almost romantic survey.

456 Laver, Rod, and Collins, Bud. THE EDUCATION OF A TENNIS PLAYER. New York: Simon and Schuster, 1971. 318 p. Photos. ISBN 0-671-20902. LC 70-139639.

This is an account of Laver's second grand slam year (1969), interspersed with instructional tips, portraits of leading op-ponents, and flashbacks to the author's own tennis develop-ment.

Laver, Rod, and Pollard, Jack. HOW TO PLAY CHAMPIONSHIP TEN-NIS.

See 643A.

457 Lichtenstein, Grace. A LONG WAY BABY: BEHIND THE SCENES IN WOMEN'S PRO TENNIS. New York: William Morrow, 1974. 239 p. Photos. ISBN 0-688-00263-3. LC 74-1166.

Beginning and ending with the Riggs versus King extravaganza, Lichtenstein describes what life was like on the women's pro-fessional tennis tour in 1973. She gives portraits of many of the leading women tennis players and paints a convincing pic-ture of the importance of the tour to the women's movement.

McPhee, John. LEVELS OF THE GAME.

See 845.

458   Medlycott, James. 100 YEARS OF THE WIMBLEDON TENNIS CHAM-
PIONSHIPS. New York: Crown, 1977. 93 p. Photos., dwgs. ISBN
0-517-224259. LC 77-72783.

The Wimbledon story is told in words and pictures. The history is given in chronological order first, followed by a chapter on leading personalities. There is some repetition in this
coffee table item and one particular delight; the famous
"proof" that Spencer Gore, the 1877 champion, would have
defeated Bjorn Borg, the 1976 champion, is detailed.

459   Metzler, Paul. TENNIS STYLES AND STYLISTS. New York: Macmillan, 1970. 217 p. Photos., dgrms., dwgs. LC 77-114328.

This presents a description of the styles of play and court
tactics used by great players from the first Wimbledon through
1969. The author makes his case for Jack Kramer as the
greatest player of them all.

460   Minton, Robert. FOREST HILLS: AN ILLUSTRATED HISTORY. Philadelphia: J.B. Lippincott, 1975. 240 p. Photos., dwgs. ISBN 0-397-
01094-X. LC 75-14461.

This begins with a text and photographic portrait of the atmosphere
at Forest Hills when the U.S. Open was played there (a different picture can be found in Bell's CARNIVAL AT FOREST
HILLS (see 432), and then gives a quick overview of the
founding of the West Side Tennis Club in Manhattan and its
move to Queens. The bulk of the text is about the greats
who have played there. The illustrations include several cartoons.

461   Potter, Edward. THE DAVIS CUP. Cranbury, N.J.: A.S. Barnes, 1969.
142 p. Photos. ISBN 0-498-06665-7. LC 68-27208.

Potter provides a straight narrative history of the cup, year by
year and player by player, from its beginnings through 1968.
Pictures of leading players are included. Potter concludes
that ". . . the Davis Cup, as a symbol of the universality of
the game of 'lawn tennis,' has reached the end of its useful-
ness."

462   _____. KINGS OF THE COURT: THE STORY OF LAWN TENNIS.
New York: A.S. Barnes, 1963. 342 p. Photos. LC 63-9368.

This is a history of the game from its beginnings through the
early 1960s. In addition to chronological narrative, there
are chapters on such topics as doubles and professional tennis.

The photographs are primarily portraits rather than shots of
the players in action. (The dust jacket of the book refers to
it as a "Revised edition," but that statement does not appear
in the book itself and no evidence of an earlier edition could
be found.)

463 Riessen, Marty, and Evans, Richard. MATCH POINT: A CANDID
VIEW OF LIFE ON THE INTERNATIONAL TENNIS CIRCUIT. Englewood
Cliffs, N.J.: Prentice-Hall, 1973. 285 p. Photos. ISBN 0-13-560128-
2. LC 73-1173.

This covers what life was like on the men's professional tour
in 1971-72 as well as the story of Riessen's life--the under-
the-table amateur payments, the decision to turn professional,
and the one deliberate throwing of a match. The book concludes with some doubles instructional tips and discusses which
players have the strokes to watch.

464 Riggs, Bobby, and McGann, George. COURT HUSTLER. Philadelphia:
J.B. Lippincott, 1973. 203 p. Photos. ISBN 0-397-00893-7. LC 73-
13818. The book is also available to blind and other physically handicapped readers through a national network of libraries. To obtain the
name and address of the closest one, write to the National Library Service, Division for the Blind and Physically Handicapped, Library of Congress, Washington, D.C. 20542.

Riggs tells his story through his first battle-of-the-sexes win
over Margaret Court. He also offers views on women's tennis,
why tennis is a better game than golf, blacks in tennis, and
more. From childhood marbles to tennis championships, there
was always something on the line when Riggs played.

Rosewall, Ken, and Barrett, John. PLAY TENNIS WITH ROSEWALL.
See 683.

465 Rowley, Peter. KEN ROSEWALL: TWENTY YEARS AT THE TOP. New
York: G.P. Putnam's Sons, 1976. 252 p. Photos. ISBN 0-399-11683-
4. LC 75-42773.

"The finest tennis player who ever existed" is Rowley's claim,
and his supporting evidence is the statistics of "the Little
Master's" more than twenty-year top flight record. Extensive
quotes from his subject on other players are given in words
that sometimes sound more literary than the conversational
items they are supposed to be.

466 Schickel, Richard. THE WORLD OF TENNIS. New York: Random,
1975. 251 p. Photos., dwgs. ISBN 0-394-49940-9. LC 75-10331.

This is a portrait of tennis, both its evolution and how it was

in 1974. Although not a definitive history, it does comment
on those aspects of the past that Schickel chooses to emphasize: for example, the importance of King, Lenglen, and
Tilden to the game, the Hopman era in Australia, and more.

467 Smith, Stan. IT'S MORE THAN JUST A GAME. New Life Ventures.
Old Tappan, N.J.: Fleming Revell, 1977. 63 p. Paperbound. ISBN
0-8007-9002-2. LC 77-14287.

Smith tells his life story up to 1977 with emphasis on his
beliefs as a practicing Christian. It's a straightforward narrative told in an even-tempered manner, particularly his account of the famous Davis Cup match against Rumania in
1972, when Smith's resistance to the tactics of Ion Tiriac in
particular and those of the linesmen in general earned him
well-deserved respect in the tennis world.

Tilden, William [T.]. MATCH PLAY AND THE SPIN OF THE BALL.

See 711.

468 Tingay, Lance. TENNIS: A PICTORIAL HISTORY. New York: Hastings, 1977. 168 p. Photos., dwgs. ISBN 0-8038-7167-8. LC 76-
51842.

Pictures, ranging from early prints to modern cartoons, are a
prime part of this history, which tends to be a bit rushed in
the modern era. There is a nice light touch throughout the
text--"King Henry VIII was tennis champion of England--who
would have dared beat him?"

469 Tinling, Ted, and Humphries, Rod. LOVE AND FAULTS: PERSONALI-
TIES WHO HAVE CHANGED THE HISTORY OF TENNIS IN MY LIFE-
TIME. New York: Crown 1979. 314 p. Photos. ISBN 0-517-53305-
7. LC 78-23276.

Tinling has been associated with tennis from the 1920s, when
he played with and umpired for Suzanne Lenglen, to the present (he designs tennis wear for players of both sexes). He
gives portraits of many players he has known with special concentration on those he feels have changed tennis history. The
illustrations are fascinating.

470 Vines, Ellsworth, and Vier, Gene. TENNIS: MYTH AND METHOD.
New York: Viking, 1978. 320 p. Photos., dwgs., gloss. ISBN 0-
670-69665-X. LC 77-18544.

The authors choose ten players active since World War II, discuss in great detail how they played the game, and rank
them--Don Budge number one, Jack Kramer number two. A
prime purpose is to dispel the "myth" that the big game of
serve and volley is the only way to play top-flight tennis.

Instructional tips for intermediate to advanced players are also given.

471 Wade, Virginia, and Mellace, Mary. COURTING TRIUMPH. New York: Mayflower, 1978. 191 p. Photos. ISBN 0-8317-1800-5.

Woven through this autobiography of Virginia Wade is a detailed description of her final round match with Betty Stove at Wimbledon in 1977 when she won her home country's title. Some detailed philosophical speculations on her personality form an important part of this self-portrait.

472 Whitington, Richard. AN ILLUSTRATED HISTORY OF AUSTRALIAN TENNIS. New York: St. Martins, 1975. 126 p. Photos., dwgs. ISBN 0-312-40810. LC 75-27001.

This is a detailed account of the abilities and great matches of leading players from Norman Brooks through Evonne Goolagong. The pros and cons of the Hopman era are discussed, and there are many illustrations of players in and out of match situations. Adrian Quist's rankings of the Australians--Rod Laver is number one--conclude the text.

473 Whitman, Malcolm. TENNIS: ORIGINS AND MYSTERIES. New York: Derrydale Press, 1932. Reprint. Detroit: Singing Tree, 1968. 258 p. Photos., dwgs., bibliog. ISBN 0-8013-3542-5. LC 68-58970.

This is an account of the origins of court and lawn tennis with a thorough bibliography of both games through 1931 by Robert Henderson. Chapters deal with such topics as how it came about that there are two serves, the why of 15-30-40-game scoring, and how zero came to be called "love."

474 Wind, Herbert Warren. GAME, SET, AND MATCH: THE TENNIS BOOM OF THE 1960S AND 1970S. New York: E.P. Dutton, 1979. 229 p. ISBN 0-525-11140-9. LC 78-26895.

A series of essays which, while concentrated in the period of the subtitle, range as far back as the beginnings of the game. The first open Wimbledon, the increased participation in tennis by average players, a Harry Hopman portrait, Pancho Gonzales and Ken Rosewall during the first U.S. Open tournament (entitled appropriately "September Song") are just a few of these superbly crafted pieces.

Fiction

The attempt here was to make this as complete a list of fiction in English as possible, and so in-print and out-of-print items, books published in Great Britain as well as in the United States and Canada, and juvenile books have been included. There may be criticism of some of the titles found here. They include books in which tennis is the whole story, and books in which it is minimal. In John Carr's book (see 483) a body is found on a tennis court with only one set of footprints leading to it; Daveson's book (see 490) has tennis on the cover and hardly any place else; and Morris's book (see 522) has little more than a chapter on a game. Yet all of them are found here: Carr's because it's a good mystery, Daveson's because every bibliography deserves a Harlequin Romance, and Morris's because every bibliography ought to have a work of "literature" in it. And it may be a surprise to some readers that the five little Peppers played tennis (see 517). In short, this is an opinionated list that took an enormous amount of thoroughly enjoyed time to compile. This editor would welcome correspondence from enthusiasts on any titles missed.

Collections of short stories in which only one or two items are about tennis are not included: for example, Kent Nelson's THE TENNIS PLAYER AND OTHER STORIES (Urbana: University of Illinois Press, 1977). Collections in which every story is about tennis are included--the works by Sherman (540) and by Tilden (546-48). In some cases the authors used pseudonyms. The pseudonym is given after the author's real name. Searchers for these books in second-hand stores should realize that they will be alphabetized under the pseudonyms, while searchers in library catalogs should look under the real name.

475   Allen, Alex. THE TENNIS MENACE. Chicago: Whitman, 1975. 64 p.

      Juvenile.

476   Barker, Robert. LOVE FORTY. Philadelphia: J.B. Lippincott, 1975. 216 p.

477   Barrett, Richmond. TRUANT. New York: E.P. Dutton, 1944. 336 p.

478   Boyar, Jane, and Boyar, Burt. WORLD CLASS. New York: Random House, 1975. 402 p.

479   Braddon, Russell. THE FINALISTS. New York: Atheneum, 1977. 224 p.

480   Brandner, Gary. THE PLAYERS. New York: Pyramid, 1975. 256 p. Paperbound.

480A Brennan, Dan. DOUBLE FAULT. New York: Norden, 1979. 346 p. Paperbound.

481   Brennan, Peter. SUDDEN DEATH. New York: Rawson Associates, 1978. 335 p.

482   Brinkley, William. BREAKPOINT. New York: William Morrow, 1978. 324 p.

483   Carr, John Dickson. THE PROBLEM OF THE WIRE CAGE. New York: Harper, 1939. 296 p.

484   Christopher, Matt. THE PIGEON WITH THE TENNIS ELBOW. Boston: Little Brown, 1975. 116 p.

       Juvenile.

485   Clavering, Molly. RESULTS OF THE FINALS. London: Hodder, 1957. 192 p.

       Claymore, Tod. See Hugh Clevely.

486   Clevely, Hugh [Tod Claymore]. REUNION IN FLORIDA. London: Cassell, 1952. 210 p.

487   _____. THIS IS WHAT HAPPENED. New York: Simon and Schuster, 1939. 301p.; YOU REMEMBER THE CASE. Toronto: Nelson, 1939. 306 p.

488   Courtier, Sidney. SWING HIGH, SWEET MURDER. London: Hammond, 1962. 205 p.

489   Cox, William. GAME, SET AND MATCH. New York: Dodd, Mead, 1977. 182 p.

       Juvenile.

490   Daveson, Mons. THIS TOO I'LL REMEMBER. Stratford, Ontario: Harlequin, 1970. 186 p. Paperbound.

491   Delman, David. SUDDEN DEATH. New York: Doubleday, 1972. 174 p.

491A Demers, Ralph. THE CIRCUIT. New York: Viking, 1976. 261 p.

491B Ellery, Jan. THE LAST SET. New York: Kensington Publishing Corp., 1979. 207 p. Paperbound.

492   Ellin, Stanley. THE VALENTINE ESTATE. New York: Random House, 1968. 274 p.

493   Etter, Les. COOL MAN ON THE COURT. New York: Hastings House, 1969. 125 p.

       Juvenile.

       Everett, Gail. See Arlene Hale.

494   Fadiman, Edwin. THE PROFESSIONAL. Greenwich, Conn.: Fawcett

Crest, 1973. 351 p. Paperbound.

495 Friend, Alona. MIXED DOUBLES. New York: Greystone, 1940. 313 p.

Gilbert, Nan. See Mildred Gilbertson.

496 Gilbertson, Mildred [Nan Gilbert]. CHAMPIONS DON'T CRY. New York: Harper and Row, 1960. 198 p.
   Juvenile.

497 Goodchild, George. DEATH ON THE CENTER COURT. New York: Green Circle Books, 1936. 317 p.

498 Grahame, Jean. PERDITA FINDS HERSELF. London: Eyre and Spottis- woode, 1944. 223 p.

Haggard, Paul. See Stephen Longstreet.

499 Hale, Arlene [Gail Everett]. LOVE IS THE WINNER. New York: Bouregy, 1960. 233 p.

500 Harkins, Philip. THE BIG SILVER BOWL. New York: William Morrow, 1947. 218 p.
   Juvenile.

501 _____. GAME, CAROL CANNING! New York: William Morrow, 1958. 221 p.
   Juvenile.

502 Harris, Peter. THE FINAL SET. London: John Long, 1965. 184 p.

503 Hoppe, Art. THE TIDDLING TENNIS THEORUM. New York: Viking, 1977. 182 p.

504 Hutto, Nelson. VICTORY VOLLEY. New York: Harper and Row, 1967. 249 p.
   Juvenile.

505 Jackson, Caary [Jack Paulson]. MATCH POINT. Philadelphia: West- minster, 1956. 188 p.
   Juvenile.

506   Jacobs, Helen. CENTER COURT. New York: A.S. Barnes, 1950. 239 p.
      Juvenile.

507   _____. JUDY, TENNIS ACE. New York: Dodd, Mead, 1951. 212 p.
      Juvenile.

508   _____. THE TENNIS MACHINE. New York: Charles Scribner's Sons,
      1972. 220 p.
      Juvenile. The book is also available to blind and other
      physically handicapped readers through a national network of
      libraries. To obtain the name and address of the closest one,
      write to the National Library Service, Division for the Blind
      and Physically Handicapped, Library of Congress, Washington,
      D.C. 20542.

509   Jacobs, Linda. IN TENNIS LOVE MEANS NOTHING. St. Paul,
      Minn.: EMC Corp., 1974. 38 p.
      Juvenile.

510   Entry deleted.

511   Klein, Norma. IT'S OK IF YOU DON'T LOVE ME. New York: Dial,
      1977. 202 p.
      Juvenile.

512   Lambert, Derek. GRAND SLAM. London: Arlington, 1971. 220 p.

513   Leigh, Roberta. LOVE MATCH. Garden City, N.Y.: Doubleday,
      1979. 216 p. (This is bound with two other novels that do not deal
      with tennis in a volume labeled "Doubleday Romance Library.")

514   Lenglen, Suzanne. LOVE GAME: BEING THE LIFE STORY OF MAR-
      CELLE PENROSE. New York: Adelphi, 1925. 300 p.

515   Levene, Philip. AMBROSE IN LONDON. London: Robert Hale, 1959.
      190 p.

516   Longstreet, Stephen [Paul Haggard]. DEAD IS THE DOORNAIL. Phila-
      delphia: J.B. Lippincott, 1937. 315 p.

517   Lothrop, Harriet [Margaret Sidney]. FIVE LITTLE PEPPERS AT SCHOOL.
      Boston: Lothrop, Lee and Shepard, 1903. 435 p.
      Juvenile.

518 Lunemann, Evelyn. TENNIS CHAMP. Westchester, Ill.: Benefic, 1972. 68 p.

    Juvenile.

519 Marx, Arthur. THE ORDEAL OF WILLIE BROWN. New York: Simon and Schuster, 1951. 279 p.

520 Meggs, Brown. SATURDAY GAMES. New York: Random House, 1974. 178 p.

521 Meynell, Laurence. DOUBLE FAULT. London: Collins, 1965. 224 p.

522 Morris, Wright. THE HUGE SEASON. New York: Viking, 1954. 306 p.

523 Neigoff, Mike. HAL, TENNIS CHAMP. Chicago: Whitman, 1971. 126 p.

    Juvenile.

524 Newman, Bernard. CENTRE COURT MURDER. London: Gollancz, 1951. 303 p.

525 November, Penny. THE TENNIS FAIRY. N.p.: Published by the author, 1976. Unpaged. Paperbound.

    Juvenile.

526 O'Donnell, Lillian. DEATH ON THE GRASS. New York: Arcadia House, 1960. 224 p.

527 Ogan, Margaret, and Ogan, George. TENNIS BUM. Philadelphia: Westminster, 1976. 122 p.

    Juvenile.

528 Oldham, Archie. A RACE THROUGH SUMMER. New York: Dell, 1975. 174 p. Paperbound.

Paulson, Jack. See Caary Jackson.

529 Peters, Ludovic. TWO SETS TO MURDER. New York: Coward-McCann, 1963. 189 p.

530 Petrocelli, Orlando. MATCH SET. New York: Pinnacle, 1977. 370 p. Paperbound.

531 Pici, J.R. THE TENNIS HUSTLER. Canoga Park, Calif.: Major Books, 1978. 256 p. Paperbound.

532 Platt, Kin. MATCH POINT FOR MURDER. New York: Random House, 1975. 185 p.

533 Porter, Mark. SET POINT: A WIN HADLEY SPORT STORY. New York: Simon and Schuster, 1960. 224 p.

Juvenile.

534 Potter, Jeremy. HAZARD CHASE. London: Constable, 1964. 192 p.

As the title indicates, this book uses court tennis.

535 Ray, Robert. THE HEART OF THE GAME. New York: Berkley, 1975. 219 p. Paperbound.

536 Sanderlin, Owenita. TENNIS REBEL. New York: Franklin Watts, 1978. 95 p.

Juvenile.

537 Schayer, E. Richard. THE GOOD LOSER. Philadelphia: David McKay, 1917. 59 p.

Juvenile.

538 Schulman, Janet. JENNY AND THE TENNIS NUT. New York: Greenwillow, 1978. 56 p.

Juvenile.

539 Scott, Leroy. THE TRAIL OF GLORY. Boston: Houghton Mifflin, 1926. 206 p.

540 Sherman, Harold. THE TENNIS TERROR AND OTHER TENNIS STORIES. Chicago: Goldsmith, 1932. 244 p.

Short stories.

Sidney, Margaret. See Harriet Lothrop.

541 Sklar, George. THE PROMISING YOUNG MEN. New York: Crown, 1951. 304 p.

542 Slote, Alfred. LOVE AND TENNIS. New York: Macmillan, 1979. 163 p.

Juvenile.

543   Spain, Nancy. POISON IN PLAY. London: Hutchinson, 1946. 168 p.

544   Streatfeild, Noel. TENNIS SHOES. New York: Random House, 1938. 290 p.

        Juvenile.

545   Tilden, William T. GLORY'S NET. Garden City, N.Y.: Doubleday, 1930. 296 p.

546   _____. IT'S ALL IN THE GAME. Garden City, N.Y.: Doubleday Page, 1922. 245 p.

        Short stories.

547   _____. THE PHANTOM DRIVE AND OTHER TENNIS STORIES. New York: American Lawn Tennis, 1924. 235 p.

        Short stories.

548   _____. THE PINCH QUITTER AND OTHER TENNIS STORIES FOR JUNIOR PLAYERS. New York: American Lawn Tennis, 1924. 202 p.

        Short stories. Juvenile.

549   Towne, Mary. FIRST SERVE. New York: Atheneum, 1976. 214 p.

        Juvenile.

Trent, Michael. See William Underhill.

550   Tunis, John R. AMERICAN GIRL. New York: Book League Monthly, 1930. 237 p.

551   _____. CHAMPION'S CHOICE. New York: Harcourt Brace, 1940. 300 p.

        Juvenile.

552   Underhill, William [Michael Trent]. YOUNG TENNIS PLAYER. London: Constable, 1961. 159 p.

        Juvenile.

553   Walden, Amelia. HEARTBREAK TENNIS. Philadelphia: Westminster, 1977. 168 p.

        Juvenile.

554   Wallop, Douglass. MIXED SINGLES. New York: Norton, 1977. 185 p.

555 Welch, Timothy. THE TENNIS MURDERS. New York: Popular Library, 1976. 224 p. Paperbound.

556 Wilkinson, Burke. LAST CLEAR CHANCE. Boston: Little Brown, 1953. 252 p.

557 Wills, Helen, and Murphy, Robert. DEATH SERVES AN ACE. New York: Charles Scribner's Sons, 1939. 317 p.

> Two plays are listed below. They are imaginative works of literature and deserve mention here.

558 Reach, James. THE TENNIS CLUB MYSTERY: A MYSTERY IN ONE ACT. New York: Samuel French, 1941. 32 p.

559 Trow, George. THE TENNIS GAME. This play was never published. It opened off Broadway in New York in February 1978, closed shortly thereafter, reopened in November 1978, and again closed after a short run.

Instruction

There are many, indeed too many, instruction books, each repeating what every other one has said. An annotation could be written that would apply to most books below as follows: "This book gives information on grips, how to hit the strokes, and how to use them, that is, tactics and strategy. Illustrations cover most points, and there are chapters on conditioning, equipment, doubles play, and practice drills. The rules (or a summary of them) are given as of the publication date." In the annotations that follow, therefore, the reader can assume that most of such information is covered, unless the title of the book clearly indicates a different scope.

560 ALL ABOUT TENNIS. Chicago: Rand McNally, [1975]. 194 p. Photos., dgrms. Paperbound. ISBN 0-528-84052-5.

> This is a book for the beginner. The anonymous author shows an occasional gleam of humor, makes a few minor errors, and indicates that opinions differ on certain instructional points. An unusual photograph on page 134 makes Billie Jean King a left-hander.

561 Allen, James. LEARN TO PLAY TENNIS. Chicago: Rand McNally, 1968. 72 p. Photos., dgrms., line dwgs., gloss. Paperbound. ISBN 0-528-81025-1. LC 68-20416.

> This is a short, beginner's guide covering the basic rules and the strokes, with sequence line drawings illustrating the latter. The glossary contains some inadequate definitions.

562   Annarino, Anthony. TENNIS: INDIVIDUALIZED INSTRUCTIONAL PRO-
GRAM. Englewood Cliffs, N.J.: Prentice-Hall, 1973. 72 p. ISBN
0-13-903328-9. LC NUC 74-88309.

> This is similar to the same author's book on badminton (see
> item 57). It is a lesson plan approach to instruction, with
> written and skill demonstration tests on strokes and strategy.

563   Barnaby, Jack. ADVANTAGE TENNIS: RACKET WORK, TACTICS,
AND LOGIC. Boston: Allyn and Bacon, 1975. 237 p. Photos.,
dgrms. ISBN 0-205-04686-X. LC 74-22246.

> This is an immensely detailed book emphasizing racket skills.
> It is very thorough on the whys of instruction: for example,
> why the Eastern grip is best for the beginner, why it is impor-
> tant to bend the knees, and so on. There is a chapter on
> half-court play, a topic not often covered in instruction books
> in such detail.

564   _____. GROUND STROKES IN MATCH PLAY. United States Tennis
Association Instructional Series. New York: Doubleday, 1978. 152 p.
Dwgs. ISBN 0-385-12705-7. LC 77-16897.

> Barnaby's claim is that most texts teach ground strokes in iso-
> lation rather than in the context in which they will be used--
> actual play. It is play and the level of the player that deter-
> mines whether the closed or open stance should be used, how
> much backswing, and more.

565   _____. TENNIS IN BRIEF. Center Harbor, N.H.: Privately published
by the author, 1963. Available from Barnaby at Bean Road, RD 1, Center
Harbor, N.H. 03226.

> A pamphlet summarizing essentials of all elements of the
> singles and doubles game from grips through strategy, this
> includes brief sequence photographs for slice and chop, as
> well as the usual top spin drives.

566   Bassett, Glen, and Galanoy, Terry. TENNIS: THE BASSETT SYSTEM.
Chicago: Regnery, 1977. 106 p. Photos., gloss. ISBN 0-8092-7916-9.
LC 76-55670.

> Bassett, a successful coach at UCLA, describes his system which
> consists of a four-count emphasis on backswing, step, hit, and
> follow-through, with the last being the most important.

567   Bockus, William. CHECKLIST FOR BETTER TENNIS. Garden City,
N.Y.: Doubleday, 1973. 152 p. Dgrms., dwgs. Paperbound. ISBN
0-385-04612-X. LC 72-97268.

> Standard instruction is given in detail in the front of this book
> and then condensed into one-sentence key points for each stroke

in back. Information on handicap games one can play and how to build one's own court is included.

568 Boltin, Alan. BATHROOM TENNIS: 8 MINUTES A DAY TO LEARN, IMPROVE & MAINTAIN YOUR TENNIS GAME AT HOME. New York: Ballentine, 1978. 54 p. Photos., dgrms., line dwgs. Paperbound. ISBN 0-345-27619-1. LC 78-52212.

The title of this one caused reviewers to treat it as a joke. Actually it is standard instruction written in "rich beautiful prose." For example: "Once you blend proper movement with consistent strokes and give them a chance to ferment, your tennis game will be like a rich tasting, rare wine." Why the title? Boltin recommends that his conditioning exercises and mind training program be performed in that location.

569 Braden, Vic, and Bruns, Bill. VIC BRADEN'S TENNIS FOR THE FUTURE. Boston: Little Brown, 1977. 274 p. Photos., dgrms. ISBN 0-316-10510-4. LC 77-5603.

This is an exhaustively detailed book reflecting Braden's approach, which consists of emphasis on the loop rather than straight backswing, the importance of topspin, the necessity of knowing court measurements and angles, and humor. Outstanding photographs are included.

570 Bradlee, Dick. INSTANT TENNIS: A NEW APPROACH BASED ON THE COORDINATION, RHYTHM AND TIMING OF CHAMPIONS. New York: Devin-Adair, 1962. 107 p. Photos., dwgs. ISBN 0-8159-5811-0. LC 62-13467.

The author's contention is that standard instruction books are wrong, and that name players teach one way but play another. Principles of motion economy and moving pictures of top players show that one should not stand sideways to the net but with the feet parallel, and for forehand and backhand should step forward with the right foot (if one is right-handed) prior to the hit.

571 Brecheen, Joel. TENNIS MADE EASY: COUNT ONE TO TOP TENNIS TECHNIQUE. North Hollywood, Calif.: Wilshire, 1969. 111 p. Photos., dgrms., dwgs. Paperbound. In the original hardcover edition the subtitle was the title. Tuscon: Palo Verde, 1969. LC 70-95603.

Brecheen's method emphasizes the use of the whole body and continuous movement once the racket motion starts. He believes that two beginners can teach others enough so that they can have a good game if they follow his method.

572 Brent, R. Spencer. PATTERN PLAY TENNIS. Garden City, N.Y.: Doubleday, 1974. 140 p. Dgrms., dwgs. ISBN 0-385-05874-8. LC 72-89295.

> Brent offers a book for the tennis teacher. The basic idea is that tennis is a game of repeated patterns (serve to backhand, backhand return to backhand volley, backhand volley to backhand) and that it should be taught by repetition of such patterns in practice situations. He also feels that instruction should begin with the volley, since that's the easiest stroke for the beginner to see improvement.

573 Brown, Jim. TENNIS: TEACHING, COACHING, AND DIRECTING PROGRAMS. Englewood Cliffs, N.J.: Prentice-Hall, 1976. 192 p. Photos., dgrms., bibliog. ISBN 0-13-903344-0. LC 75-33047.

> This is a point-by-point instruction manual on recognizing stroke flaws, drills, conducting clinics and tournaments, and how the teacher can develop professionally, as well as the differences in teaching children, adolescents, and adults. It is a combination and expansion of several magazine articles by Brown.

574 _____. TENNIS WITHOUT LESSONS. Englewood Cliffs, N.J.: Prentice-Hall, 1977. 154 p. Photos., gloss., bibliog. ISBN 0-13-903252-5. LC 76-18801.

> Brown's thesis is that one can learn tennis without formal instruction by reading this book and applying its principles of understanding how to hit and being able to analyze and correct errors. He also discusses what one can learn by watching and reading about the game.

Budge, Don. DON BUDGE: A TENNIS MEMOIR. See 436.

575 Cantin, Eugene. TOPSPIN TO BETTER TENNIS. Mountain View, Calif.: World, 1977. 200 p. Photos., dgrms. ISBN 0-89037-075-3. LC 77-73877.

> Topsin all the time on all ground strokes except the backhand approach is Cantin's idea, which he explicates thoroughly while telling how to groove strokes for tournament play. No hit and giggle tennis here; it's war in which the player should " . . . leave the court strewn with the wreckage of his opponent's game."

576 Casewit, Curtis. AMERICA'S TENNIS BOOK. New York: Charles Scribner's Sons, 1975. 214 p. Photos., gloss., bibliog. ISBN 0-684-13900-6. LC 74-10714.

> This is a primer in every sense, with its many one-sentence

paragraphs and some strokes introduced in quotes: for example, "volley" is presented as if it were almost a foreign language. In addition to instruction, careers in tennis, injuries and their treatment, and tennis camp information are included. A few inaccuracies were noted.

577 Charles, Allegra. HOW TO WIN AT LADIES' DOUBLES. New York: Arco, 1975. 151 p. Photos., dgrms., gloss., bibliog. ISBN 0-688-03797-0. LC 75-3780.

Emphasis is placed on not playing one-up one-back doubles but on being together (preferably at the net) at every opportunity--standard doubles instruction that Charles feels needs stressing for women, who are more reluctant to play that way. The inevitable sex and tennis chapter is here too.

578 Chase, Edward. COVERING THE COURT. United States Tennis Association, Tennis Instructional Series. Garden City, N.Y.: Doubleday, 1976. 63 p. Dgrms., dwgs. ISBN 0-385-05502-1. LC 74-12679.

If one can't get to where the ball is--that is, cover the court --and get set to make the shot, one will not win no matter how good the strokes are. That point made, Chase spends the rest of the book discussing what other texts call tactics and strategy.

579 Collins, Ed. WATCH THE BALL, BEND YOUR KNEES, THAT'LL BE $20 PLEASE. Ottawa, Ill.: Green Hill, 1977. 216 p. Dwgs. Paperbound. ISBN 0-916054-50-0. LC 76-55626.

This is a compilation of one hundred newspaper instructional columns with a table of contents by subject that pulls similar items together. Drills are included in most columns to practice points made. This book should win a prize for the most imaginative title for an instruction manual.

580 Conroy, John, and Kraft, Eve. THE TENNIS WORKBOOK: UNIT TWO FOR INTERMEDIATE AND ADVANCED PLAYERS. Rev. ed. New York: Scholastic Coach, 1976. 72 p. Dgrms., bibliog. Paperbound.

This is the sequel to Kraft's Unit One (see 633) and is more of the same for the higher level player. It gives instruction followed by a series of exercises. A skill test is included; those who pass are eligible for United States Tennis Association badges and certificates.

581 Cox, Mark. LAWN TENNIS: HOW TO BECOME A CHAMPION. Challenge Series. London: William Luscombe, 1975. Distributed in the United States by Hippocrene Books, New York. 123 p. Photos., dgrms. ISBN 0-86002-023-1. LC 77-351916.

This is standard instruction. The strong points are a clear explanation of spin, the pros and cons of using two-handed strokes, and a discussion of who should play the deuce court and who the ad court in doubles.

582 Cutler, Merritt. THE TENNIS BOOK. New York: McGraw-Hill, 1967. 111 p. Dwgs. ISBN 0-07-014991-7. LC 67-18323.

Cutler, an artist and 1930 indoor doubles champion, wrote and illustrated this oversize book. The emphasis is on the illustrations. The instruction is standard, although the author did leave out the backhand underspin stroke.

583 Devereux, Rick. NET RESULTS: THE COMPLETE TENNIS HANDBOOK. Boston: Pathfinder, 1974. 182 p. Photos., dgrms., gloss. Paperbound. ISBN 0-913390-07-0. LC 74-80452.

Devereux has read many other instruction books, and he quotes and incorporates information from them in his own presentation. One unusual chapter describes a doubles set, giving the characteristics of each player's game, and then does post-match analysis--useful information for more informed tennis watching.

584 Doerner, Peter; Doerner, Cynthia; and Ozier, Dan. WINNING TENNIS DOUBLES. Chicago: Contemporary Books, 1978. 111 p. Photos., dgrms., line dwgs. ISBN 0-8092-7697-6. LC 77-91151.

The authors emphasize the triangle concept as essential to a winning game--establishing a court position in which the partners are the side-by-side base with the ball the third point. The book also covers mixed doubles from male and female viewpoints and left-handers as partners and opponents.

585 Driver, Helen. TENNIS FOR TEACHERS. Enl. ed. of the international ed. Madison, Wis.: Monona-Driver, 1970. 219 p. Photos., dgrms., gloss., bibliog. ISBN 0-910982-00-7.

This book has been through many editions since its first publication in 1936, but it is outdated. Silk, instead of nylon, is mentioned for racket strings, and the Continental grip is not covered for ground strokes (it is for the serve and is called "the service grip"). There is sound and thorough advice in the book for teachers on how to instruct.

586 _____. TENNIS SELF-INSTRUCTOR. Enl. ed. Madison, Wis.: Monona-Driver, 1971. 109 p. Photos., dgrms., dwgs., gloss. Paperbound.

This is a companion volume to the author's TENNIS FOR TEACHERS (see 585). While it does not have as dated a tone as the other, most illustrations are from an earlier era of the game. Some sections are repeated verbatim from the other book.

587 Durr, Francoise. DOUBLES STRATEGY: A CREATIVE AND PSYCHO-
LOGICAL APPROACH TO TENNIS. New York: David McKay, 1978.
112 p. Dgrms. ISBN 0-679-20350-8. LC 77-21194.

> This is a book for the thinking advanced player. After intro-
> ductory sections comparing doubles and singles in terms of the
> effects of the alley and strategy and tactics, Durr analyzes
> the game thoroughly.

588 Eldred, Vince. TENNIS WITHOUT MISTAKES. New York: G.P. Putnam's Sons, 1975. 224 p. Photos., dgrms. ISBN 0-399-11309-6. LC
74-16589.

> For every topic covered--footwork, concentration, and prac-
> tice, as well as the standard strokes and tactics--the chapter
> devoted to it begins with a list of common errors, continues
> with a detailed discussion of those errors, and concludes with
> tips for special concentration. Photographs of Eldred show
> the wrong and the right way to do it.

589 Ellwanger, Rico. TENNIS--UP TO TOURNAMENT STANDARD. EP
Sport Series. Wakefield, Engl.: EP Publishing, 1973. Distributed in
the United States by Charles River Books, Boston. 118 p. Photos.,
dwgs. ISBN 0-7158-0579-7.

> Many illustrations are the distinguishing feature of this volume,
> which was translated from German and on occasion shows a
> certain awkwardness of expression. Standard instruction is
> given.

590 Everett, Peter, and Skillman, Virginia. BEGINNING TENNIS. Rev.
ed. Sports Skills Series. Belmont, Calif.: Wadsworth, 1968. 58 p.
Dgrms., line dwgs., gloss., bibliog. Paperbound. LC 68-25413.

> Standard instruction is given with written and skills tests in-
> cluded.

591 Fannin, Jim, and Mullin, John. TENNIS AND KIDS: THE FAMILY
CONNECTION. Garden City, N.Y.: Doubleday, 1979. 194 p.
Dwgs. ISBN 0-385-14378-8. LC 78-22317.

> Fannin uses tennis as a framework to make a larger philoso-
> phical statement. His message is that we must teach attitudes
> more than skills, and those attitudes--summed up in the acro-
> nym SCORE, which stands for self-discipline, concentration,
> optimism, relaxation, and enjoyment--are ". . . the guide-
> posts . . . on the road to a solid self esteem." Many spe-
> cific exercises are given to develop good SCOREs on the court
> and in life.

592 Faulkner, Edwin, and Weymuller, Frederick. ED FAULKNER'S TENNIS:

HOW TO PLAY IT--HOW TO TEACH IT. New York: Dial, 1970. 294 p. Photos. Paperbound. ISBN 0-8037-2244-3. LC 70-76967. A-bridged ed. New York: Dell, 1974. 287 p. Paperbound. ISBN 0-440-03192-150.

> This book explains how to learn and how to teach all elements of the game. Trouble spots for each stroke, as well as what the player and the teacher should do to correct them, are given in clear text and shown in good, detailed sequence photographs.

593   Fiske, Loring. HOW TO BEAT BETTER TENNIS PLAYERS. New York: Doubleday, 1970. 296 p. Dgrms. ISBN 0-385-00346-3. LC 74-97660.

> This is instruction for the average player on how to make the most of what he or she has. Fiske repeats himself a lot and leaves out discussion of the grip in his chapter on the serve.

594   Forer, Bernard. A NEW PRACTICAL TENNIS BOOK: STROKES, STRAT-EGY, AND SUCCESSFUL PLAY. New York: Vantage, 1974. 127 p. Dgrms., dwgs. ISBN 0-533-00768-2.

> This is instruction for all levels from beginner to advanced, and the text varies with the audience. The chapters for beginners are written in simple language, while those for higher levels are quite technical. Drawings are not always well placed; the drop shot, for example, is pictured on page 24 but not discussed until page 98.

595   Fotre, Vincent. WHY YOU LOSE AT TENNIS. New York: Barnes and Noble, 1973. 103 p. Photos., dgrms. Paperbound. ISBN 0-06-463326-8. LC 72-9913.

> This book goes beyond the title and explains not only why one loses, but also what one can do about it. Topics covered include percentage tennis, how to play different opponents (retriever, big hitter, and so forth), one's first tournament and how to handle it, and how to play on different court surfaces.

596   Fraser, Neale. SUCCESSFUL TENNIS: FROM BEGINNER TO EXPERT IN FORTY LESSONS. New York: Pitman, 1974. 79 p. Photos., dgrms., dwgs., gloss. ISBN 0-273-07089-4. LC 74-15570.

> This book presents forty brief lessons in seventy-nine pages. They reflect the Australian approach to the game, which in-cludes minimal change between forehand and backhand grip because there isn't time to change up at the net where one will be most of the time, and hard physical exercises to get and keep in shape.

597   Gallwey, W. Timothy. THE INNER GAME OF TENNIS. New York: Random House, 1974. 141 p. ISBN 0-394-49154-8. LC 73-20582.

> "It's not that I don't know what to do, it's that I don't do what I know." How to do what one knows is the subject of this best-selling book on "zen tennis." Gallwey's thesis is that the body will follow the correct method of stroking automatically if one will just let it do so and not let the self-correcting verbal "you" interfere. See also 332.

598   _____. INNER TENNIS: PLAYING THE GAME. New York: Random House, 1976. 173 p. ISBN 0-394-40043-7. LC 76-14199.

> The author takes the principle described in the annotation above and applies it to other life situations ranging from sex to washing dishes. He provides practical exercises, both mental and physical, to help people attain inner serenity. While tennis still provides the bulk of examples chosen, the book is really more a philosophical manual than an instruction book.

599   Garner, Stan. THE STAN GARNER TENNIS IMPROVEMENT METHOD. New York: Tactical Marketing, 1977. Unpaged. Dgms., line dwgs. Paperbound.

> This is a privately published item with some of the problems such books are heir to--no page numbers, no index, and many typos. Some Garner points are to play with any grip that feels comfortable, two hands are better than one on the backhand, and one should not worry about serve toss variations as long as the hit is made at the arm's full extension.

600   Gautschi, Marcel. TENNIS: PLAYING, TRAINING, WINNING. New York: Arco, 1979. 144 p. Dgrms., dwgs., gloss., bibliog. ISBN 0-688-04692-9.

> Written in outline format, this book contains basic points written on the left side and discussion on the right. Standard instruction is given with poor sequence drawings, and the bibliography cites out-of-date editions of works. There is a useful section on pages 138-42 discussing a method of analyzing play that is helpful for fault correction.

601   Gensemer, Robert. TENNIS. 2d ed. Physical Activities Series. Philadelphia: W.B. Saunders, 1975. 108 p. Dgrms., line dwgs., gloss., bibliog. Paperbound. ISBN 0-7216-4110-5. LC 74-6682.

> Clear text, informal style, and thorough standard instruction are presented here with points illustrated by drawings. In two instances the last drawing of a series shows the player left-handed where heretofore he had been right-handed.

602 Gonzales, Pancho, and Bairstow, Jeffrey. TENNIS BEGINS AT 40: A GUIDE FOR ALL PLAYERS WHO DON'T HAVE WRISTS OF STEEL OR A CANNONBALL SERVE, DON'T ALWAYS RUSH THE NET OR HAVE A DEVASTATING OVERHEAD BUT WANT TO WIN. New York: Dial, 1976. 180 p. Photos., dgrms. ISBN 0-8037-5945-2. LC 76-9416.

Gonzales stresses the importance of good physical fitness and devotion to practice. This text is intended for the older player who has no tournament ambitions but still wants to win.

603 Gonzales, Pancho, and Hawk, Dick. TENNIS. Introduction by Gladys Heldman. New York: Crown, 1962. 123 p. Photos., dgrms., dwgs. ISBN 0-517-12842-X. LC 62-8027.

Standard instruction is given by the former U.S. national champion. Gonzales adds the necessary corollary to the famous "Never change a winning game--always change a losing one," when he says "never switch to a game you do not know how to play. If you are basically a baseliner don't become a net rusher . . . Try change of pace."

604 Gonzales, Pancho, and Hyams, Joe. WINNING TACTICS FOR WEEKEND SINGLES. New York: Holt, Rinehart and Winston, 1974. 136 p. Photos. ISBN 0-03-013136-7. LC 74-4805.

This question and answer format manual covers more than the title's "tactics"--stroke instruction, tennis past age forty, and more are included. The lack of an index is a problem. For example, information about blister prevention is found in a section labeled "Pregame."

605 Gordon, Barbara. IMPROVING YOUR TENNIS GAME. New York: Hawthorn, 1976. 136 p. Photos., dgrms., line dwgs. Paperbound. ISBN 0-8015-3978-1. LC 73-9305.

This book is organized as a dialogue between a pupil and teacher based on a "Here is my problem, what can I do about it?" situation. The pupil has most of the problems an intermediate player experiences. There is no index, but chapter titles give clues to what is covered.

606 Gould, Dick. TENNIS ANYONE? 3d ed. Palo Alto, Calif.: Mayfield, 1978. 101 p. Photos., dgrms., dwgs., gloss. Paperbound. ISBN 0-8474-438-X. LC 78-51946.

This is an extremely well-organized standard instruction book. Topics include when to use cross court and when to use down the line shots, strategy in advanced doubles, and more.

607 Graebner, Clark; Graebner, Carole; and Prince, Kim. MIXED DOUBLES TENNIS. New York: McGraw-Hill, 1973. 107 p. Dgrms., line dwgs.

ISBN 0-07-023879-0. LC 72-10043.

The authors present the mixed game for average players and stress the use of each person's strengths and weaknesses to form an effective combination. An amusing section on how to psych one's opponent is included along with a piece on life on the big-time circuit.

608 Grafton, Charlene. HOW TO TEACH TENNIS . . . FOR THURSDAYS CHILDREN. Cover title: DIAGNOSTIC AND PRESCRIPTIVE METHODS: A TEXT FOR TENNIS AND OTHER RELATED SPORTS. Oklahoma City: Winning Ways, n.d. Unpaged. Photos., dgrms. Paperbound.

This is the only instruction book that covers teaching tennis to children and adults with learning disabilities--primarily physical but also behavioral. It discusses how one diagnoses the problems, identifies and builds on the strengths the pupils have, and uses various teaching strategies. Teaching aids that will be helpful for such pupils are also covered.

609 Greene, Robert. TENNIS DRILLS: ON--AND OFF--COURT DRILLS AND EXERCISES FOR BEGINNERS, INTERMEDIATE PLAYERS, AND TEACHING PROFESSIONALS. New York: Hawthorn, 1976. 233 p. Photos., dgrms., gloss. ISBN 0-8015-7525-7. LC 75-28689.

All drills given can be performed by one person or with partners. They are illustrated, as well as described.

610 _____. TENNIS TACTICS: MATCH PLAY STRATEGIES THAT GET IMMEDIATE WINNING RESULTS. New York: G.P. Putnam's Sons, 1978. 149 p. Photos., dgrms., gloss. ISBN 0-399-12120-X. LC 77-26216.

Flexibility is a keynote in this book; the author considers individual strengths and weaknesses when he makes a recommendation for a particular strategy. Only the singles game is considered, and topics include scouting one's opponent, energy saving tactics, the effect of different court conditions, and much more.

611 Groppel, Jack, and Patterson, Jeff. THE SOLID BALL: AN OFFENSIVE WEAPON: A FUNDAMENTAL AND MECHANICAL APPROACH TO HITTING EFFECTIVE GROUNDSTROKES. Tallahassee, Fla.: Privately published by the author, 1976. Available from Patterson at P.O. Drawer 20469. Tallahassee, Fla. 32304. 7 p. Dwgs. Paperbound.

This pamphlet tells what the term "heavy ball" means--an example might be any backhand drive hit by Don Budge--and how to hit it.

612 Harman, Bob. USE YOUR HEAD IN DOUBLES. New York: Charles Scribner's Sons, 1979. 115 p. Dgrms., dwgs. ISBN 0-684-16135-4. LC 78-31524.

Twenty-nine chapters on doubles with the usual Harman characteristics--clear explanations and sensible advice with some humor for the average player. For example: "Lady MacBeth might have been very good in doubles. She had the killer instinct, and she knew how to get her partner to follow suggestions." Topics include "What To Do When One Player Doesn't Show Up" and "How Unevenly Matched Partners Can Still Have Fun."

613 Harman, Bob, and Monroe, Keith. USE YOUR HEAD IN TENNIS. Rev. ed. New York: Crowell, 1974. 230 p. Dgrms., dwgs. ISBN 0-690-00584-9. LC 74-10715.

The authors tell the average player how to make the most of what he or she has when playing opponents at the same level, and how to enjoy the game at the same time. The theme is: "strategy is better than strength." This book was first published in 1950 and is a classic in tennis instruction.

614 Herzog, Billy Jean. TENNIS HANDBOOK. 3d ed. Dubuque, Iowa: Kendall Hunt, 1977. 83 p. Photos., dgrms., gloss., bibliog. Paperbound. ISBN 0-8403-0682-2.

This handbook reinforces learning done in an individual or group instruction program. It is one of the few books giving details on both nine and twelve point tie-breakers.

615 Hopman, Harry. LOBBING INTO THE SUN. Indianapolis: Bobbs-Merrill, 1975. 129 p. Dgrms., line dwgs. ISBN 0-672-51420-6. LC 73-11794; HARRY HOPMAN'S WINNING TENNIS STRATEGY. Indianapolis: Bobbs-Merrill, 1978. 129 p. Paperbound. ISBN 0-672-52530-5. LC 78-19185.

This is not a basic guide on how to play, but a commentary on those aspects of instruction that interest the author. For example, it discusses what to concentrate on during the pre-match warmup, handling the opponent who chops, and much more. His comments on women's tennis will not appeal to the liberated reader.

616 Huang, Bob, and Shay, Arthur. TEACHING YOUR CHILD TENNIS. Chicago: Contemporary Books, 1979. 71 p. Photos. ISBN 0-8092-7546-5. LC 78-57474.

This is teaching advice from the professional at Chicago's Midtown Tennis Club. After some general hints--for example, vary the introductory lessons and don't try to "teach one thing until they get it right,"--the authors give ten lessons beginning with palm tennis. The emphasis is on various games used to make learning easier.

617 Hunt, Lesley. INSIDE TENNIS FOR WOMEN. Chicago: Contemporary Books, 1978. 126 p. Photos., dgrms. ISBN 0-8092-7715-8. LC 77-91157.

Hunt says that most instruction books are written for men, but women play a different game and need a different book. Standard instruction is included with large illustrations. There is a good section in the beginning on limbering exercises.

618 Huss, Sally Moore. HOW TO PLAY POWER TENNIS WITH EASE. New York: Harcourt Brace Jovanovich, 1979. 95 p. Line dwgs. Spiral bound. ISBN 0-15-236836. LC 78-20569.

Real power in tennis stroking comes from swinging the head of the racket freely. In text and drawings the author shows how the player can teach herself or himself to do just that for ground strokes, serve, volley, and smash. A final chapter offers tips on finding "mental freedom"--playing for the fun of it.

619 INSTANT TENNIS LESSONS. Norwalk, Conn.: Tennis Magazine, 1978. 191 p. Dwgs. Paperbound. ISBN 0-914178-18-0. LC 77-92905.

"Lesson" is too broad a word for what is here; "tip" would be more accurate. Each page highlights a problem, and a member of the United States Professional Tennis Association provides the answer. A difference in opinion was noted. "Keep your other arm at your side for better backhands," says Dave Kozlowski (p. 81). On the other hand, "Use your other arm like a tightrope walker," says Lee Draisin (p. 91). Illustrations for each tip are given.

620 Jacobs, Helen. THE YOUNG SPORTSMAN'S GUIDE TO TENNIS. New York: Nelson, 1961. 93 p. LC 61-12638; BEGINNER'S GUIDE TO WINNING TENNIS. North Hollywood, Calif.: Wilshire, 1975. 91 p. Photos., dgrms., gloss., bibliog. Paperbound. ISBN 0-87980-283-9.

Wilshire, the paperbound publisher, made an error in choice of title; there is much here about court angles and spin aimed at the intermediate. Much detail is packed into a few pages. "Bounce, hit" appears here, long before Tim Gallwey.

621 Jaeger, Eloise, and Leighton, Harry. TEACHING OF TENNIS FOR SCHOOL AND RECREATIONAL PROGRAMS. Minneapolis: Burgess, 1963. 142 p. Photos., dgrms., line dwgs., bibliog.

Beginning with simple tossing exercises and body control skills as a lead-in to formal tennis, this book covers how to teach beginners and varsity players. There is a suggested lesson plan. Statements such as "Steel rackets always come with wire stringing" date the book, but a new edition has been promised for the near future.

622 Johnson, Joan, and Xanthos, Paul. TENNIS. 3d ed. Physical Education Activities Series. Dubuque, Iowa: William C. Brown, 1976. 96 p. Photos., dgrms., gloss., bibliog. Paperbound. ISBN 0-697-07071-9. LC 76-11103.

A description of the graduated length method of learning is a feature of this standard instruction book.

623 Joint Committee of the United States Lawn Tennis Association and the American Association for Health, Physical Education and Recreation. TENNIS GROUP INSTRUCTION. Washington, D.C.: American Alliance for Health, Physical Education and Recreation, 1963. 64 p. Photos., dgrms., bibliog. Paperbound. LC 63-14002.

This book emphasizes equipment such as ball machines, as well as utilizing what might be at hand: for example, floor markings, walls, and mats. A sample lesson plan is included. A few minor errors exist in text and photographs.

624 Jones, C.M. IMPROVING YOUR TENNIS: STROKES AND TECHNIQUES. London: Faber and Faber, 1973. Distributed in the United States by Transatlantic Arts, New York. 132 p. Dgrms., dwgs. ISBN 0-571-10148-8. LC 73-165611.

A basic thrust of this book for intermediate and above players is the application of scientific formulas to stroking, and readers may find some of that material highly technical. Close students of the game will find the detailed analysis of the Rod Laver versus Ken Rosewall 1972 World Championship of Tennis final (see 326) of great interest.

625 _____. MATCH-WINNING TENNIS: TACTICS, TEMPERAMENT AND TRAINING. London: Faber and Faber, 1971. Distributed in the United States by Transatlantic Arts, New York. 166 p. Dgrms. ISBN 0-571-09289-6. LC 79-589150.

This is a combination theoretical and practical book for the advanced player at the tournament level. It includes analyses of several top-level matches. Very long quotes from other sources are presented.

626 _____. TENNIS: HOW TO BECOME A CHAMPION. 2d ed. London: Faber and Faber, 1970. Distributed in the United States by Transatlantic Arts, New York. 146 p. Photos., dgrms., line dwgs. ISBN 0-571-04714-9. LC 68-106276.

Anyone who wonders why the Eastern forehand grip is wrong for serving should read Jones. He goes on for pages about it and for most other topics as well in this detailed book for those who want to go all the way, whether at Wimbledon or at a local club championship. A strong stress on the mental as well as the physical needs to that end is included.

627 Jones, C.M., and Buxton, Angela. STARTING TENNIS. London: Ward Lock, 1975. Distributed in the United States by Transatlantic Arts, New York. 96 p. Photos., dgrms., line dwgs. ISBN 0-7063-1972-9.

> In the very beginning of this book, the pictures and text are aimed at children, but the vocabulary level throughout and later portions of the text (for example, the mixed doubles chapter) are not for children. As in all Jones's books, British English is used and references are made to local conditions in England.

628 Kenfield, John. TEACHING AND COACHING TENNIS. 3d ed. Dubuque, Iowa: William C. Brown, 1976. 141 p. Photos., dgrms., bibliog. Paperbound. ISBN 0-697-07413-7. LC 75-35433.

> Section 1 covers teaching the individual with a list of problems and how to correct them for each stroke. Section 2 deals with group teaching and covers children of different ages, school classes, and clinics. The final section is on coaching a team and goes into administrative necessities, as well as on-court coaching.

629 _____. THE VOLLEY AND THE HALF-VOLLEY: THE ATTACKING GAME. United States Tennis Association, Tennis Instructional Series. New York: Doubleday, 1978. 62 p. Dgrms., dwgs., bibliog. ISBN 0-385-12633-6. LC 76-56310.

> Attack is the name of the topnotch game, and Kenfield describes how to get to the net, as well as two of the strokes one needs to know to cope with the opponent's passing attempts. Kenfield includes practice tips and quickness drills.

630 King, Billie Jean, and Chapin, Kim. TENNIS TO WIN. New York: Harper and Row, 1970. 157 p. Dgrms., dwgs. ISBN 0-06-012393-1. LC 70-95969.

> This is instruction following the King personality: be bold, hit out even if a baseliner, and never play pat ball. There are good sections on serve return, the lob, and percentage tennis.

631 King, Billie Jean, and Hyams, Joe. BILLIE JEAN KING'S SECRETS OF WINNING TENNIS. New York: Holt, Rinehart and Winston, 1974. 116 p. Photos. ISBN 0-03-01341-3. LC 74-5095.

> In question and answer format (no index but chapter heads serve as guides), King tells her secrets from racket selection through strategy. A chapter on female questions is included.

632 Kleiman, Carol, and Stephens, Russell. YOU CAN TEACH YOUR CHILD TENNIS: A 30 DAY GUIDE TO TENNIS READINESS. New York: Faw-

cett, 1979. 127 p. Photos., dgrms. Paperbound. ISBN 0-445-04403-9. LC 79-114859.

> This is a how-to-do-it guide for parents with a detailed thirty-day lesson plan. Some might quarrel with Kleiman's reward system--milkshakes, McDonald's, and sodas for good performance--but she gives reasons for using it. The instruction begins with hitting the ball with the palm and continues on from there.

633 Kraft, Eve. THE TENNIS WORKBOOK: UNIT ONE FOR BEGINNERS AND ADVANCED BEGINNERS. Rev. ed. New York: Scholastic Coach Athletic Services, 1976. 64 p. Photos. Paperbound.

> This workbook is a step-by-step self-instruction guide in two parts; the first part for third- to sixth-grade pupils, the second part for advanced and older beginners who have completed part 1. The text consists of a series of exercises beginning with ball bouncing and going through skill and understanding tests. Pupils passing the tests are eligible for United States Tennis Association badges. There is a sequel to the book (see 580).

634 Kraft, Eve, and Conroy, John. THE TENNIS TEACHER'S GUIDE: GROUP INSTRUCTION AND TEAM COACHING. Rev. ed. New York: Scholastic Coach Athletic Services, 1976. 96 p. Photos., dgrms. Paperbound.

> This book is designed to be used as a teacher's guide to the instruction presented in the TENNIS WORKBOOKS (see 580, 633) by the same authors. Beginning a group program, teacher preparation, and class organization and motivation are covered.

635 Kraft, Virginia. TENNIS INSTRUCTION FOR FUN AND COMPETITION. New York: Grosset and Dunlap, 1976. 176 p. Photos., gloss. ISBN 0-448-11698-7. LC 73-18527.

> This is the story of a noncoordinated, over thirty years old, absolute beginner who learned to play well enough in one summer to be competitive in a local tournament. The writing and illustrations are clear and valuable to similar beginners in giving them encouragement.

636 Kramer, Jack, and Sheehan, Larry. HOW TO PLAY YOUR BEST TENNIS ALL THE TIME. New York: Atheneum, 1977. 178 p. Dgrms., dwgs. ISBN 0-689-10757-9. LC 76-534.

> The man who epitomized percentage tennis writes for the intermediate and advanced player. The strong points are his discussion of the idea of developing one's own style of play based on what works, coverage of the two-handed backhand,

and how to match the kind of racket one uses to the game one plays.

637 Lardner, Rex. THE COMPLETE BEGINNER'S GUIDE TO TENNIS. New York: Doubleday, 1967. 126 p. Dgrms., line dwgs., gloss. ISBN 0-385-04101-2. LC 67-17265.

Standard instruction is included for the most part. In one startling exception, Lardner recommends that in doubles for beginners the receiver's partner should stand halfway between the baseline and service line, a recommendation not seen in any other instruction book.

638 _____. FINDING AND EXPLOITING YOUR OPPONENT'S WEAKNES-SES. United States Tennis Association, Tennis Instructional Series. New York: Doubleday, 1978. 80 p. Dwgs. ISBN 0-385-09103-6. LC 74-12730.

The attacking player has the advantage, says Lardner, so attack on the approach shot, on one's own serve at least half the time, and even on return of the serve if possible. The various attacking strokes--groundstrokes, volley, smash--are illustrated in full-page sequence drawings.

639 _____. TACTICS IN WOMEN'S SINGLES, DOUBLES, AND MIXED DOUBLES. United States Tennis Association, Tennis Instructional Series. New York: Doubleday, 1975. 135 p. Dgrms., dwgs. ISBN 0-385-09044-7. LC 74-12731.

Topics covered include handling and playing with left-handers, when and how to poach, the Australian formation and when to use it, receiving serve in singles and doubles, and much more. It is not clear why this information is directed only to women.

640 Laver, Rod. 228 TENNIS TIPS. Chicago: Follett, 1977. 80 p. Line dwgs. Paperbound. ISBN 0-695-80716-1. LC 76-50752.

The tips are arranged in no particular order--the table of contents is the unifying device, indicating on what pages one can get return of serve help, backhand help, and so forth. Some tips are for beginners, some for intermediates, some for advanced players, but there is no way of telling which is which until one reads them.

Laver, Rod, and Collins, Bud. THE EDUCATION OF A TENNIS PLAYER. See 456.

641 _____. ROD LAVER'S TENNIS DIGEST. Chicago: Follett, 1973. 288 p. Photos., dwgs. Paperbound. ISBN 0-695-80387-5. LC 72-97511.

642 _____. ROD LAVER'S TENNIS DIGEST. 2d ed. Chicago: Follett, 1975. 288 p. Photos., dgrms., dwgs., gloss. Paperbound. ISBN 0-695-80527-4. LC 75-311253.

These two digests (see 641 and 642) are a compilation of articles from WORLD TENNIS magazine (see 876) by different authors covering a wide range of topics--instruction, personalities, tournament results, and more. There is no repetition in the two editions.

643 Laver, Rod; Emerson, Roy; and Tarshis, Barry. TENNIS FOR THE BLOODY FUN OF IT. New York: Quadrangle, 1976. 158 p. Photos. ISBN 0-8129-0590-3. LC 75-11479.

The authors engage in cheerful badinage (for example, reminding each other of disastrous losses) mixed with thorough instruction. Particularly useful are the many photographs of Laver hitting strokes. In most instruction books left-handers are told to reverse instructions. Here they can see Laver doing it the way it should be done.

643A Laver, Rod, and Pollard, Jack. HOW TO PLAY CHAMPIONSHIP TENNIS. New York: Macmillan, 1965. 148 p. Photos. ISBN 0-02-569150-3. LC 64-18193.

This is a combination autobiography and instruction book. The instruction changes the usual order, since Laver begins with the serve, covers the backhand, the volley, and only then the forehand before moving on to the other strokes.

644 Leary, Don. THE TEACHING TENNIS PRO. Los Angeles: Pinnacle Books, 1979. 218 p. Dwgs., gloss. Paperbound. ISBN 0-523-40574-X.

Leary presents a compilation of instructional tips that originally appeared as a newspaper column. They are arranged under broad chapter headings and cover the groundstrokes, the serve and overhead, the volley and net play, tactics, strategy, and mental preparation. Each tip is accompanied by a "word picture," an illustration that accompanies the text to make the meaning graphic and clear.

645 Leighton, Jim. INSIDE TENNIS: TECHNIQUES OF WINNING. Englewood Cliffs, N.J.: Prentice-Hall, 1969. 192 p. Photos., dgrms. ISBN 0-13-467530-4. LC 69-14432.

This book for the teacher is divided into three sections: beginners, intermediates, and advanced. In each section, Leighton, aided by other teachers (Van der Meer, Van Horn, and others), presents the fundamentals that a player at that level should be able to accomplish with different methods of achieving them. The emphasis throughout is on tailoring the instruction to the individual.

646 Lenz, Bill. UNISEX TENNIS. Port Washington, N.Y.: Kennikat, 1977. 260 p. Photos., dgrms. Paperbound. ISBN 0-8046-9147-9. LC 76-7981.

There are differences in learning tennis for men and women, says Lenz, and a prime purpose of this book is "helping the fair sex (and nonathletic men) toward better tennis." But there is more than that here; the author has read and absorbed much of what other books have to offer, and his points about spin (going beyond Tilden, see 711), doubles, and court surfaces show a thoughtful mind at work. There are a few stylistic infelicities.

647 Litz, David. A PHOTOGRAPHIC GUIDE TO TENNIS FUNDAMENTALS. New York: Arco, 1978. 110 p. Photos., gloss. Paperbound. ISBN 0-668-04185-4. LC 77-1533.

The title indicates the scope of this book, which covers not only the usual detailed sequence photographs for strokes but also illustrates the section on tactics with pictures of players doing the right or wrong things with comment in the text.

648 Lord, Sterling. RETURNING THE SERVE INTELLIGENTLY. United States Tennis Association, Tennis Instructional Series. New York: Doubleday, 1976. 60 p. Dwgs. ISBN 0-385-05297-9. LC 73-20532.

How to return in the deuce court, in the ad court, in singles, in doubles, on different kinds of surfaces, and what one does when one's partner receives serve are discussed.

649 Lott, George, and Bairstow, Jeffrey. HOW TO PLAY WINNING DOUBLES. Norwalk, Conn.: Tennis Magazine; New York: Simon and Schuster, 1979. 144 p. Dgrms., dwgs. ISBN 0-914178-20-2. LC 77-92904.

Lott, a former great doubles player, discusses all aspects of the "thinking player's game," with many illustrations of points made. The effect of different court surfaces on doubles, a topic not often dealt with in detail in doubles books, is explained thoroughly here.

650 Lowe, Jack. WINNING WITH PERCENTAGE TENNIS. 3d ed. North Hollywood, Calif.: Wilshire, 1975. 92 p. Photos., dgrms. Paperbound. ISBN 0-87980-327-4; PERCENTAGE TENNIS. Greenville, S.C.: Keys Printing Co., 1975. 92 p. Paperbound. LC 74-176273.

In part 1, "Stroke Production," Lowe recommends the inside-out swing for ground strokes--wrist laid back, racket head the leading edge of the swing, and high follow-through. A good two-paragraph summation of the pros and cons of the two-handed backhand is presented. Part 2, "Court Strategy," covers what the percentage shot is for prospective situations.

651 Marder, Terrin. TIPS FOR BETTER TENNIS. Toronto: Coles, 1976. 94 p. Photos., dgrms., line dwgs. Paperbound.

Standard instruction is presented, but the photographs for the grip are not clear. Sequence shots for groundstrokes show a left-hander hitting the ball with some peculiar leg positions. The book is written with a nice touch of humor. There are a few minor errors.

652 Mason, R. Elaine; Walts, Kenneth; and Mott, Mary. TENNIS. Basic Concepts and Skills of Physical Activity Series. Boston: Allyn and Bacon, 1974. 146 p. Photos., dgrms., line dwgs., bibliog. Paperbound. ISBN 0-205-03844-1. LC 73-84851.

The first two sentences of the annotation for the book by Burris and Olson in the badminton chapter (see 63) apply to this book as well. This is a detailed teaching from the founder of the graduated length method of instruction.

653 MASTERING YOUR TENNIS STROKES. Edited by Larry Sheehan. New York: Atheneum, 1976. 201 p. Photos. ISBN 0-689-10718-8. LC 75-41854.

Five players--Charlie Pasarell, Tom Okker, Arthur Ashe, Tony Roche, and Harold Solomon--in text and photographs cover the serve, forehand, backhand, volley, and lob. Common errors are shown side by side with the correct method, and a final section covers strategic considerations necessary to employ the stroke with maximum effectiveness.

654 Megale, Donald, and Winkler, Bill. TENNIS: FUNDAMENTALS AND BASIC PRINCIPLES ILLUSTRATED. Corvallis: Oregon State University Bookstore, 1961. 59 p. Dgrms., gloss. Paperbound. ISBN 0-88246-071-4.

Most instruction in this book is given in step form--one, two, three, four--with accompanying illustrations. The Eastern grip is the only one covered for groundstrokes, the forehand grip is recommended for the serve, and the Continental grip (not named as such) is recommended for the volley. "Contact with ball made opposite belt buckle" is stated for forehand and backhand; most other instruction books would disagree.

655 Metzler, Paul. ADVANCED TENNIS. Rev. ed. New York: Sterling, 1972. 191 p. Photos., dgrms., line dwgs. ISBN 0-8069-4000-X. LC 68-18790.

Metzler provides information for the advanced player, covering such topics as temper and match temperament, the importance of the fingers in ball control, how to watch (Metzler's recommendation: observe champions in early rounds of tournaments), what to do against different styles of play, and more.

656 _____. FINE POINTS OF TENNIS. New York: Sterling, 1978. 208 p. Dgrms., line dwgs. ISBN 0-8069-4199-7. LC 77-93309.

The fine points are for the upper intermediate to advanced player, and they include anticipation, making one's opponent hit the shot one wants hit, how to play various opponents (including ambidextrous ones), what to do about bad days, and more.

657 _____. GETTING STARTED IN TENNIS. Athletic Institute Series. New York: Sterling, 1975. 128 p. Photos., dgrms., line dwgs. ISBN 0-8069-4051-4. LC 70-180467.

This is a book of standard instruction for the beginner.

658 _____. TENNIS: WEAKNESSES AND REMEDIES. Athletic Instruction Series. New York: Sterling, 1974. 96 p. Dgrms., line dwgs. ISBN 0-8069-4060-3. LC 73-83459.

Instruction concentrates on a "here is the weakness, here is what to do about it" approach. A guiding principle is that there are no hard and fast rules; rather "try things, experiment--but settle for what feels most effective."

659 _____. TENNIS DOUBLES: TACTICS AND FORMATIONS. Athletic Institute Series. New York: Sterling, 1975. 160 p. Photos., dgrms., line dwgs. ISBN 0-8069-4086-7. LC 74-31695.

Metzler devotes two chapters to one-up, one-back doubles before moving on to topflight all-four-at-the-net play. Thorough coverage is given to all aspects of the game. The usual Metzler stylistic problem is present--women players are sometimes "girls," but men are never "boys."

660 Mottram, Tony. PLAY BETTER TENNIS. New York: Arco, 1971. 123 p. Photos. ISBN 0-668-02502-6. LC 70-161213.

The unique feature of this book is a series of photographs on the sides of the pages. As one flips these pages one gets a sequential series of such strokes as Evonne Goolagong's backhand, John Newcombe's overhead, and so forth. Eight strokes in all are shown in this fashion. Standard instruction is given.

661　Murphy, Bill. COMPLETE BOOK OF CHAMPIONSHIP TENNIS DRILLS. West Nyack, N.Y.: Parker, 1975. 228 p. Dgrms. ISBN 0-13-156026-3. LC 74-23175.

> Murphy includes drills for all strokes, for doubles, and for conditioning. There is a chapter on drills for beginners, and another on games that can be used for younger players.

662　Murphy, Bill, and Murphy, Chet. LIFETIME TREASURY OF TESTED TENNIS TIPS: SECRETS OF WINNING PLAY. West Nyack, N.Y.: Parker, 1978. 240 p. Dgrms., line dwgs. ISBN 0-13-536441-8. LC 77-17048.

> Over two hundred tips are organized under main headings-- groundstrokes, overhead, miscellaneous strokes (not all tips in that last section are stroke related; many are tactical points), and more. Analogies are often used as an instruction method, and some of them are repetitive, for example, "Use a candy cane swing," says number four; "Use an egg shaped swing," says number eight.

663　_____. TENNIS HANDBOOK. New York: Ronald, 1962. 345 p. Photos., dgrms. ISBN 0-8260-6515-5. LC 62-9758.

> This is a compilation of periodical articles and chapters from books, some of which are written by the Murphys and others by different authorities. The articles were written from the 1930s through the 1950s, and, as might be expected, on occasion contradict each other. There is much repetition, most notably in the section on doubles.

664　Murphy, Chet. ADVANCED TENNIS. 2d ed. Physical Education Activities Series. Dubuque, Iowa: William C. Brown, 1976. 101 p. Photos., dgrms., gloss. ISBN 0-697-07070-0. LC 75-23608.

> "There is more than one correct way to play" might be the key sentence in this book, which is devoted to instructing intermediate players on methods of improving their games. Questions throughout the text test readers to see if they remember points made.

665　Murphy, Chet, and Murphy, Bill. TENNIS FOR THE PLAYER, TEACHER AND COACH. Philadelphia: Saunders, 1975. 274 p. Photos., dgrms., gloss., bibliog. ISBN 0-7216-6620-5. LC 74-17759.

> This is a detailed how-to-teach manual aimed at instructors in high schools and colleges. The basic concept is that there is a "range of correctness" for all strokes, within which teachers may allow considerable variations. There is thorough discussion of the mechanics behind teaching and the psychological aspects of instruction. Points are often repeated as they occur in different contexts.

666 Murray, Henry. TENNIS FOR BEGINNERS. 1961. Reprint. North
Hollywood, Calif.: Wilshire, 1974. 124 p. Dgrms. Paperbound.
ISBN 0-87980-263-4. Originally published as TIGER TENNIS IN ONE
SEASON. Kingswood, Surrey, Engl.: Elliot, 1961. 124 p.

Murray begins many chapters by listing contradictory advice
of "experts" (never identified by name). His own approach
is summarized in ten points ("The TENnis Commandments").
The most basic point is given a chapter to itself--"Look over
your shoulder at the approaching ball which you intend to
hit."

667 Newcombe, John; Newcombe, Angie; and Mabry, Clarence. THE FAM-
ILY TENNIS BOOK. New York: Quadrangle, 1975. 157 p. Photos.,
line dwgs. ISBN 0-8129-0544-X. LC 74-26011.

Ball sense, movement, and racquet control are the basics for
good tennis which can be a game for family recreation.
There are numerous photographs of the Newcombe family.

668 Orantes, Manolo, and Tarshis, Barry. THE STEADY GAME. New York:
Bantam, 1977. 117 p. Photos. Paperbound. ISBN 0-553-11146-9.

This is essentially a book on tactics. Its main concept is
that only topnotch players can overpower their opposition, so
the average club competitor should use an approach emphasizing a series of shots based on control, variety, and strategy
geared toward the opponent's game. Eventually that opponent
will make a weak shot that the player can put away.

669 Palfrey, Sarah. TENNIS FOR ANYONE! Rev. ed. New York: Cornerstone, 1972. 172 p. Photos., gloss. Paperbound.

A former champion mixes instruction with reminiscences of the
greats she has known from Maurice McLoughlin through Chris
Evert. There is a focus shift; at times she seems to be address-
ing young people, at other times, adults.

670 Patterson, Jeff. HOW TO HIT TWO-HANDED BACKHANDS. Tallahassee, Fla.: Privately published by the author, 1976. Available from
Patterson at P.O. Drawer 20469, Tallahassee, Fla. 32304. 17 p. Photos. Paperbound.

A thorough explanation of the stroke is given in this pamphlet.
The writing mixes the scholarly with the informal: for example, "It is almost impossible to mess up the motion of a
one-hand backhand by experimenting with a semi-two-hander;
in fact it should even improve your power and accuracy by
developing proper upper body rotation."

671 Pearce, Wayne, and Pearce, Janice. TENNIS. Sport Series. Englewood Cliffs, N.J.: Prentice-Hall, 1971. 98 p. Dgrms., line dwgs., gloss., bibliog. ISBN 0-13-903443-9. LC 79-149307.

Standard instruction is included with a rather unusual bibliography at the end. Of the twenty-one items listed, only four relate directly to tennis. The remainder deal with psychology and physical and motor skills.

672 Pelton, Barry. TENNIS. 2d ed. Physical Activities Series. Pacific Palisades, Calif.: Goodyear, 1973. 84 p. Photos., dgrms., gloss., bibliog. Paperbound. ISBN 0-87620-891-X. LC 72-91476.

This is suggested as an introductory text for the college student. There is a student-teacher tear-cut section featuring instructional objectives for the various strokes and another section on how to measure achievement. The most recent book in the bibliography is 1963.

673 Petty, Roy. CONTEMPORARY TENNIS. Chicago: Contemporary Books, 1978. 104 p. Photos., dgrms., line dwgs., gloss. ISBN 0-8092-7548-1. LC 78-157.

This book covers the fundamentals. The author believes in wrist rotation for topspin and backspin shots and advises against the two-handed backhand. He makes one or two minor errors; for example, the drawings illustrative of the overhead show the player facing the net rather than side-on to it. The photographs were taken by Arthur Shay, and every one of them can be found in Shay's own book annotated further on in this section (see 690).

674 Plagenhoef, Stanley. FUNDAMENTALS OF TENNIS. Englewood Cliffs, N.J.: Prentice-Hall, 1970. 130 p. Dgrms., dwgs. ISBN 0-13-344606-9. LC 77-101530.

This is a technical account of the mechanics of stroking. The author says "The firmness of grip at impact is the single most important factor in hitting a tennis ball," and goes on to describe in great detail how each stroke should be hit for maximum effectiveness.

675 Platt, Don. TENNIS: PLAYING A WINNING GAME. Toronto: McGraw Hill Ryerson, 1977. 103 p. Photos. Paperbound. ISBN 0-07-082511-4. LC C77-001082-2.

Standard instruction is included but it is incomplete. The sections on the grip and hitting the ball leave important points out, and the author's service advice--". . . the racquet goes down while the ball goes up,"--contradicts the more standard "down together, up together."

676 Pollard, Jack, ed. LAWN TENNIS: THE AUSTRALIAN WAY. New York: Drake, 1973. 128 p. Photos., dgrms., dwgs. ISBN 0-87749-368-5. LC 72-6835.

Twenty-four short chapters by recognized Australian stars like Frank Sedgman, Lew Hoad, and Evonne Goolagong, give standard instruction. Although the date of publication is 1973, at least one chapter--"The Greats of Australian Lawn Tennis"--only goes up to 1962.

677 Pons, Fred. TENNIS MADE (SOMEWHAT) EASIER. New York: Exposition, 1973. 63 p. Photos. ISBN 0-682-47829-6. LC 73-90469.

The author provides instruction in strokes (except for the lob and smash) only. He recommends bent knees, racket back to five o'clock (assuming twelve o'clock directly in front), weight transfer at moment of impact, racket head going through the ball and finishing high, forward foot moving away from flight of the ball, and semi-open stance at the conclusion.

678 Professional Tennis Registry--USA. INSTRUCTOR'S MANUAL. Vol. 2. Oakland, Calif.: Professional Tennis Registry, 1978. 105 p. Photos. Paperbound.

Volume 2 is available to the general public; volume 1 is available only to those willing to take the Professional Tennis Registry (see 274) instructor's examination. The manual is primarily illustrations and shows registry president Dennis Van der Meer demonstrating correct methods of hitting strokes from forehand through drop shot. Succinct textual advice is given on strategy and common faults and their correction, and twenty-five pages are devoted to teaching "myths,": for example, that one must keep one's racket head above one's wrist at all times.

679 Ralston, Dennis, and Tarshis, Barry. SIX WEEKS TO A BETTER LEVEL OF TENNIS. New York: Simon and Schuster, 1977. 106 p. Photos. ISBN 0-671-22580-4. LC 77-3289.

The author claims that there are three keys to on-court success--early preparation, body control, and letting the racket head do most of the work. A questionnaire is included to help players find their present level of ability, and those aspects of their games that need special work. By concentrating on those aspects and the three keys, one can raise the grade of one's game by one level.

680 Ramo, Simon. EXTRAORDINARY TENNIS FOR THE ORDINARY PLAYER. Rev. ed. New York: Crown, 1977. 158 p. Dgrms. ISBN 0-517-55032-5. LC 76-30349.

Ramo says there are two kinds of players: professional and

ordinary. His book is aimed at the latter, telling her or
him how to beat other ordinary players. Chapters such as
"Botches and Sons of Botches" make points with humor. The
revised edition of the book is a reprint of the original edition; the only difference is that the former has a foreword
by Gene Scott.

681 Riessen, Clare, and Cox, Mark. TENNIS: A BASIC GUIDE. New
York: Lothrop, Lee and Shepard, 1969. 128 p. Photos., gloss. ISBN
0-688-51088-4. LC 69-15859.

Using his playing son Marty as one of his models, Riessen
gives the reader a guide to how to hit the strokes in words
and pictures. As the publication date might indicate, the
two-handed backhand is not included.

Riessen, Marty, and Evans, Richard. MATCH POINT. See 463.

682 Rosewall, Ken. KEN ROSEWALL ON TENNIS. New York: Frederick
Fell, 1978. 173 p. Photos. Paperbound. ISBN 0-8119-0309-5. LC
78-18730.

The Library of Congress calls this a juvenile book, and the
first chapter reads that way. Succeeding chapters do not,
however, and while it certainly is a book for beginners, it
is basically an adult text on how to hit the strokes. There
are fine sequence photographs of Rosewall.

683 Rosewall, Ken, and Barrett, John. PLAY TENNIS WITH ROSEWALL.
North Hollywood, Calif.: Wilshire, 1975. 160 p. Photos., dwgs.
Paperbound. ISBN 0-87980-305-3. LC 75-350013 (English ed.).

This is a combination of instruction and reminiscence that also
appeared, in WORLD OF TENNIS (see 817) for 1972 and 1973.
The instruction emphasizes how to play on different court surfaces. The reminiscence is in part historical and in part a
discussion of famous opponents from John Bromwich through
Rod Laver.

684 Roy, Harcourt. TENNIS FOR SCHOOLS. London: Pelham Books, 1974.
Distributed in the United States by Transatlantic Arts, New York. 226 p.
Dgrms., line dwgs., bibliog. ISBN 0-7207-0610-6. LC 74-186347.

This is written for teachers of tennis in English schools, so
addresses, information, and vocabulary apply to that country.
Strong points include a detailed explanation of the differences
between slice, cut, and chop, and the various methods of
giving instruction to pupils.

685 Scharff, Robert. QUICK AND EASY GUIDE TO TENNIS. Quick and Easy Series. New York: Collier, 1962. 94 p. Dgrms., line dwgs., gloss. Paperbound. LC 62-16970.

This is a clear exposition of standard instruction. As the publication date indicates, some sections are out of date--"Most, if not all, good racket frames are made with laminated strips of wood . . ."--and there is nothing about tie breakers in the scoring rules.

686 Schultz, Nikki. TENNIS FOR EVERYONE. Good Life Books. New York: Grosset and Dunlap, 1975. 96 p. Photos., gloss. ISBN 0-448-13231-1. LC 74-7544.

The standard instruction here is marred by a number of minor errors: for example, " . . . on the return of serve, your best volley is . . . "; grass is not, as the author claims, a slower surface than clay; "For the first serve, aim right for your opponent . . ."--true on occasion but not true all the time.

687 Schwed, Peter. THE SERVE AND THE OVERHEAD SMASH. United States Tennis Association, Tennis Instructional Series. Garden City, N.Y.: Doubleday, 1976. 86 p. Dgrms., dwgs. ISBN 0-385-11487-7. LC 76-10521.

Information on how the serve acts on different court surfaces is not here, but everything else is--mixing the flat, slice, and twist serves to gain maximum advantage, when to take the overhead on the bounce, the backhand smash, and more. This is written in a relaxed, lightly humorous style.

688 _____. SINISTER TENNIS: HOW TO PLAY AGAINST AND WITH LEFT-HANDERS. United States Tennis Association, Tennis Instructional Series. Garden City, N.Y.: Doubleday, 1975. 94 p. Dgrms., dwgs. ISBN 0-385-06706-2. LC 73-20530.

Schwed estimates that one of six tennis players is left-handed, and while the left-hander is accustomed to playing right-handers, the reverse is not true. His book tells what to do while playing with and against left-handers in singles or doubles. The basic advice is obvious; think opposite the usual playing pattern.

689 Segura, Pancho, and Heldman, Gladys. PANCHO SEGURA'S CHAMPIONSHIP STRATEGY: HOW TO PLAY WINNING TENNIS. New York: McGraw Hill, 1976. 180 p. Dwgs., gloss. ISBN 0-07-056040-4. LC 75-43500.

"Unless you're a beginner you need not start this book at Chapter 1 and read straight through," the authors say. " . . . at least 90% of American players today are beginners." The

90 percent then, who will read this book from start to finish,
will find it an outstanding volume covering all aspects of strategy. Most chapters are divided into sections for beginning,
intermediate, and advanced players.

690 Shay, Arthur. 40 COMMON ERRORS IN TENNIS AND HOW TO COR-
RECT THEM. Chicago: Contemporary Books, 1978. 100 p. Photos.
ISBN 0-8092-7825-1. LC 77-23708.

The forty errors (actually forty-one) are divided into chapters
--"Grips and Body Position," "Strokes," "Service," "Volleying," "Doubles"--and in all instances the error is shown in
pictures and described in text on the left-hand side of the
page with the correction on the right. It is interesting to
note that identical pictures are shown on pages 33 and 36,
but one is labeled an error while the other is called correct.
Also see the last sentence in the annotation of the book by
Petty in this section (see 673).

691 Shingleton, Jack. HOW TO INCREASE YOUR NET VALUE: A SIMPLI-
FIED GUIDE TO BETTER TENNIS. New York: Winchester, 1975. 152 p.
Photos., line dwgs., gloss. ISBN 0-87691-165-3. LC 74-16871.

This is standard instruction for the how-to-beat-other-ordinary-
players audience. Cartoons and photographs both illustrate
and comment upon points made.

692 Sirota, Bud, and Gray, Howard. DIRECT TENNIS. New York: Play-
more, 1978. 96 p. Photos., dgrms., line dwgs., gloss. Paperbound.

The authors believe that beginners bring prior experience to
tennis instruction (running, following a moving object); the
main new concept is the racket and the arm extension that
the racket allows. Groundstrokes should first be taught with
open stance and shoulder turn; only after repeated racket and
ball contact in that position should the instructor move to the
classic side-to-the-net stance.

693 Smith, Stan; Lutz, Bob; and Sheehan, Larry. MODERN TENNIS
DOUBLES. New York: Atheneum, 1975. 150 p. Dwgs. ISBN 0-689-
10687-4. LC 75-13514.

The principles on which successful doubles are based--the
importance of the net, getting the first serve in, chipping
the backhand return of serve, who should play the ad court
and who the deuce--are covered in great detail by one of
America's most successful doubles teams.

694 Smith, Stan, and Sheehan, Larry. STAN SMITH'S GUIDE TO BETTER
TENNIS. New York: Grosset and Dunlap, 1975. 48 p. Photos.,
dwgs. ISBN 0-448-13278-8. LC 75-621.

Color photographs and text show what Smith feels are the mistakes commonly made by the average player, for example, lobbing too short. During the warmup the player hits lobs so that the net person can practice overheads, and this carries over when play starts. Advice on how to correct such errors is given.

695 _____. STAN SMITH'S SIX TENNIS BASICS. New York: Atheneum, 1974. 48 p. Photos. ISBN 0-689-10636-X. LC 74-176280.

The six basics are to relax, be ready, get the racket back soon, keep eyes on the ball (and bend low enough so that the eye can see the ball in the plane of its movement), hit in front of the body, and have a full follow-through. Color sequence photographs of leading players hitting shots (Charlie Pasarell serve, Tom Gorman backhand) are included.

696 Smith, Stan, and Valentine, Tom. INSIDE TENNIS. Inside Sports Series. Chicago: Regnery, 1974. 91 p. Photos., dgrms., line dwgs., gloss. ISBN 0-8092-8887-7. LC 73-20692.

Standard basic instruction is presented. In one or two cases the text beneath an illustration is not really related to what is being shown.

697 Snyder, Dave. TENNIS. Sports Techniques Series. Chicago: Athletic Institute, 1971. 48 p. Photos., gloss. ISBN 0-87670-049-0. LC 79-109498.

This is a brief book on strokes, rules, and etiquette.

698 Sonneman, Donald. THE COMPLEAT POCKET TENNIS STRATEGIST. Rev. ed. San Diego, Calif.: Privately published by the author, 1974. Available from The Compleat Tennis Strategist, 4362 Clairmont Mesa, No. 53, San Diego, Calif. 92117. 34 p. Dgrms., line dwgs. Paperbound. ISBN 0-9601478-1-0.

Information is offered on strategy in singles and doubles condensed into a short booklet that will fit in a pocket or tennis case.

699 Strong, Mark. THE MAGIC PLUS: THE KEY TO BEING A HITTER IN TENNIS. Cincinnati: Privately published by the author, 1973. Available from Strong at 1100 Fourth and Walnut Building, Cincinnati, Ohio 45202. 40 p. Dgrms. Paperbound.

The most important element in hitting the ball is "the magic plus": placing the face of the racket on the moving ball in the correct manner and continuing to focus on that contact point until well after the racket has moved through it. That is the author's message, and he concludes with a discussion of the three ways to place the face--topspin, level, underspin --and how to use the magic plus in the forecourt and the backcourt.

700 Summerfield, Sidney. TENNIS--LEARN TO VOLLEY FIRST. New York: Vantage, 1970. 120 p. Dwgs., line dwgs., gloss.

Summerfield believes that one should give the student confidence by reversing the usual order of instruction and start with the volley. The book contains a useful series of line drawings on the serve with front and side views of correct motion. There is also a most unusual glossary. One of the terms defined is "a sucker for a short ball" alphabetized under "a."

701 Talbert, Peter, and Fishman, Lew. SECRETS OF A WINNING SERVE AND RETURN. Englewood Cliffs, N.J.: Prentice-Hall, 1977. 191 p. Photos., dgrms. ISBN 0-13-797589-9. LC 77-122.

Front and side view photographs of the flat, slice, and twist serves are shown. On the return Talbert recommends the Continental grip. He discusses running around the return and how to analyze the approaching serve.

702 Talbert, William. SPORTS ILLUSTRATED TENNIS. Rev. ed. Philadelphia: J.B. Lippincott, 1972. 96 p. Photos., dgrms., dwgs., gloss. ISBN 0-397-00863-5. LC 72-37609.

Three chapters--"Singles," "Doubles," "Mixed Doubles"--summarizes the basics. The chapter on the mixed game advises that the male needs to feel he is boss, and she should treat him so even if she is the better player.

703 Talbert, William, and Greer, Gordon. BILL TALBERT'S WEEKEND TENNIS: HOW TO HAVE FUN AND WIN AT THE SAME TIME. New York: Doubleday, 1970. 225 p. Line dwgs., gloss. ISBN 0-385-08771-3. LC 77-103779.

This is another book for the average player who wants to make the most of his or her abilities. Common and easily correctable errors are discussed, fundamentals are reviewed, one is told how to psych ". . . yourself up your opponent down," and more. Big names are dropped, good jokes are told, and sound advice is given.

704 Talbert, William, and Old, Bruce. THE GAME OF DOUBLES IN TENNIS. 4th ed. Philadelphia: J.B. Lippincott, 1977. 214 p. Dgrms. ISBN 0-397-00529-6. LC 77-35333.

The first edition of this book was the first book entirely devoted to doubles, and it has long been a standard in the field.

All aspects of the game are covered, backed up by statistical data taken from observing many matches, and there are diagrams of actual points played in championships. A regrettable error occurs in the introduction to both the third and fourth editions in referring to the first diagram. The offender is not player A as it says on page 13, but the diagram itself is correct.

705 _____. THE GAME OF SINGLES IN TENNIS. Rev. ed. Philadelphia: J.B. Lippincott, 1977. 158 p. Dgrms., dwgs. ISBN 0-397-01181-4. LC 76-40118.

The same techniques used in the book above are found here--statistics indicating what percent of the time what shots will win points, and numerous easy-to-follow albeit crowded diagrams of actual points played. Some pages--for example, those showing Billie Jean King hitting the overhead and Clark Graebner the forehand--are reprinted verbatim from the authors' STROKE PRODUCTION IN THE GAME OF TENNIS.

705A _____. STROKE PRODUCTION IN THE GAME OF TENNIS. Philadelphia: J.B. Lippincott, 1971. 136 p. Dgrms., dwgs. ISBN 0-397-00718-3. LC 77-151489.

The method used in this in-depth analysis was to take films of major players making strokes--for example, the Don Budge, Ken Rosewall, Billie Jean King backhands--and then make sequential drawings from those films and comment upon them. There is a chapter on teaching strokes to the beginner.

706 TENNIS: HOW TO PLAY, HOW TO WIN. Norwalk, Conn.: Tennis Magazine, 1978. 222 p. Photos., dgrms., dwgs. ISBN 0-914178-18-9. LC 77-92906.

These are articles (with some reworking) from the Instructional Portfolio series in TENNIS magazine (see 31) that were published between April 1975 and January 1978. For a similar volume, see 709. All the strokes, including such rarely seen ones as the lob volley and the backhand overhead, are shown both in drawings and in full sequence pictures. The book also includes sections on strategy, practice and conditioning, and left-handers (what they can do and what right-handers can do to counteract). Unlike item 709 this book is written in one voice.

707 TENNIS DRILLS FOR SELF-IMPROVEMENT. Edited by Steven Kraft. United States Tennis Association, Tennis Instructional Series. New York: Doubleday, 1978. 82 p. Dgrms. ISBN 0-385-12632-8. LC 77-78516.

Ten coaches offer drills for the intermediate to advanced player on the strokes. All drills are clearly marked as to purpose, method, and possible variations, and all are for one to four players in normal playing situations.

708 TENNIS FOR WOMEN. Edited by Ford Hovis. New York: Doubleday, 1973. 245 p. Photos. ISBN 0-385-06727-5. LC 73-75416.

Ten professional women players offer advice to beginners and intermediates of their own sex. Rosie Casals, Francoise Durr, Nancy Gunter, Wendy Overton, and Valerie Ziegenfus are among the authorities present.

709 TENNIS STROKES AND STRATEGIES. New York: Simon and Schuster, 1975. 216 p. Photos., dgrms., dwgs. ISBN 0-671-22073-X. LC 75-14065.

This volume is a compilation of some of the instructional articles appearing in TENNIS magazine (see 31) between 1972 and March 1975. The chapters are written by players and teachers, and the final chapter in each section by John Alexander relates the topic under discussion to the professional game. Fine drawings and illustrations are included, but there is no index and having one would have helped: for example, points on doubles are made in sections of the book other than the one devoted to doubles.

710 Tilden, William T. HOW TO PLAY BETTER TENNIS. New York: Simon and Schuster, 1950. 191 p. LC 50-7349. New York: Cornerstone, 1972. 144 p. Dgrms., line swgs. Paperbound. ISBN 0-346-12115-9.

This is Tilden's last book, and one of his two still in print in paperbound version. He offers a lifetime of writing and thinking about the game in this summary of how to play. His feelings on mixed doubles would be a male chauvinist's delight: for example, "Once in a while you find a girl who really gets into the game and plays her one third of the match, which is all any sane man would allow her to play."

711 _____. MATCH PLAY AND THE SPIN OF THE BALL. New York: American Lawn Tennis, 1925. 355 p. Photos. LC 25-4179. Reprints. (1) Port Washington, N.Y.: Kennikat, 1960. 177 p. Photos. LC 76-333; (2) New York: Arno, 1975. 177 p. Photos. ISBN 0-405-06679-1. LC 75-33763.

This is considered Tilden's best book on the game. It still can be useful for its complete discussion of the various spins and how to handle them. It includes a long biographical section on Tilden by Stephen Merrihew, and many comments by Tilden on players of the 1920s.

712 Tilmanis, Gundars. ADVANCED TENNIS FOR COACHES, TEACHERS AND PLAYERS. Philadelphia: Lea and Febiger, 1975. 126 p. Photos., dgrms., gloss. Paperbound. ISBN 0-8121-0511-7. LC 74-13856.

This book presents thorough instruction on tennis principles as the author sees them and is aimed primarily at teachers of adults, on such topics as coaching methodology, class control, and tactics for various court situations.

713 Trabert, Tony, and Hyams, Joe. WINNING TACTICS FOR WEEKEND TENNIS. New York: Holt, Rinehart and Winston, 1972. 128 p. Dgrms., gloss. ISBN 0-03-091468-8. LC 77-185343.

The title should have added the word "doubles," because that is the concern of the authors. A series of questions and answers is organized under broad topics--the warm-up, how to lob, and so forth. Liberated persons will not enjoy the chapter on mixed doubles.

714 Trengove, Alan, ed. HOW TO PLAY TENNIS THE PROFESSIONAL WAY. New York: Simon and Schuster, 1964. 160 p. Photos. ISBN 0-671-21335-0. LC 64-12480.

Ten professional male players write chapters on how to play the game their way. In the course of so doing they praise some of their contemporaries, criticize others, and disagree with each other. Don Budge, Pancho Gonzales, Lew Hoad, Frank Sedgman, and Tony Trabert are some of the professionals and Jack Kramer provides an introductory overview of the game.

715 United States Lawn Tennis Association. Education and Research Committee. TENNIS: TEACHING TENNIS TO GROUPS. Princeton, N.J.: U.S. Lawn Tennis Association, 1974. 16 p. Paperbound.

This is a compilation of articles on the title subject first published on pages 25-40 of the May 1974 issue of the JOURNAL OF HEALTH, PHYSICAL EDUCATION AND RECREATION. Topics include what to do about the "too many students, too few courts" situation, useful instructional aids for both individual and group teaching, and more.

716 Varn, Ben, and Jungle, Hank. STAIRSTEPS TO SUCCESSFUL TENNIS. Travelers Rest, S.C.: Tennis Services Co., 1974. 120 p. Photos., dgrms., gloss. Paperbound.

After a presentation of standard instruction points, the authors present their stairstep concept; the "levels of a plan by which the students can progress from a beginner to a national class player." There are five: putting and keeping the ball in play, keeping the opponent from attacking, putting the opponent on the defensive, attacking, and defending.

Vines, Ellsworth, and Vier, Gene. TENNIS: MYTH AND METHOD. See 470.

717 Willis, DeWitt. LEARN TO PLAY TENNIS AT HOME. New York: McGraw-Hill, 1976. 118 p. Photos., dgrms., dwgs. Paperbound. ISBN 0-07-070625-5. LC 76-5941.

The author calls his method "rhythmetonics," a system in which the aspiring player is given a method of muscle training and practicing stroke movements before going on the court. The idea is to fix those movements in what might be called "muscle memory" without the distraction of the ball. The illustrations form the bulk of the book.

718 Wilson, Craig. HOW TO IMPROVE YOUR TENNIS: STYLE, STRATEGY, AND ANALYSIS. Cranbury, N.J.: A.S. Barnes, 1974. 205 p. Photos., dgrms. ISBN 0-498-01483-5. LC 73-17465.

Beginning with a review of basics of grip and strokes, the main body of this text is devoted to analysis of the various types of serve, and the best responses of the receiver to those serves. It concludes with Wilson's method of scoring the progress of a given player, both in general and in a specific match.

719 Winnett, Tom, and Fay, Marion. TENNIS IS AN UNNATURAL ACT. Berkeley, Calif.: Wilderness, 1977. 99 p. Photos., dgrms., bibliog. Paperbound. ISBN 0-911824-60-X. LC 77-71716.

In contrast to Tim Gallwey's claim that given a proper good example one can trust one's body to do the correct thing naturally (see 597), Winnett and Fay state that proper stroking is highly artifical and must be learned. They agree with Gallwey on the importance of inner calm to be able to play at one's best, and offer suggestions for attaining that calm.

720 WINNING TENNIS: STROKES AND STRATEGIES OF THE WORLD'S TOP PROS. Edited by Bob Gillen. Radnor, Pa.: Chilton, 1978. 154 p. Photos., dgrms., bibliog. ISBN 0-8019-6648-5. LC 77-26831.

A collection of articles that originally appeared in TENNIS USA (see 874) when that newsletter was a magazine, this book gives a complete discussion of each stroke followed by sequence photographs of the detailed execution of that stroke by a leading female and male player. Dick Stockton and Wendy Overton give a thorough analysis of those players' strokes, telling where they follow the ideal and where and why they depart from it.

721 Woods, Ronald. YOUR ADVANTAGE: A TEXTBOOK FOR STUDENTS
AND TEACHERS OF TENNIS. Dubuque, Iowa: Kendall Hunt, 1976.
78 p. Dgrms., dwgs., gloss., bibliog. Spiral bound. ISBN 0-8403-
1325-X.

> This book gives instruction with key points in one, two,
> three outline form. There is also a chapter on teaching pro-
> gressions--first thing to teach, second, and so on--and on
> evaluation and testing techniques that will be of use to the
> instructor.

722 Yale, Virginia, and Lewis, Morey. SOLO TENNIS. New York: Drake,
1976. 94 p. Photos., dgrms. Paperbound. ISBN 0-8473-1062-0. LC
75-36142.

> The basic idea here is that practice against a backboard--solo
> tennis--will improve one's game, and the text shows how.
> The book is marred by several misprints, and a style of writ-
> ing that will irritate some.

723 Young, Gloria. MECHANICS OF TENNIS. Riverside, Calif.: Tennis
Ink, 1978. 85 p. Photos., bibliog. Spiral bound.

> Young supplies a discussion of each tennis stroke in terms of
> the mechanics of movement involved, the aspects of motor
> perception that apply (for example, space adjustments in strok-
> ing), and the application of such principles as Newton's First,
> Second, and Third Laws of Motion. The author often states
> the obvious--"When attempting overhead smashes, the player
> should be instructed to position herself so the sun is not
> directly in the path of the ball flight" (p. 56).

724 Zweig, John. COURTSIDE COMPANION: A TENNIS WORKBOOK FOR
THE SERIOUS PLAYER. San Francisco: Chronicle, 1973. 93 p. Photos., gloss. Paperbound. ISBN 0-87701-042-0. LC 73-77334.

> Sequence photographs show each stroke, and then a step-by-
> step photographic review with text commentary on each ele-
> ment of the sequence is given. Tips on how to practice,
> conditioning, how to win, and a few drills are also included.

Juvenile

The assignment of grade levels to the books below (and to a few others in the
badminton, racquetball, and table tennis chapters) was done by Marla Peele,
elementary school librarian at the Horace Mann-Barnard School in New York
City. Her judgments do not necessarily coincide with those of the publishers.

The books discussed here range from grades one through "young adult," that
mysterious period of life that the Young Adult Services Division of the American

Library Association refused to assign ages to in 1978.[1] A useful guide not only for tennis but for all sports books in the juvenile area is the book by Barbara Harrah, annotated earlier in this volume (see 9).

725 Ashe, Arthur, and Robinson, Louie, Jr. GETTING STARTED IN TENNIS. New York: Atheneum, 1977. 102 p. Photos., gloss. ISBN-0-689-10826-5. LC 77-5199.

> Ashe covers strokes, footwork, how to play a game, court conduct, practicing, what to do if one wants to go on seriously in the game, and more. There are some minor problems-- using the word "extruded" without definition, insufficient information on the two-handed style, and insufficient photographs in the serving sequence. Grades four and up.

726 Baker, Eugene. I WANT TO BE A TENNIS PLAYER. Chicago: Children's Press, 1973. 31 p. Dwgs. ISBN 0-516-01746-2. LC 73-738.

> This book describes a boy and girl watching a match and then taking instruction and finally playing in a tournament. The diagram of the court is a bit advanced for the audience's age level, and instruction does not normally begin with the serve as the text does here. The drawings are clear, but the forehand pictured gives a wrong idea of the correct execution of that stroke. See the filmstrip with the same title (337). Grades one to three.

727 Baker, Jim. BILLIE JEAN KING. New York: Grosset and Dunlap, 1974. 90 p. Photos. Paperbound. ISBN 0-448-07436-2. LC 74-7690.

> This is a longer biography than most for young people. Highlights of King's career, her work for equal rights for women, some of her matches (including a whole chapter on the one with Riggs), and her somewhat unusual marriage are all here. Many black and white photographs are included. Grades four and up.

728 Batson, Larry. JIMMY CONNORS. Mankato, Minn.: Creative Educational Society, 1975. 31 p. Dwgs. ISBN 0-87191-438-7. LC 75-1459.

> This is a brief biography emphasizing Connors's determination from boyhood to be a great player. The story is carried through 1974, his great year, when he overwhelmingly won Wimbledon and Forest Hills. The drawings are decorative only. Grades four to six.

729 Braun, Thomas. BILLIE JEAN KING. Superstars Series. Mankato, Minn.: Creative Educational Society, 1976. 31 p. Dwgs. Paperbound. ISBN 0-87191-275-9. LC 76-12090.

---

1. See AMERICAN LIBRARIES, July-August 1978, p. 436.

It should be noted that the ISBN printed in this book is identical to the one in the Olsen biography of King (see item 777), and the illustrations by John Nelson are also the same. The text is quite different, however, beginning with Riggs, and telling King's life story with emphasis on her aggressive style of play and on her efforts to change women's tennis. Grades four to six.

730 Burchard, Marshall. SPORTS HERO: JIMMY CONNORS. Sports Hero Biographies. New York: G.P. Putnam's Sons, 1976. 93 p. Photos. ISBN 0-399-60993-8. LC 76-6148.

Connors's life story is chronologically told from the first tennis lesson at age three to the "new Jimmy" at the indoor championships in Philadelphia in early 1976. The author is incomplete on occasion: for example, the explanation of Connors's exclusion from the French Open in 1974. Burchard says it was because he had skipped playing in other tournaments; he does not say it was also because he had played in World Team Tennis matches. Grades three to six.

731 Burchard, Marshall, and Burchard, Sue. SPORTS HERO: BILLIE JEAN KING. Sports Hero Biographies. New York: G.P. Putnam's Sons, 1975. 93 p. Photos., dwgs. ISBN 0-399-60907-5. LC 74-16623.

This is a well-written account of King, emphasizing her determination to be the best in a male-dominated sport, and what she had to do to accomplish that goal. Grades three to six.

731A Burchard, Sue. JOHN McENROE: SPORTS STAR! Sports Star Series. New York: Harcourt Brace Jovanovich, 1979. 63 p. Photos. ISBN 0-15-278007-3. LC 79-87509.

This is a straightforward chronological life of McEnroe through his September 1979 victory in the U.S. Open. The narrative emphasizes victories--the story of his reaching the semifinals at Wimbledon in 1977 when he was ranked 270 in the world is told in some detail; his first round loss in that same tournament one year is given one sentence. Grades four and up.

732 _____. SPORTS STAR: CHRIS EVERT. Sports Star Series. New York: Harcourt Brace Jovanovich, 1976. 64 p. Photos. ISBN 0-15-278007-6. LC 76-18156.

This presents highlights of the Evert career--what she gave up to be a champion, the hard work it involved, the strong family ties, the style of play. There are good black and white photographs. The one-sentence paragraphs make for a choppy writing style. Grades two to four.

733 Church, Carol. BILLIE JEAN KING: QUEEN OF THE COURTS. Focus on Famous Women Series. Minneapolis: Greenhaven, 1976. 65 p. Photos. A "read-along cassette" is available for purchase with the book. ISBN 0-912616-41-5.

> A good selection of photographs, many of King in her younger days, is a highlight of this book. Blank space on many text pages makes for a choppy appearance, and the book tells more about what she won than about the qualities of her lifestyle and play that may indicate how she won. Page 10 repeats page 3 almost as if the latter hadn't been written. Grades five and up.

734 Cook, Joseph. FAMOUS FIRSTS IN TENNIS. New York: G.P. Putnam's Sons, 1978. 63 p. Photos. ISBN 0-399-61111-8. LC 77-21855.

> Cook takes some leading events and players from tennis history and uses the device of "first" as a framework on which to hang the stories. At times this leads him astray: for example, he calls Roy Emerson "The First Doubles Star." Each "first" takes about one page of text and is accompanied by a black and white picture. Grades five and up.

735 Coombs, Charles. BE A WINNER IN TENNIS. New York: Morrow, 1975. 128 p. Photos., gloss. ISBN 0-688-32020-1. LC 74-23262.

> This is a general introduction to the game that includes pointers on equipment selection, warming-up exercises, hitting strokes, plus a description of a typical set. On occasion the text does not match the illustrations. Grades five and up.

736- Deegan, Paul. THE BASIC STROKES. Vol. 1. SERVING AND RE-
38 TURNING SERVICE. Vol. 2. VOLLEYING AND LOBS. Vol. 3. Creative Education Sports Instructional Series. Mankato, Minn.: Creative Educational Society, 1976. 31 p. each. Dwgs. Vol. 1: ISBN 0-87191-502-2. LC 75-41383. Vol. 2: ISBN 0-87191-495-6. LC 75-31813. Vol. 3: ISBN 0-87191-496-4. LC 75-35614.

> This is a series of books on the basics. Volume 3 also includes the half-volley and overhead. With few exceptions illustrations are for right-handed people, which might be more frustrating for younger left-handers than the same situation in adult books. A rather advanced vocabulary is used. Grades four to six.

739 Dickmeyer, Lowell, and Chappell, Annette. TENNIS IS FOR ME. Sports for Me Books. Minneapolis: Lerner, 1978. 46 p. Photos., gloss. ISBN 0-8225-1077-4. LC 77-92300.

> This book is written from the point of view of a child first learning the game, and it goes from that point to playing in the city championships. Elementary lessons on the forehand, backhand, and serve are included. Grades three to six.

740 Dolan, Edward, Jr., and Lyttle, Richard. MARTINA NAVRATILOVA. Garden City, N.Y.: Doubleday, 1977. 81 p. Photos. ISBN 0-385-12525-9. LC 76-56282.

The authors present the life of the Czechoslovakian star from her early days of banging a ball against a garage through her year as a Cleveland Net for World Team Tennis. The temper, occasional appetite binges, sense of humor, rivalry with and liking for Chris Evert, and the story of her defection from her homeland are all included in the authors' sympathetic portrait, which includes many full-page photographs. Grades five and up.

741 Duroska, Lud. TENNIS FOR BEGINNERS. New York: Grosset and Dunlap, 1975. 90 p. Photos. ISBN 0-448-13236-2. LC 74-94.

After brief information on history, scoring, and the different kinds of rackets, the bulk of this book gives detailed stroking instruction with sequence photographs showing a boy and girl hitting each shot correctly followed by other photographs in which they make errors. Unfortunately, the "correct" picture of the girl on the serve shows her making an obvious foot fault. Tips on practice and information on doubles is also included. Grades five and up.

742 Frayne, Trent. FAMOUS TENNIS PLAYERS. New York: Dodd, Mead, 1977. 192 p. Photos. ISBN 0-396-07470-7. LC 77-6501.

Brief sketches of their lives, descriptions of memorable matches, comments by other players, and Frayne's own views on the careers of some leading male players from Bill Tilden through Bjorn Borg are presented here. Young adult.

743 _____. FAMOUS WOMEN TENNIS PLAYERS. New York: Dodd, Mead, 1979. 223 p. Photos. ISBN 0-396-07681-5. LC 78-22428.

It turned out to be a protested mistake for Frayne to title his other book FAMOUS TENNIS PLAYERS (see 742) without including any women. In this book he makes up for it in twelve chapters beginning with Suzanne Lenglen and ending with Martina Navratilova. Frayne has a nice writing style, and his portraits come alive. Young adult.

744 Gemme, Leila. KING ON THE COURT: BILLIE JEAN KING. Milwaukee: Raintree, 1976. 47 p. Photos. ISBN 0-8172-0128-9. LC 75-42488.

Beginning with her 1975 "first retirement" victory at Wimbledon, the author tells the King story with emphasis on her fight for monetary equality with men and on ending "shamateurism." There are numerous color photographs and several one-sentence paragraphs that make reading a bit disjointed. Grades four and up.

745   Glickman, William. WINNERS ON THE TENNIS COURT. Picture Life
      Series. New York: Franklin Watts, 1978. 48 p. Photos. ISBN 0-
      531-02912-3. LC 77-21188.

      The lives of Evonne Goolagong, Jimmy Connors, Bjorn Borg,
      Arthur Ashe, Chris Evert, and Billie Jean King are given in
      brief here. Good full-page photographs show them in action.
      Grades two and up.

746   Hahn, James, and Hahn, Lynn. BJORN BORG: THE COOLEST ACE.
      Champions and Challengers Series 2. St. Paul, Minn.: EMC Corpora-
      tion, 1979. 39 p. Photos., gloss. ISBN 0-88436-478-X. LC 78-
      13127.

      This book begins with Borg's exciting win over Jimmy Connors
      at Wimbledon in 1977 and then flashes back to cover his
      early years with their dedication to tennis. Comments on
      his style of play and comments by other players about him
      are included in this brief but good biography. Grades four
      to seven.

747   _____. TRACY AUSTIN: POWERHOUSE IN PINAFORE. Champions
      and Challengers Series 1. St. Paul, Minn.: EMC Corporation, 1979.
      39 p. Photos., gloss. ISBN 0-88436-439-9. LC 78-18902.

      This is the life story of tennis's wonder child. Many photo-
      graphs show her in action on the court and in repose else-
      where. Grades four to seven.

748   Haney, Lynn. CHRIS EVERT: THE YOUNG CHAMPION. New York:
      G.P. Putnam's Sons, 1976. 127 p. Photos., gloss. ISBN 0-399-61037-
      5. LC 76-26716.

      Her early years, the strong family influence, some of her
      major matches, her romance with Jimmy Connors and dates
      with Jack Ford, the "Ice Maiden" reputation, and portraits,
      both verbal and photographic, of her friends and rivals on
      the circuit, as well as life on that circuit, are covered.
      Grades six and up.

749   Hasegawa, Sam. STAN SMITH. Superstars Series. Mankato, Minn.:
      Creative Educational Society, 1975. 31 p. Dwgs. ISBN 0-87191-474-3.
      LC 75-23448.

      Beginning with an account of his well-deserved famous victory
      over Ion Tiriac in the 1972 Davis Cup finals, this book brief-
      ly reviews highlights and lowlights of the Smith career, end-
      ing with his bad period in 1974. The illustrations are decora-
      tive only. Grades five and up.

750 Herda, D.J. FREE SPIRIT: EVONNE GOOLAGONG. Milwaukee: Raintree, 1976. 47 p. Photos. ISBN 0-8172-0147-5. LC 76-16197.

The Goolagong story from aboriginal beginnings in Barellan, Australia, to victory at Wimbledon is told. Her "walk-abouts," her lack of killer instinct, and the Vic Edwards influence are all covered. Herda's writing style is a bit choppy, but there are good, though uncaptioned, photographs. Grades five and up.

751 Higdon, Hal. CHAMPIONS OF THE TENNIS COURT. Englewood Cliffs, N.J.: Prentice-Hall, 1971. 60 p. Photos., gloss. ISBN 0-13-125419-7. LC 76-148490.

This contains brief, declarative sentence biographies of leading players past and present from Suzanne Lenglen to Arthur Ashe. The glossary is sometimes too brief: for example, "Spin: A player puts spin on the ball by hitting it with a slicing motion. When the ball lands it will bounce high, low, or to the side and be hard to return." Grades five and up.

752 Hopman, Harry. BETTER TENNIS FOR BOYS AND GIRLS. New York: Dodd, Mead, 1972. 95 p. Photos., gloss. ISBN 0-396-06365-9. LC 76-165672.

The author uses some Australian expressions that may baffle a younger American reader--"This gives the ball a little runaway to the off . . ."--but otherwise this is a fine instruction book covering physical fitness, match preparation, and practicing with a wall and with an opponent, as well as the strokes. Many illustrations, with those on the serve particularly thorough. Young adult.

753 Jacobs, Linda. ARTHUR ASHE: ALONE IN THE CROWD. Black American Athletes Series. St. Paul, Minn.: EMC Corp., 1976. 38 p. A "Read Along Cassette" is available. Photos. ISBN 0-88436-263-9. LC 76-000015.

This book begins with Ashe winning Wimbledon in 1975 and then goes back to the early years of struggle and "whites only" tournaments. There is no mention of his first great triumph, the U.S. Open title in 1968. Grades four and up.

754 _____. CHRIS EVERT, TENNIS PRO. Women Who Win, Series 4. St. Paul, Minn.: EMC Corp., 1974. 40 p. "A "Read Along Cassette" is available. Photos. ISBN 0-88436-128-4. LC 74-2300.

This is more a portrait of Evert in 1974 than a biography, although there are some flashbacks. Emphasis is on her calm attitude and dedication to the game. Grades four and up.

755 _____. EVONNE GOOLAGONG: SMILES AND SMASHES. Women Who Win, Series 2. St. Paul, Minn.: EMC Corp., 1975. 38 p. A "Read Along Cassette" is available. Photos. ISBN 0-88436-158-6. LC 74-31267.

> The focus here is on Goolagong's personality and personal life rather than on strokes and style of play. Some photographs are uncaptioned. Grades four and up.

756 _____. MARTINA NAVRATILOVA: TENNIS FURY. Women Who Win, Series 4. St. Paul, Minn.: EMC Corp., 1976. 40 p. A "Read Along Cassette" is available. Photos. ISBN 0-88436-236-X. LC 76-8421.

> A readable style and good photographs mark this biography of the star. Beginning with her first victory over Chris Evert, the story goes back to the early years and ends with her seeking asylum in the United States. Grades four and up.

757 _____. ROSEMARY CASALS: THE REBEL ROSEBUD. Women Who Win, Series 3. St. Paul, Minn.: EMC Corp., 1975. 40 p. A "Read Along Cassette" is available. Photos. ISBN 0-88436-166-7. LC 75-4646.

> The many facets of Casals are portrayed--activist in women's causes, tireless scrambler and retriever on court, always trying but never able to reach the top, devotion to the game, and sense of humor. Grades five and up.

758 Jones, C.M. YOUR BOOK OF TENNIS. Your Book Series. London: Faber and Faber, 1970. Distributed in the United States by Transatlantic Arts, New York. 64 p. Photos., dgrms. ISBN 0-571-08767-1. LC 77-523600.

> This is an instruction book with emphasis on the practical. Those who want theory can move up to the author's next level text, TENNIS: HOW TO BECOME A CHAMPION (see 626), which is not a juvenile book. Only the strokes are covered in this one. Young adult.

Jones, C.M., and Buxton, Angela. STARTING TENNIS.

> See 627.

759 Lawrence, Andrew. TENNIS: GREAT STARS, GREAT MOMENTS. New York: G.P. Putnam's Sons, 1976. 127 p. LC 76-11008.

> Short chapters (including several typographical errors) discuss the lives and careers of leading players from Bill Tilden to Jimmy Connors. An analysis of the playing style is usually included. Grades five and up.

760 Leighton, Harry. JUNIOR TENNIS. Athletic Institute Series. New
York: Sterling, 1974. 128 p. Photos., dgrms., gloss. ISBN 0-8069-
4072-7. LC 73-93589.

The text covers grips and strokes in detail. Leighton uses the
graduated length method for the latter--hitting first with the
palm, then a paddle, and finally the racquet. Other teachers
may disagree with some of his methods: for example, he has
beginners serving six inches behind the baseline to avoid foot
faults. Grades five and up.

761 Libman, Gary, and Deegan, Paul. BJORN BORG. Superstars Series.
Mankato, Minn.: Children's Book Co., 1979. 32 p. Photos. Paperbound. ISBN 0-87191-721-1. LC 79-11046.

This small book contains a lot of information about the Swedish
star. His life-style, personal characteristics, and how he plays
the game are all reported. Young adult.

762 McCormick, Bill. TENNIS. First Book Series. New York: Franklin
Watts, 1973. 66 p. Photos., gloss. ISBN 0-531-00803-7. LC 73-3407.

Short chapters discuss the origins, equipment, scoring, fundamental strokes, tactics, doubles, and great names of the game.
Many illustrations of players hitting shots are included, with
the smash picture being a bad choice since the smasher is
not looking at the ball. Grades five and up.

763 May, Julian. ARTHUR ASHE: DARK STAR OF TENNIS. Sports Close-
Up Books. Mankato, Minn.: Crestwood House, 1975. 48 p. Photos.
ISBN 0-913940-31-3. LC 75-28932.

This is Ashe's life story through his upset of Jimmy Connors
at Wimbledon in 1975. Emphasis is on the events of his life
rather than on his playing style. Grades four and up.

764 _____. BILLIE JEAN KING: TENNIS CHAMPION. Sports Close-Up
Books. Mankato, Minn.: Crestwood House, 1974. 46 p. Also available from EMC Corp. with a "Read Along Cassette." Photos. ISBN
0-913940-09-7. LC 74-82744.

This is a well-written biography with good photographs on
King's life and personality. It ends with a description of the
Riggs match and what it meant. Grades four and up.

765 _____. CHRIS EVERT: PRINCESS OF TENNIS. Sports Close-Up Books.
Mankato, Minn.: Crestwood House, 1975. 46 p. Photos. ISBN 0-
913940-19-4. LC 75-28936.

Evert's life and personality, with well-chosen quotes and appropriate photographs, are presented. Grades four and up.

766 _____. EVONNE GOOLAGONG: SMASHER FROM AUSTRALIA.
Sports Close-Up Books, Mankato, Minn.: Crestwood House, 1975. 46 p.
Also available from EMC Corp. with a "Read Along Cassette." Photos.
ISBN 0-913940-19-4. LC 74-31951.

This is another good, brief biography by May, who stresses
Goolagong's aboriginal origins and her most important matches.
Good photographs on and off the court are included. Grades
four and up.

767 _____. FOREST HILLS & THE AMERICAN TENNIS CHAMPIONSHIP.
Sports Classic Series. Mankato, Minn.: Creative Educational Society,
1976. 45 p. Photos. ISBN 0-87191-505-7. LC 76-4481.

This book gives portraits in brief (one to three pages) of some
of the famous players who won at Forest Hills from Bill Tilden
to Chris Evert with full-page photographs of many. It includes
a list of all singles champions from 1915 to 1975. Grades
four and up.

768 _____. WIMBLEDON: WORLD TENNIS FOCUS. Sports Classic Series.
Mankato, Minn.: Creative Educational Society, 1975. 47 p. Photos.
ISBN 0-87191-444-1. LC 75-17779.

This is an illustrated history of some of the high points at
Wimbledon from Victoria's time through the joint victories of
Chris Evert and Jimmy Connors in 1974. Gussie Moran and
her lace panties are discussed and depicted, and there is a
reversed image of Rod Laver hitting the ball right-handed.
A list of singles champions from 1877 to 1974 is included.
Grades four and up.

769 Meade, Marion. WOMEN IN SPORTS: TENNIS. New York: Harvey
House, 1975. 78 p. Photos. ISBN 0-8178-5402-9. LC 75-15066.

Short biographies of Billie Jean King, Rosie Casals, Chris
Evert, Evonne Goolagong, and Margaret Court are presented
from a feminist viewpoint. The sketches emphasize the frus-
trations over discrimination, the real achievements of the five,
and the progress toward full recognition of those achievements
by the outside world. Grades five and up.

770 Miklowitz, Gloria. TRACY AUSTIN. New York: Gorsset and Dunlap,
1978. 87 p. Photos. ISBN 0-448-26268-1. LC 77-92168.

This is a biography of the star emphasizing the factors that
led to her success—her drive and dedication, the chance to
practice with her family of good players, and superior instruction from Vic Braden and Robert Lansdorp. The final chapter
gives tips to other young players. The margins are very narrow. Grades four and up.

771 Morse, A[nn]. TENNIS CHAMPION, BILLIE JEAN KING. Mankato, Minn.: Creative Educational Society, 1976. 30 p. Photos. ISBN 0-87191-479-4. LC 75-38966.

> Alternate pages of text and pictures give a fan magazine portrait of King. Grades three and up.

772 Morse, Charles, and Morse, Ann. ARTHUR ASHE. Superstars Series. Mankato, Minn.: Amecus Street, 1974. 31 p. Dwgs. ISBN 0-87191-340-2. LC 74-954.

> This book emphasizes Ashe's determination and the prejudices he had to overcome. The copyright date is confusing, since the story goes through his Wimbledon victory over Jimmy Connors in 1975. Decorative color illustrations are included. Grades four to six.

773 _____. EVONNE GOOLAGONG. Superstars Series. Mankato, Minn.: Amecus Street, 1974. 31 p. Dwgs. ISBN 0-87191-339-9. LC 74-796.

> There is some description of important matches in this book, but in the main it is a personality study. The illustrations are decorative only. Grades four to six.

774 _____. PANCHO GONZALES. Superstars Series. Mankato, Minn.: Amecus Street, 1974. 31 p. Dwgs. ISBN 0-87191-341-0. LC 74-1359.

> The authors emphasize the Gonzales desire to win and his determination to play in his early years. Some of the great matches are described, and one famous Gonzales (originally from Roy Emerson) tip is given: cut pockets from shorts to be faster because sweat-soggy pockets add weight. The illustrations are decorative only. Grades four to six.

775 Ogan, Margaret, and Ogan, George. SMASHING: JIMMY CONNORS. Milwaukee: Raintree, 1976. 45 p. Photos. ISBN 0-8172-0140-8. LC 76-10356.

> This portrait concentrates on a few of his big matches, his mercurial temperament, his opinions of his fellow players, as well as the influence of his mother, grandmother, and Bill Riordan on his career. The short paragraphs make for a choppy writing style. Grades four and up.

776 Okker, Tom. TENNIS IN PICTURES. New York: Sterling, 1970. 160 p. Photos., gloss. ISBN 0-8069-4089-1. LC 74-31696.

> The basic strokes are covered and illustrated with Okker in rather grainy sequence shots. There is an interesting chapter on referees and linesmen; Okker does not think highly of them and says so. The text was translated from the Dutch and shows it; the English is occasionally awkward. Grades six and up.

777 Olsen, James. BILLIE JEAN KING: THE LADY OF THE COURT. Superstars Series. Mankato, Minn.: Creative Educational Society, 1974. 31 p. Dwgs. ISBN 0-87191-275-9. (See the statement accompanying the Braun biography of King in 729). LC 73-12438.

> Emphasis is on her personal life and on her as a model for women making the most of themselves. A textual error is seen with "Wimbledon Cup" on page 18 when "Wightman Cup" was meant. The illustrations are decorative only. Grades four to six.

778 Entry deleted.

779 O'Shea, Mary Jo. WINNING TENNIS STAR: CHRIS EVERT. Mankato, Minn.: Creative Educational Society, 1977. 30 p. Photos. Paperbound. ISBN 0-87191-588-X. LC 76-44410.

> Alternating color with black and white pictures and text pages give a fan magazine portrait of Evert. Grades four to six.

780 Paulson, Gary. FOREHANDING AND BACKHANDING--IF YOU'RE LUCKY. Milwaukee: Raintree, 1978. 31 p. Photos. ISBN 0-8172-1158-6. LC 77-27046.

> This is a commentary on different aspects of tennis using color photographs of leading players in funny positions. The large print is deceptive; the humor is adult. Grades five and up.

781 Phillips, Betty. CHRIS EVERT: FIRST LADY OF TENNIS. New York: Julian Messner, 1977. 189 p. Photos. ISBN 0-671-32890-5. LC 77-14398.

> This is Evert's life story in detail with numerous, almost novelistic, injections of what her feelings were on various occasions. The photograph on page 59 is badly mislabeled; it shows Billie Jean King hitting a backhand volley over the caption "Billie Jean's forehand becomes a frightening weapon." Grades five and up.

782 Ravielli, Anthony. WHAT IS TENNIS? New York: Atheneum, 1977. Unpaged. Dwgs. ISBN 0-689-30505-9. LC 77-1062.

> The clear text and drawings on the history of the game are the highlights. It also covers the basic drives with sequence drawings and discusses the volley, lob, smash, and how to serve. Grades four to six.

783 Reardon, Maureen. MATCH POINT. Venture Series. Milwaukee: Advanced Learning Concepts, 1975. 75 p. Photos. ISBN 0-8172-0234-X. LC 75-22012.

> This book takes a look at various aspects of the game--beginning tennis and first tournament experience told from the parti-

cipant's point of view, history, great players, Wimbledon, and Bobby Riggs discussed in a breezy, informal style. A text for reluctant readers, but nonreluctant ones will also find it interesting. Grades five and up.

784 Robinson, Louie, Jr. ARTHUR ASHE, TENNIS CHAMPION. Garden City, N.Y.: Doubleday, 1970. 144 p. Photos. LC 79-10387.

This is the Ashe story told by a black writer with considerable sympathy for the early years of discrimination and the difficulties he faced due to the death of the mother. There is much detail on his determination and stubbornness, as well as why and how he plays the way he does. The story is carried through his U.S. Open victory in 1968. Grades five and up.

785 Robison, Nancy. TRACY AUSTIN: TEENAGE SUPERSTAR. New York: Harvey House, 1978. 63 p. Photos., gloss. ISBN 0-8178-5807-5. LC 78-105533.

Beginning with a chapter-long account of Austin at Wimbledon in 1977, this book tells her story in nonchronological order through the end of that year. Her personality, as well as her matches, are discussed in some detail, and brief portraits of friends and competitors are given. Grades four and up.

Rosewall, Ken. KEN ROSEWALL ON TENNIS.

See 682.

786 Sabin, Francene. JIMMY CONNORS: KING OF THE COURTS. New York: G.P. Putnam's Sons, 1978. 159 p. Photos. ISBN 0-399-61115-0. LC 77-11688.

"On a scale of one to ten, Jimmy Connors is an eleven." That comment by a reporter quoted by Sabin sums up her attitude in this long biography of Connors. Details on many of his great matches, his life story through his victory over Bjorn Borg at Forest Hills in 1976, and a sympathetic personality portrait are given. Grades five and up.

787 _____. SET POINT: THE STORY OF CHRIS EVERT. New York: G.P. Putnam's Sons, 1977. 127 p. Photos. ISBN 0-399-61073-1. LC 76-41819.

This presents a straightforward chronological life through early 1976, when Evert signed to play World Team Tennis with the Phoenix Racquets. Her style of play and personality are covered as are her on-off romance with Jimmy Connors and the beginnings of independence from her family. Grades five and up.

788   Schmitz, Dorothy. CHRIS EVERT: WOMEN'S TENNIS CHAMPION. Pros Series. Mankato, Minn.: Crestwood House, 1977. 46 p. Photos. ISBN 0-913940-64-X. LC 77-70891.

> Evert's life, event by event, is covered with little discussion of playing style. Some photographs are uncaptioned. Grades three and up.

789   Seewagen, George, and Sullivan, George. TENNIS. All-Star Sports Series. Chicago: Follett, 1968. 127 p. Photos., dgrms., line dwgs. LC 68-4142.

> This gives instruction on strokes, strategy, and tournament play for young people. The text is clear, but some of the drawings and photographs are misleading and inadequate. Specific price information is given for items at their cost in 1968. Grades five and up.

790   Smith, Jay. CHRIS EVERT. Superstars Series. Mankato, Minn.: Creative Educational Society, 1975. 31 p. Dwgs. ISBN 0-87191-439-5. LC 75-8739.

> Beginning with a comparatively long account of Evert's first Wimbledon championship in 1974, the author concentrates on some famous matches in the Evert career and gives information on her style and personality. The decorative illustrations are not helpful; no one could tell anything about the two-handed backhand after seeing its depiction on page 12 here. Grades four to seven.

791   Sullivan, George. QUEENS OF THE COURT. New York: Dodd, Mead, 1974. 111 p. Photos., gloss. ISBN 0-396-06973-8. LC 74-3777.

> The author presents short biographies of leading women players --Rosie Casals, Margaret Court, Chris Evert, Evonne Goolagong, Billie Jean King, and Virginia Wade--with the tournament records of each one. A historical chapter discusses previous greats from Hazel Wightman through Althea Gibson. The information is more interestingly presented than in most collections of this type. Grades six and up.

792   Sweeney, Karen. ILLUSTRATED TENNIS DICTIONARY FOR YOUNG PEOPLE. Illustrations by David Ross. Englewood Cliffs, N.J.: Prentice-Hall, 1979. 125 p. Dwgs. Paperbound. ISBN 0-13-451278-2. LC 78-73758.

> An introductory section of this book summarizes rules, and a concluding chapter gives one-paragraph summaries of the lives of some great players. The main part is the dictionary, which gives many inaccurate, inadequate, and incomplete definitions. Grades five and up.

793 Talbert, Peter. TRACY AUSTIN: TENNIS WONDER. Photographs by Bruce Curtis. New York: G.P. Putnam's Sons, 1979. 46 p. Photos., gloss. ISBN 0-399-20689-2. LC 79-11914.

> A good, brief biography of the star from her days of batting a yarn ball at age two and a half through her first victory as a professional in late 1978. Grades five and up.

794 Thacher, Alida. RAISING A RACKET: ROSIE CASALS. Milwaukee: Raintree, 1976. 47 p. Photos. ISBN 0-8172-0132-7. LC 75-42036.

> Beginning with a description of Casals as "bright and brassy," her life story is told with the recurring theme of Casals versus the United States Tennis Association. Her television commentary on the Billie Jean King-Bobby Riggs match is discussed. Grades four to seven.

Reference

795 Brady, Maurice, comp. LAWN TENNIS ENCYCLOPAEDIA. Cranbury, N.J.: A.S. Barnes, 1969. 221 p. Photos. ISBN 0-498-07468-4. LC 71-79755.

> Part 1, "Biographies," gives the birth date, best world ranking, and highlights of the major tournament and Davis Cup records of leading players through 1968. For many, a descriptive paragraph is also included. (One important omission noted is Stan Smith). Part 2, "Facts and Figures," lists winners of major country championships (singles, doubles, and mixed doubles) plus a smattering of miscellaneous entries-- "Fashions," "Rallies, Long," and so forth. There is no index, which sometimes necessitates reading through the entries. For example, information on the shortest match is found under the part 2 heading, "Record Happenings."

796 COMPLETE GUIDE TO TENNIS. Skokie, Ill.: New American Library, 1975. 386 p. Photos. Paperbound. LC 75-324003.

> This is a tennis handbook containing instruction, injuries and what to do about them, equipment and how to choose it, resorts and camps, and a selection of statistics. In several places a duplicate picture is shown with slight variations in the text beneath.

797 Duggan, Moira, and Scott, Eugene. THE TENNIS CATALOG. New York: Macmillan, 1978. 256 p. Photos., gloss. Paperbound. ISBN 0-02-028350-4. LC 77-17869.

> This is a guide to the tennis marketplace: brand name descriptions of clothes, equipment, supplies; information on possible careers in tennis; resorts and camps; a selection of books, films,

and periodicals; a list of mail order houses with their specialties; and an index of manufacturers.

798   Fiott, Steve. TENNIS EQUIPMENT. Newly rev. and enl. ed. Radnor, Pa.: Chilton, 1978. 158 p. Photos. Paperbound. ISBN 0-8019-6716-3. LC 77-014726.

These are specifics in text and pictures about the manufacture and playability of different brands of rackets, shoes, balls, strings, and a brief section on fashion and accessories. Some general considerations on purchasing those items are given, but the purpose is not to provide a CONSUMER REPORTS "best buy" list, but to give the weak and strong points of the products in the opinion of the author.

799   Hedges, Martin. THE CONCISE DICTIONARY OF TENNIS. New York: Mayflower, 1978. 278 p. Photos., dwgs., gloss., bibliog. Two different ISBNs are given: in the book 0-86124-012-X; on the dust jacket 0-8317-1765-3.

Part 1, "Players and Venues," gives brief biographies of living and deceased players, information about famous tennis locations, and associations. Some omissions are noted--Renee Richards (under either her or his name), Carole Graebner (under either of her names), and Joe Hunt. Part 2, "Terms," is a glossary (Australian or tandem formation not defined), and part 3, "Results," the winners and runners-up of major championships. In conclusion, this is Brady's book (see 795) expanded and updated.

800   Kelly, Julie, and Kirwan, Nancy. THE TENNIS LEAGUE HANDBOOK. Hinsdale, Ill., and Dallas: Finn Hall Enterprises, 1975. 83 p. Photos. Paperbound.

Here are all the necessary factors to consider in organizing and operating a tennis league: Sample draw schedules for an even or odd number of players or teams; expenses that will be incurred; a sample of ladder rules; different methods of scoring; player responsibilities, and more.

801   Klein, Jerome. THE TENNIS PLAYER'S VACATION GUIDE. New York: Interbook, 1974. 154 p. Photos. Paperbound. ISBN 0-913456-71-6. LC 74-80059.

Some "107 tennis centers in 22 states and 21 countries" is what will be found here--numbers of courts, name of the professional, if tournaments are run, costs and other features of the hotel or area that might be of interest. This guide may be compared with the books by Richards (804), Rosenbaum (806), Tarshis (808), TENNIS DIRECTORY (809), and Van Daalen (816), with the date of publication an important factor in how current the information is.

802   Owens, Eleanor. TENNIS: EASY ON--EASY OFF. Rev. 4th ed.
Princeton, N.J.: United States Tennis Association, 1977. 70 p. Paperbound.

> This book mainly provides charts of methods of scheduling
> doubles games for a given number of players on a given
> number of courts--for example, eleven players, two courts.
> The charts show who plays, who sits out, and how the rota-
> tion can be accomplished so that each player has equal time.

803   Powel, Nick. "THE CODE." Princeton, N.J.: United States Tennis
Association, 1978. Unpaged. Paperbound.

> In an unofficiated match, player A says "I can't be sure if
> it was in or out; therefore the point is yours." Player B in
> the same situation says "Let's play a let." The purpose of
> this pamphlet is to cover all such situations and provide a
> means for players to solve them in a fair manner. It is the
> unofficial rules.

804   Richards, Gilbert. TENNIS FOR TRAVELERS. 4th ed. Cincinnati:
Gilbert Richards, 1973. 254 p. Paperbound. LC 74-17109.

> This guide claims it covers more than 7,500 court locations in
> 156 countries. The information varies: sometimes just a name
> and address; other times number of courts; whether or not they
> are lighted; name of the professional; and costs in low and
> high season. See also the annotation under Klein above (see
> 801).

805   Robertson, Max, and Kramer, Jack. THE ENCYCLOPEDIA OF TENNIS.
New York: Viking, 1974. 392 p. Photos., dgrms., dwgs. ISBN 0-
670-29408-X. LC 73-10776.

> Here we have one large volume divided into three sections.
> Part 1 gives the history of the game through 1973 with sec-
> tions on instruction and on great matches and great players.
> Part 2 is the encyclopedia: short alphabetically arranged
> articles of different lengths (some signed) about players, courts,
> countries, tournaments, and major organizations. Part 3 is a
> list of records of the important championships. The volume is
> copiously illustrated, with an emphasis on things British.

806   Rosenbaum, Helen. TENNIS VACATIONS. New York: Popular Library,
1977. 331 p. Photos. Paperbound. ISBN 0-445-08591-6.

> This is the same sort of book as the Richards guide above (see
> 804), but no number of inclusions is given. There is a sec-
> tion on tennis fashions and a useful article by Vic Braden on
> what to expect from a tennis camp.

807 STAHRE DECISIS. 6th ed. Riverside, Calif.: Tennis Ink, 1978. Several sets of pagings. Spiral bound.

For more than a decade, tennis umpire Jack Stahr has written a column for WORLD TENNIS magazine (see 876) called "Decisions" in which he offers guidance to players asking questions about the interpretation of both official and unofficial rules (see Powel above, 803) that govern tennis. This book publishes both sets of rules with Stahr's decisions and also republishes Stahr's A FRIEND AT COURT (see 860), a guide for umpires and reprints of other materials to assist those who run tournaments.

Sweeney, Karen. ILLUSTRATED TENNIS DICTIONARY FOR YOUNG PEOPLE.

See 792.

808 Tarshis, Barry, and Tennis Magazine. THE TRAVELERS GUIDE TO TENNIS. Norwalk, Conn.: Tennis Magazine, 1976. 142 p. Photos., line dwgs., maps. Paperbound. ISBN 0-914178-10-5. LC 76-25369.

This is a listing of facilities where one can find a genuine tennis program (not merely courts). Arranged by state, the information includes facilities, fees, instructional programs, other recreational programs, accommodations and rates, and how to get there. It covers the United States primarily, but nearby islands, Canada, Mexico, and Spain are also included. See also the annotation under Klein above (see 801).

809 TENNIS DIRECTORY. Boston: Ski Earth Publications, 1977-- . Semiannual. Photos.

This directory gives reference information on rackets, shoes, nets, lighting, and other products. The information is quite detailed; for example, for shoes one can find out about sole construction, outer construction, price and size ranges, and manufacturer's comments. Each issue contains feature articles on some aspect of the game and a detailed listing of camps and resorts in the Americas.

809A Tennis Magazine. THE TENNIS PLAYER'S HANDBOOK. Norwalk, Conn.: Tennis Magazine, 1980. 318 p. Photos., dwgs. Paperbound. ISBN 0-914178-32-6. LC 79-65033.

This one concerns itself with practical information on topics other than how to hit the ball. Choosing proper equipment, clothing, a tennis professional, a tennis camp; injuries, their avoidance and treatment; private versus group lessons are only some of the subjects covered.

810 United States Tennis Association. COLLEGE TENNIS GUIDE. Princeton, N.J.: 1978-- . Biannual.

A total of 1,450 colleges and junior colleges are arranged alphabetically by state with information on teams (men's and/ or women's), number of courts, names of coaches, if scholarship aid is available and if it is based on athletic and/or scholarly ability, and the schools' tennis ranking.

811 _____. OFFICIAL ENCYCLOPEDIA OF TENNIS. Edited by Bill Shannon with the staff of the USTA. Rev. and updated. New York: Harper and Row, 1979. 497 p. Photos., dgrms., gloss. ISBN 0-06-014478-5. LC 77-3777.

This is a vast compendium which includes history, rules, tournament results, instruction, records of great players, how to lay out a court, things to look for in choosing a camp, and more. There is a run-on table of contents, which makes the location of individual items difficult. The index does not include personal names.

812 _____. THE OFFICIAL YEARBOOK AND TENNIS GUIDE WITH THE OFFICIAL RULES. Lynn, Mass.: H.O. Zimman, 1903-- . Annual. Photos.

This guide includes information about the United States Tennis Association--its officers, committees, sections, constitution-- and the tennis record for the past year in detail and for years past in sum of leading players, plus tournament records, and so forth.

813 _____. PLAYER RECORDS. Princeton, N.J.: 1975-- . Annual.

This is a detailed record of the tournament results of leading men and women players over the previous year. The information includes the dates and names of the tournament, how far the individual player got, and who he or she defeated or was defeated by in each round, and the prize money won.

814 UNITED STATES TENNIS CLUB REGISTRY. Irvine, Calif.: 1976. 144 p. Photos., line dwgs.

This out-of-print item is listed here because it contains unique information, and copies do turn up in secondhand stores. It is a list of names and addresses of clubs and resort hotels in the Bahamas, Canada, Mexico, and the United States. The tennis magazines and local city magazines will, on occasion, publish lists of local clubs, but this was the only attempt to do it on a national basis.

815   United States Tennis Survey. OFFICIAL U.S. TENNIS TOURNAMENT DIRECTORY. Ann Arbor, Mich.: 1977-- . Annual. Paperbound.

This is a directory of tournaments by state and by circuit. Each listing includes the name, address, and phone number of the organizer, the court surface, the dates and location, if the tournament was closed or open, types of competition offered (junior, veterans, and so forth), and sanctioning body. After the basic volume is purchased, supplements listing additional tournaments will be sent.

816   Van Daalen, Nicholas. THE NEW INTERNATIONAL TENNIS GUIDE. Toronto: Pagurian, 1976. 191 p. Photos. Paperbound. ISBN 0-88932-033-0. LC 77-362103.

One hundred thirty resorts, hotels, camps, and schools are listed for tennis playing around the world, providing such information as numbers of courts, hours and costs of play, name of the professional, and other features of the area that might be of interest. See also the annotation for Klein above (see 801).

Whitman, Malcolm. TENNIS: ORIGINS AND MYSTERIES.

See 473. Listed here because of the complete bibliography that is included.

817   WORLD OF TENNIS. Edited by John Barrett. New York: Two Continents, 1971-- . Annual. Photos. Paperbound.

This yearbook reviews the tennis scene of the previous year with special attention to Great Britain and the United States. Tournament results, the professional tours, rankings by several authorities of leading players, and one-paragraph biographies of past and present greats are always included. Special feature articles are also published.

Miscellaneous

818   Aaron, Robert. THE TENNIS ENEMY: A COMPENDIUM OF THE VARIOUS UNPLEASANT TYPES TO BE FOUND ON THE OPPOSITE SIDE OF THE NET. Danbury, Conn.: Rampage, 1976. Unpaged. Dwgs. Paperbound. ISBN 0-914690-07-8.

The various types one may meet on the court--the gloater, the sulker, the hothead, the sport (". . . 'Great point' he shouts, following a long rally ending in his favor. As great as you were, he was, of course, just a little bit greater") are illustrated by Jeb Brady.

819   Anderson, Alan. HOW TO BUILD YOUR OWN TENNIS COURT. New York: Dutton, 1977. 182 p. Dgrms., dwgs. Paperbound. ISBN 0-87690-251-4. LC 77-6623.

The author actually built his own nonporous surface court, and he tells how one can do the same or build a porous surface court, and sets down the advantages and disadvantages of each. Diagrams are well integrated with text, and for each step the tools and work force needed, as well as the amount of time it will take, are given.

820   Bright, James. THE TENNIS COURT BOOK: A PLAYER'S GUIDE TO HOME TENNIS COURTS. Andover, Mass.: Andover Publishing Group, 1979. 108 p. Photos., dgrms. ISBN 0-933122-02-0. LC 79-51373.

Beginning with some color photographs showing glamorous completed home courts, this one presents a guide to what one needs to know about both the social (what to serve guests, scheduling play, and so forth) and construction aspects (assuming a contractor will do the work) of owning such courts. Lighting, fencing, and necessary care are also covered. A final section gives some case studies of actual courts with prices as of 1979.

821   Campbell, K. Gordon. PLAYING TENNIS WHEN IT HURTS. Millbrae, Calif.: Celestial Arts, 1976. 109 p. Photos., line dwgs., gloss. Paperbound. ISBN 0-89087-155-8. LC 75-28753.

Campbel, a tennis-playing orthopedist, recognizes that fanatics will do what his title says they'll do. His book tells how to make those hurts as slight as possible. Clear illustrations on bandaging and various helpful exercises of different types are included.

822   Cath, Stanley; Kahn, Alvin; and Cobb, Nathan. LOVE AND HATE ON THE TENNIS COURT: HOW HIDDEN EMOTIONS AFFECT YOUR GAME. New York: Charles Scribner's Sons, 1977. 178 p. ISBN 0-684-14925-7. LC 77-476.

Two psychiatrists and a journalist discuss all aspects of psychology and tennis--the different types who play (the equipment freak, the continual apologizer) and such manifestations as cheating, choking, aggression, and more. The authors do not lay all difficulties on psychological problems and give advice on overcoming hangups.

823   Champion, Rick. YOGA TENNIS: AWARENESS THROUGH SPORTS. Phoenix, Ariz.: A.S.I.A., 1973. 222 p. Photos. Paperbound.

Tennis instruction is given in yoga terms. Yoga is defined as the unity of the body, mind, and spirit forces which is attained in tennis via mantras (racket back, wait, hit), breath

control, relaxation techniques, exercises oriented on the ki
(navel), and more. Sequence photographs show standard tennis stroking.

824 Cosby, Bill. BILL COSBY'S PERSONAL GUIDE TO TENNIS POWER,
OR--DON'T LOWER THE LOB, RAISE THE NET. New York: Random
House, 1975. 93 p. Photos. Paperbound. ISBN 0-394-73056-9. LC
74-29609.

Cosby has done for "The Tennis Man" what Fernandel did for
the FRENCHMAN in Philipe Halsman's 1949 book with that
title (New York: Simon and Schuster). Under such headings
as "Illustrated Tennis Strokes for the Mediocre Player" are
shown photographs of a contorted, terror-stricken Cosby as
he sees the ball coming to his backhand. There is some text,
but the illustrations are the main interest.

825 Cutler, Bert. SO YOU THINK YOU KNOW TENNIS! Los Angeles:
Price Stern Sloan, 1977. 79 p. Dwgs. Paperbound. ISBN 0-8431-
0427-9. LC 77-9457.

"Player A serves to player B. His serve hits the net, then
hits B. B is standing between the service and base lines.
Is it server's point, a let, receiver's point, a fault?" This
book is a series of similar cartoon-illustrated questions on some
of the tougher aspects of the rules.

826 Ferguson, Don. LOVE IS ALWAYS LOSING AT TENNIS. Los Angeles:
Price Stern Sloan, 1976. 79 p. Dwgs. Paperbound. ISBN 0-8431-
0404-X.

In answer to the question "Why has tennis become so popular
in America?", three reasons are given. The third is "A tennis court is a great place to get sick because there are usually more doctors on a tennis court than in a hospital." This
book abounds with such humor.

827 Fox, Allen, and Evans, Richard. IF I'M THE BETTER PLAYER, WHY
CAN'T I WIN? Norwalk, Conn.: Tennis Magazine, 1979. 155 p.
ISBN 0-914178-28-8. LC 79-63332.

This book contains psychological factors and strategy points to
help players do better on the court. Topics discussed include
the personality factors of champions, proper preparation for a
match, how to psych and avoid being psyched, getting the
most from one's professional, and coping mentally with such
problems as fatigue, injuries, and advancing age. Fox was
a top-ranked player and has a Ph.D. degree in psychology.

828 Fox, John, and Vasil, Elizabeth. WHEN DO WE GET TO PLAY, COACH? TENNIS LEAD-UP GAMES AND DRILLS FOR STUDENTS, TEACHERS AND COACHES. N.p.: n.p., 1976. Available from the United States Tennis Association, 729 Alexander Road, Princeton, N.J.: 08540. 55 p. Photos., dgrms., line dwgs. Paperbound.

> Each game and drill is given a page and is in sequential steps. There is no index, but a table of contents locates particular items. It includes drills for a player versus a ball machine. Diagrams are given for every item.

829 Frazier, Claude, ed. MASTERING THE ART OF WINNING TENNIS: THE PSYCHOLOGY BEHIND SUCCESSFUL STRATEGY. Toronto: Pagurian, 1974. 151 p. Photos., bibliog. ISBN 0-919364-63-2. LC 74-79518.

> This is a compilation of articles by tennis playing M.D.s, Ph.D.s, and other educators on tennis psychology. Topics discussed include pulling oneself out of a slump, why it helps to mentally picture oneself successfully performing shots, how to relax on court, and many more.

Gallwey, W. Timothy. INNER TENNIS: PLAYING THE GAME.
See 598.

830 Geist, Harold, and Martinez, Cecilia. TENNIS PSYCHOLOGY. Chicago: Nelson-Hall, 1976. 127 p. Photos., gloss. ISBN 0-88229-120-3. LC 75-17651.

> This book is a collection of tennis miscellany, offering suggestions on strategy in singles and doubles, some points on tennis psychology, how to seed a draw, and what life is like on the professional circuit.

831 Gologor, Ethan. PSYCHODYNAMIC TENNIS: YOU, YOUR OPPONENT, AND OTHER OBSTACLES TO PERFECTION. New York: William Morrow, 1979. 227 p. ISBN 0-668-03466-7. LC 78-31247.

> Applying psychology to tennis means resisting being psyched out, not losing when one is the better player, and using one's strengths to one's advantage. The author discusses how to do all this and brings in such comparatively recent phenomena as risky shift and biorhythms. He applies the former to specific on-court situations and tells why he believes the latter is wrong.

832 Gordon, Bob. BASIC TENNIS. Watertown, Mass.: American, 1972. 96 p. Photos., dwgs. Paperbound.

> Although this book is listed under the author of the text, it is not for the prose that purchasers will obtain a copy. It is an

instruction book for the tired male chauvinist that may not
pick up his game but will certainly pick up his interest, since
the model wears tennis shoes and nothing else. Male friends
have expressed deep regret that the front cover model was
not used for more of the instructions.

833 Gray, Marvin. WHAT RESEARCH TELLS THE COACH ABOUT TENNIS.
What Research Tells the Coach Series. Washington, D.C.: American
Alliance for Health, Physical Education and Recreation, 1974. 56 p.
Dgrms., line dwgs., bibliog. Paperbound. LC 74-21759.

This is one of a series of publications designed "to make
available to coaches pertinent research findings with interpre-
tations for practical applications." Gray concentrates on the
competitive tennis player's sociological, psychological, physical, and physiological characteristics. Each chapter concludes
with a summary of findings, and the final section indicates
areas where there is a need for additional research.

834 Haynes, Connie; Kraft, Eve; and Conroy, John. SPEED, STRENGTH,
AND STAMINA: CONDITIONING FOR TENNIS. United States Tennis Association, Tennis Instructional Series. Garden City, N.Y.: Doubleday, 1975. 94 p. Dgrms., dwgs., bibliog. ISBN 0-385-09758-1.
LC 74-12691.

Four conditioning plans (for adults, elementary school children,
secondary school children, and advanced players) give on-
court and off-court exercises to develop the three words in
the title. A chapter on diet and simple first aid conclude
the book.

835 Hines, Henry, and Morgenstern, Carol. QUICK TENNIS. New York:
Dutton, 1977. 113 p. Photos. Paperbound. ISBN 0-525-04275-X.
LC 77-3402.

Hines teaches how to run--the method for discovering one's
best stride, the importance of forward lean, drills to sharpen
reflexes and help the player take off for the necessary short
bursts of speed. Several exercises for loosening and stretching
muscles are given.

836 Howorth, Beckett, and Bender, Fred. A DOCTOR'S ANSWER TO TEN-
NIS ELBOW: HOW TO CURE IT, HOW TO PREVENT IT. New York:
Chelsea House, 1977. 94 p. Dwgs. Paperbound. ISBN 0-87754-052-7.
LC 77-4145.

Howorth begins with questions, the answers to which will indicate whether one is particularly vulnerable to the problem,
continues with a thorough discussion of the arm and how it
works, and then discusses the subtitle of the book. He concludes with warnings against such methods as copper bracelets,
acupuncture, bands and braces, and the "play it out myth."

837 Hull, Gordon. THE SIX INSIDIOUS TRAPS OF COLLEGE TENNIS--AND HOW TO AVOID THEM. Mineola, N.Y.: Goodworth, 1979. 206 p. LC 78-78177.

> Far too many good college players transfer from one college to another, says Hull, and he begins his book with ten case studies of students who did just that. He devotes one chapter to each of the six prime reasons for such failures--not knowing enough about the school, the tennis program, the team, the coach, the scholarship situation, and not finishing in four years--and concludes with advice from eleven college coaches, advice that tends to be repetitive.

838 Kaufman, Axel. PARDON ME, YOUR FOREHAND IS SHOWING: A COLLECTION OF INSIDE AND OUTSIDE INFORMATION ABOUT TENNIS. New York: World Tennis, 1956. 86 p. Dwgs.

> A collection of stories, articles, poems, and drawings about tennis, many in the humorist Stephen Potter tongue-in-cheek style, is presented here. Most delightful is the one entitled "Fundamentals of Tennis." Any reader of instruction books, particularly Gallwey's (see 597, 598), should enjoy that one.

839 Keane, Bill. DEUCE AND DON'TS OF TENNIS. Phoenix, Ariz.: O'Sullivan Woodside, 1975. Unpaged. Line dwgs. Paperbound. ISBN 0-89019-045-3. LC 75-14107.

> The cartoonist for "The Family Circus" takes a pictorial look at some common tennis situations and irritations.

Kelly, Julie, and Kirwan, Nancy. THE TENNIS LEAGUE HANDBOOK. See 800.

840 King, Billie Jean, and Hoffman, Greg. TENNIS LOVE. New York: Macmillan, 1978. 164 p. Line dwgs. ISBN 0-02-563210-8. LC 77-25864.

> With the character Snoopy as a model in illustrations, this is a parent's guide to tennis--how to encourage family interest, what to do about lessons (unless one is Jimmy Evert, one should not give them oneself), how to deal with the emotions it arouses, and how and why not to be a tennis mother or father in the pejorative sense of that expression. Dialogues similar to those in Haim Ginott's BETWEEN PARENT AND CHILD (New York: Macmillan, 1965) are used to make points.

841 Lardner, Rex. THE FINE ART OF TENNIS HUSTLING. New York: Hawthorn, 1975. 125 p. Dwgs. Paperbound. ISBN 0-8015-2638-8. LC 75-10427.

> Over half of this book relates to the title, describing ploys

to psych out opponents. The rest describes imaginative
matches played and great shots hit by the author, parodies
Jack Stahr's "Decisions" column in WORLD TENNIS magazine
(see 876), and describes how various professions would indicate an out ball ("Actor 'Out! Out! See the damned spot.'").

842 _____. THE UNDERHANDED SERVE: OR HOW TO PLAY DIRTY TEN-
NIS. New York: Hawthorn, 1968. 122 p. Dgrms., line dwgs. ISBN
0-8015-8142-7. LC 68-30708.

"Q: Where should I serve if the sun gets in my eyes? . . .
A: Northern Sweden." More of the same kind of humor and
more gambits to upset opponents in friendly competition are
presented.

843 Leedy, Jack, and Malkin, Mort. PSYCHING UP FOR TENNIS. New
York: Basic, 1977. 178 p. Photos. ISBN 0-465-06518-X. LC 76-
43467.

The first part of this book deals with such topics as motivation, anxiety, and concentration. The style is that of a
medical textbook. Beginning with chapter eight, suggestions
are given to apply this information to one's game. Some of
this material is similar to the strategy section of standard instruction books. The rest of the book discusses topics such
as drug use, and sex and tennis.

844 Luszki, Walter. PSYCH YOURSELF TO BETTER TENNIS. Hollywood,
Calif.: Creative Editorial Service, 1971. 146 p. Photos., line dwgs.
Paperbound. ISBN 0-88409-008-6.

The early chapters of this book deal with tactics. They are
marred by misprints, poor English, and some obvious advice:
for example, "One should have a plan for serving. You
should plan to hit to the backhand, straight at the opponent,
or to the forehand." The psychological elements begin with
chapter 6 and cover such elements as how behavior modification can improve tennis, and the application of Freudian pre-
cepts to players.

845 McPhee, John. LEVELS OF THE GAME. New York: Farrar, Straus and
Giroux, 1969. 150 p. ISBN 0-374-18568-9. LC 76-87219. The book
is also available to blind and other physically handicapped readers through
a national network of libraries. To obtain the name and address of the
closest one, write to the National Library Service, Division for the Blind
and Physically Handicapped, Library of Congress, Washington, D.C. 20542.

This is a sociological study of a match between Arthur Ashe
and Clark Graebner played at the U.S. Open tournament in
1968. The two discuss each other and are commented on by
friends and relations. The narration flashes back between

points to show how the early lives of the two men made them
and their games what they are. The book first appeared in
the 7 June (pp. 45-111) and 14 June (pp. 44-81) 1969 issues
of the NEW YORKER.

846   McPhee, John, and Eisenstaedt, Alfred. WIMBLEDON: A CELEBRA-
TION. New York: Viking, 1972. 120 p. Photos. ISBN 0-670-
77079-5. LC 71-182266.

This is a portrait in words by McPhee and pictures by Eisenstaedt of a sports event that is an institution. Vignettes
about the players and spectators, and a long article on Robert
Twynam, the head groundskeeper, make up the text.

847   Mead, Shepherd. HOW TO SUCCEED IN TENNIS WITHOUT REALLY
TRYING: THE EASY TENNISMANSHIP WAY TO DO ALL THE THINGS
NO PRO CAN TEACH YOU. New York: David McKay, 1977. 181 p.
Gloss. ISBN 0-679-50749-3. LC 77-1522.

A comment on this book under the heading "Really?" on page 10
of the 19 September 1977 issue of SPORTS ILLUSTRATED, points
out that it advises one to ". . . run at least 3 miles a day,
do 20 minutes of calisthenics, practice half an hour on the
backboard and play at least two hours." "The contents,"
Sports Illustrated points out, "do not exactly agree with the
title." Practical exercises advice like that is mixed with
anecdotes about top players, an excuse list one can use when
losing, sex and tennis, and more.

848   Neal, Charles. BUILD YOUR OWN TENNIS COURT: CONSTRUCTING,
SUBCONTRACTING, EQUIPPING AND MAINTAINING INDOOR AND
OUTDOOR COURTS. Radnor, Pa.: Chilton, 1977. 163 p. Photos.,
dgrms., gloss. ISBN 0-8019-6573-X. LC 76-51303.

The subtitle tells the story. Legal requirements, cost estimates,
electrical and plumbing installations, fencing, and a few side
topics such as how to build a backboard are discussed. The
book includes a section on platform tennis court construction,
and a sample of supplier's names and addresses is included.

849   Poppenberg, Mary, and Parrish, Marlene. THE I'D RATHER PLAY TEN-
NIS HOROSCOPE: A KARMIC BOOK. Sewickley, Pa.: MPM Productions, 1975. 101 p. Line dwgs. Paperbound.

The authors follow a year of zodiac signs and tell what they
mean in tennis terms. An example: "Aries is given to quick,
although sometimes inaccurate, appraisals of people and should
exercise caution when choosing a doubles partner."

850 _____. I'D RATHER PLAY TENNIS THAN COOK . . . A COOK-
BOOK FOR TENNIS BUFFS. 2d ed. Sewickley, Pa.: MPM Productions, 1975. 107 p. 3d ed., 1973. 48 p. Spiral bound.

The bibliographic data above is not a misprint; the second
edition has a later copyright date than the third and both
can be found in specialty stores. They consist of recipes
with tennis names attached for all courses from drinks (the
Har Tru Highball) through main dishes (Racquet of Lamb) to
desserts (Court Torte). The recipes are straightforward. Compare with SERVE 'EM UP below (see 859).

851 THE PRINCETON STORY 1955-1977: AN EXAMPLE OF COMMUNITY
TENNIS PLANNING AND PROGRAMMING. Princeton, N.J.: United
States Tennis Association, 1978. Unpaged.

This is a packet of material on how a community development
program is being done in Princeton. The closing date in the
title will be changed in future revisions as new material is
added or old material updated. Included are fund raising
letters, publicity releases, materials sent to students enrolling
and to teachers of those students, a history and explanation
of the program, and more. It is designed to serve as a model
for other communities.

852 Rhame, M. LeVan, and Niemeyer, Jon Chalmers. TENNIS MAGIC:
PLAYING WITH A FULL DECK. New York: Vantage, 1979. 167 p.
Dwgs., bibliog. ISBN 0-533-03742-5. LC 78-055836.

A psychologist and a tennis professional offer this book on
the mental aspects of tennis. Chapters on tennis symbolism
(the psychological meaning behind the choice of rackets,
shoes, accessories, and such customs as winner keeps the
new can of balls, loser gets the used ones), how one's game
reflects one's personality, "tennis fleas"--people who jump
from one instructor to another, are included. Cartoon-like
illustrations are provided by Jack Turner.

853 Roberts, Jack. SO YOU'RE GOING TO TAKE TENNIS SERIOUSLY?:
HOW TO DEAL WITH GUILT, BLISTERS, AND OVERACHIEVERS. New
York: Workman, 1974. 142 p. Photos., line dwgs., gloss. Paper-
bound. ISBN 0-911104-34-8.

The only book that describes "The Fronthand," a stroke not
found in most texts, but an accurate description of what
many do when they see the ball rocketing toward their mid-
sections. The humor is presented in words and pictures.

854 Robyns, Gwen. WIMBLEDON: THE HIDDEN DRAMA. New York:
Drake, 1974. 200 p. Photos. ISBN 0-87749-566-1. LC 73-10922.

The various activities that go on behind, as well as on, the scene and make Wimbledon what it is are discussed. Topics such as the logistics problems of getting two thousand pounds of strawberries to the grounds each day are intermixed with descriptions of great matches and interviews with great players. For a different picture, see the chapter on Wimbledon in Lichtenstein's A LONG WAY BABY (see 457).

855 Sanderson, J.D. TENNIS HACKER'S HANDBOOK: HOW TO SURVIVE THE GAME AND LEARN TO LOVE IT. New York: A and W, 1977. 127 p. Line dwgs. ISBN 0-89479-009-9. LC 77-74646.

Humorous portraits of tennis playing types, instructional tips, and other general comments on the game are included in this book.

856 Schulz, Charles. SNOOPY'S TENNIS BOOK, FEATURING SNOOPY AT WIMBLEDON AND SNOOPY'S TOURNAMENT TIPS. New York: Holt, Rinehart and Winston, 1979. Unpaged. Dwgs. ISBN 0-03-050581-X. LC 78-14169.

Snoopy plays mixed doubles with both the fearsome Molly Volley and the garage, makes paw faults, hits volleys that go "blap" rather than "thong," and delivers tips not found in standard instruction manuals. A sample: "Always offer to open a new can of tennis balls, but do it as slowly as reaching for a dinner check. If care is taken, one unopened can should last the entire season."

857 Scott, Eugene. TENNIS: GAME OF MOTION. New York: Crown, 1973. 256 p. Photos. ISBN 0-517-50391-3. LC 72-82972.

Here are reflections and a selection of information on the game--great matches and great stadiums, strokes of leading stylists, comments on the boom, and more. The author often makes a quotable comment. In the words of one reviewer (Linda Timms in WORLD TENNIS magazine, November 1973, p. 48), this is a book that is "not just about physical motion but about the emotion the game generates."

858 Scott, Eugene, and DiGiacomo, Melchior. THE TENNIS EXPERIENCE. New York: Larousse, 1979. 256 p. Photos. ISBN 0-88332-119-X. LC 79-7519.

This is a survey in text by Scott and pictures by DiGiacomo of what the experience of playing tennis is all about. Topics include beginning the game, the problems of running a tournament, verbal and picture portraits of top professionals in action, repose, and expressing the passions the game arouses, and photographs of some former greats in their "twilights" contrasted with how they looked in their younger years.

859 SERVE 'EM UP: A COOKBOOK FOR TENNIS PEOPLE AND OTHER "BUSIES." Baltimore: Baltimore County Tennis Association, 1978. 85 p. Dwgs. Spiral bound.

> The recipes are contributed by players from the unknown to the famous. Aside from "Velvet Volley" (incorrectly located in the index), there are none of the tennis-related names for recipes by Poppenberg and Parrish (see 850).

Schickel, Richard. THE WORLD OF TENNIS.

> See 466.

860 Stahr, Jack. A FRIEND AT COURT: USLTA UMPIRES' HANDBOOK. Boston: H.O. Zimman, 1975. 44 p. Paperbound.

> This is a guide for umpires, referees, linespersons, and tournament chairpersons on their duties and how to carry them out, as well as their powers and how to enforce them. It also includes the official rules with comments and cases based on them.

861 Tarshis, Barry. TENNIS AND THE MIND. New York: Atheneum, 1977. 183 p. ISBN 0-689-10749-8. LC 77-76789.

> ". . . there is to the game a mental dimension that frequently transcends its purely physical, technical and intellectual demands." Thus speaks Tarshis in the middle of his first sentence, and the rest of the book explores that dimension, primarily in terms of the thoughts of some great players of today and yesterday on such topics as concentration, personality factors, and the drive to be a winner.

862 TENNIS QUESTIONS ANONYMOUS. Riverside, Calif.: Tennis Ink, n.d. 302 p. Spiral bound.

> This is a compilation and rearrangement under broad subjects of many of the queries that appeared in WORLD TENNIS magazine (see 876) beginning in 1953. Each question is answered, and the date of the issue in which the question and answer originally appeared is given. The questions are not only about rules; all aspects of the game are covered.

863 United States Tennis Association. FINANCING PUBLIC TENNIS COURTS. Rev. ed. Princeton, N.J.: 1979. 80 p. Bibliog. Paperbound.

> The first step is to find a leader who is persistent, persuasive, and able to mobilize others. Then necessary committees, selling the project, the feasibility study, and financing with private, state, and federal assistance are all described. There is a series of case studies of how other cities and counties did it.

864 _____. LIGHTING OUTDOOR TENNIS COURTS. North Palm Beach, Fla.: Tennis Foundation of North America, 1978. 56 p. Gloss., bibliog. Paperbound.

Here is what one needs to know to discuss intelligently how to light one's own court or set of courts with a professional consultant. Written in lay language (with a glossary for technical terms), it discusses all aspects of lighting from getting community approval and financing the project through problems connected with the environment and lighting. Case studies are given.

865 _____. TENNIS COURTS: CONSTRUCTION, MAINTENANCE, EQUIPMENT. Boston: H.O. Zimman, 1977. 80 p. Dgrms., gloss. Paperbound.

In contrast to Anderson and Neal (see 819, 848), this is not a real construction manual. Like Bright (see 820) it assumes that most work will be done by a contractor. It discusses factors to consider in choosing the contractor and court surface, lighting for indoor and outdoor courts, tennis bubbles, and more. There is a useful two-page chart comparing the various types of courts in terms of how often resurfacing needs to be done, drying time after rain, and so forth.

866 Van der Meer, Dennis, and Olderman, Murray. TENNIS CLINIC: PLAY THE TENNISAMERICA WAY. New York: Hawthorn, 1974. 193 p. Photos., dwgs. ISBN 0-8015-7524-9. LC 74-347.

This book shows what happened to persons who enrolled in one of the now defunct TennisAmerica one-week clinics. Specific criticisms of clinic participants are interspersed with general instructional tips, anecdotes, and a section on Bobby Riggs versus Margaret Court and Billie Jean King (Van der Meer coached both women in their matches against the master chauvinist). TennisAmerica died but Van der Meer continues to teach, and his book is useful to his pupils as a review or for someone wanting an idea of what happens on such weeks.

867 Wilson, Craig. TENNIS: BEYOND THE INNER GAME. New York: Drake, 1977. 143 p. Photos., bibliog. Paperbound. ISBN 0-8473-1361-1. LC 76-27798.

Defining the inner game as "the structure of motivation, value and social interaction which provides the foundation for physical skill," Wilson begins with a hypothetical mixed doubles match between four psychologically different people in order to show how their inner games are the essential factor in the results. (Devereux did the same thing, see 583). He gives psychological portraits of past and present champions to show that the "humble champion" is a myth; top players must exaggerate belief in themselves.

868 _____. TOTAL HEALTH TENNIS: A LIFESTYLE APPROACH. Ardmore, Pa.: Whitmore, 1979. 159 p. Photos. ISBN 0-87426-050-7. LC 79-51336.

> The title of this book refers to the concept of good tennis as a basis for total mental and physical health. Wilson stresses the importance of visualization in playing well--for example, thinking of the racket as an extension of the arm, seeing the seams as the ball comes toward one, imaging oneself hitting the good shot right into the target area. Standard instruction is also given on hitting the various strokes, with some of the photographs being rather poor illustrations of what they are intended to show.

869 Xanthos, Paul. HANDBOOK FOR ORGANIZATION AND CONDUCT OF TENNIS CLINICS AND TEACHER TRAINING WORKSHOPS. Princeton, N.J.: United States Lawn Tennis Association, 1974. 39 p. Photos., bibliog. Paperbound.

> This book takes one through the pre-planning, financing, site location, staffing, publicity, and program planning for clinics and workshops. Sample programs are given for three-hour through five-day workshops.

CAMPS

As indicated in the section on camps in the introduction to this book (p. xvii), no specific names and addresses will be given here. Unlike the other racket sports, such information is easily obtainable for tennis, so rather than providing material that tends to go rapidly out of date, the sources listed below will tell the reader where to find information.

Periodical literature on tennis camps is extensive. As an introduction to the subject this editor recommends two articles. Vic Braden's "What You Should Expect From a Top-Notch Tennis Ranch" originally appeared in the May 1975 issue of MAINLINER on pages 30-33 and was reprinted in Helen Rosenbaum's TENNIS VACATIONS (see 806). Barry Tarshis's "Can a Tennis Camp Transform Your Game? Yes, If . . .", TENNIS magazine, January 1979, pages 65-66 is another good one. Dennis Van der Meer's TENNIS CLINIC (see 866) describes what a camp with him would be like.

The principal sources of up-to-date camp information are the tennis magazines. RACQUETS CANADA (see 30), TENNIS (see 31), TENNIS WEEK (see 875), and WORLD TENNIS (see 876) each publish annual camp listings. To be as complete as possible, one would have to obtain all four; generally each magazine lists at least one camp that the others do not include.

EQUIPMENT

Basic information on this subject has been given in the equipment section of the first chapter of this book (see p. 6). In the case of tennis, two frequently asked questions deserve additional comment. In a sporting goods store dozens of racquet models line the walls, and the "How do I choose the best one for me" problem is always there.

A start toward a better than trial and error approach was described in the 11 December 1978 issue of SPORTS ILLUSTRATED in the "Sideline" column by Virginia Kraft, pages 19-20. In brief, a psychological and visual portrait of the prospective purchaser is made by means of a nine-question test given to that purchaser plus observation of such factors as age, weight, and height. A certain number of rackets are chosen as good possibilities from these observations, and the player hits with these possibilities while being observed by a "complex collection of lights, gauges and dials, the Magnificent Green Tennis Machine." (That is its actual name; it is a device invented by James Cox.) The machine will match the player to the racket that is best, claims Cox. As of now there is but one such machine, and until it gets wider trials and is produced in quantity, players will have to content themselves with advice in instruction books, the tennis magazines, or what this editor believes to be the best article on the subject, "How to Choose a Racket" by Steve Fiott, WORLD TENNIS, January 1979, pages 66-67.

The second question is what to do with used tennis balls. Junior development programs are usually glad to accept them as gifts, but for those who want a small return on their original investment the American Company, P.O. Box 355, Merrick, N.Y. 11566, paid five cents per ball and refunded postage at the time of publication. There are some conditions: the prospective seller must live within 1,500 miles of Merrick, and the balls must be in good condition. The company provides a mailing bag for the balls and a definition of "good condition," so one should write to it first.

INSTRUCTION

"I need instruction. How do I know that the person doing the teaching is any good?"

Obviously that question is one of interest to more than tennis players. The reason it is discussed in this chapter is that so much has been done with it in that sport. Both platform tennis and racquetball, for example, have an association that certifies teaching professionals and squash racquets is moving in the same direction, but tennis has at least six such organizations: Peter Burwash International Limited (see 273), Professional Tennis Registry--USA (see 274), Rick Ellstein Tennis Institute and Research Center (see 276), United States Professional Tennis Association (see 283), Van der Meer Tennis University (see 287), and the teacher training program of the Vic Braden Tennis College (see 288). An annual tennis teachers conference is held in New York City and in other locations under the auspices of the United States Professional Tennis Association, and the Professional Tennis Registry--USA holds similar conferences in various cities. The fact that a professional attended one of these conferences or graduated from one of the programs still does not guarantee knowledge, but at the very least the professional has had exposure to tennis theory, and in many cases has had to demonstrate on-court competence and teaching ability. A prospective pupil should certainly ask the teacher if he or she has participated in one of those programs. In addition, the pupil should try to obtain what this editor considers the best article on the subject, Barry Meadow's "How to Evaluate Your Tennis Instructor," which appeared in TENNIS USA (see 874) when that publication was a magazine, May 1978, pp. 45-47. Although aimed at tennis, the pointers given in the article apply to instruction in any racket sport.

PERIODICALS

In addition to the periodicals below, there are a host of regional and local magazines and newsletters. The United States Tennis Association's Education and Research Center (see 284) maintains a list of names and addresses of such publications.

It should be noted that some of the titles annotated in the periodicals section of chapter 1 of this book cover tennis (see pp. 11-12).

870   BLACK TENNIS. 3548 Rio Grande Circle, Dallas, Tex. 75233, 1977-- . Bimonthly.

> The standard annotation holds for this one (see p. xvii) with the emphasis on news items, results, and biographies of black tennis players.

871   COLLEGE AND JUNIOR TENNIS. Junior Tennis. 100 Harbor Road, Port Washington, N.Y. 11050, 1973-- . 11 per year (1 per month with a combined Oct.-Nov. issue).

> Results, rankings, biographies, scholarship information, and feature articles about the junior and college tennis scene appear here.

872   INTERNATIONAL TENNIS WEEKLY. Association of Tennis Professionals, 319 Country Club Road, Garland, Tex. 75040, 1976-- .

> This is a newspaper-format weekly with tournament results and schedules, news about the game, and signed editorials. It is the official publication of the Association of Tennis Professionals (see 255) and gives that association's computer rankings of professionals.

873 TENNIS CHAMPIONSHIPS MAGAZINE. 156 Broad Street, Lynn, Mass. 09101. 1948-- . Monthly.

This magazine appears in conjunction with leading tennis tournaments in the United States. For example, the tournament program sold at the U.S. Open championships is an issue of this magazine. The main function is to give the program for the tournament, but there are always feature articles.

874 TENNIS USA. United States Tennis Association, 1515 Broadway, New York, N.Y. 10036, 1937-- . Twenty-four issues per year.

This began as a monthly magazine and changed in June 1979 to a newsletter in newspaper format. It is the official publication of the United States Tennis Association (see 284), and includes news of the association, local and sectional events, tournament results, and personalities.

875 TENNIS WEEK. Tennis News, Inc., 120 East Fifty-sixth Street, New York, N.Y., 1974-- . Forty issues per year.

In addition to standard annotation material (see p. xvii), this magazine has editorials by Gene Scott, annual tennis camp and tennis product directories, and a list of names and addresses of racket sport organizations in some issues.

876 WORLD TENNIS. 1515 Broadway, New York, N.Y. 10036, 1953-- . Monthly.

In addition to the standard annotation material (see p. xvii), this publication has long been noted for giving the results of rounds of major tournaments. It has annual tennis camp and yearbook issues. It is "the magazine of membership in the United States Tennis Association." It also publishes TENNIS BUSINESS, a newsletter covering all aspects of the industry.

RATING SYSTEMS

A problem that plagues all racket sport players is finding terms to describe their own games. The standard words, "beginner," "intermediate," and "advanced" are never satisfactory, particularly "intermediate" since it encompasses such wide variations. Various tennis associations have established individual systems, but the beginning of a national solution appeared in 1979 when three organizations--the National Tennis Association (see 268), the United States Professional Tennis Association (see 283), and the United States Tennis Association (see 284)--jointly endorsed a new classification system. Players can either rate their own ability or have a professional do it for them on a scale of thirteen different levels of skill, with descriptions furnished of what each level can accomplish. For example, an eighth-level player ". . . has begun to master the use of power and spins; has sound footwork; can control depth of shots and is able to move opponents up and back; can hit first serves with above average power and accuracy and place the second serve; is able to rush the net with some success on serve against players of similar ability." One may write to any of the three organizations for copies of the statement for all levels.

TENNIS FOR THE HANDICAPPED

One organization and several books in this chapter have been cited as being beneficial to persons with emotional and/or physical handicaps (see 256, 429, 436, 452, 464, 508, 608, 845). In addition, the Croched Mountain Center, Greenfield, N.H. 03580, offers a program. For information, write to Jack Kennedy, Tamarack Tennis Camp, Franconia, N.H. 03580. Peter Burwash International (see 273) sends some of its pros out into the field to offer a coaching program for blind and handicapped students. Finally the United States Tennis Association (see 284) began a program in 1980 to seek information on programs for the handicapped. For details write to Julie Simon, USTA Education and Research Center, 729 Alexander Road, Princeton, N.J. 08540.

TOURNAMENTS

As stated in the first chapter (see p. 12), for most sports the national association, its affiliates on regional or state levels, and the periodicals published for each game are the best sources to keep one abreast of tournament information. The same is true for tennis, but as usual there's much more. If the reader will look through the list of associations given at the beginning of this chapter (pp. 69-77), he or she will see how often tournaments are given as one of the functions. In the reference section of this chapter, one will find an entire book that does nothing but list tournaments (see item 815).

Chapter 9

OTHER GAMES

In this chapter other games (and books about a few of them) are briefly described. Many of them are board game spin-offs from, or minor versions of, the major sports previously described, and in several instances there is little differentiation among them. Such games come and go, and the author would welcome correspondence from readers who know of others not covered here. The four major games--court tennis (see 882), paddle tennis (see 898), racquets (see 904), and squash tennis (see 909)--have been given more space.

To update information on the minor games, a useful source is the directory issue of PLAYTHINGS magazine (usually the last issue in May each year), which is published weekly at 51 Madison Avenue, New York, N.Y. 10010. In the section devoted to "Classified Product Listings" under the heading "Games--Tennis," one can find a list of manufacturers. Those that last for some time may be in the Museum and Archive of Games, 415 Phillips Street, Waterloo, Ontario.

877 ALL BALL. Tennis Resources West, 2563 Greer Road, Palo Alto, Calif. 94303.

> Foam rubber balls, short (20 inch) or intermediate (23 inch) length rackets, and a net that can be set up indoors between articles of furniture or outdoors between trees are the equipment needed for this game. Players hit the ball back and forth and keep score.

878 ANCHOR TENNIS. Childcraft Education Corporation, 20 Kilmer Road, Edison, N.J. 08817.

> A weighted anchor and a rubber ball attached to it by a string is used by one or two players who hit the ball with a paddle. For a very similar game see the description of LUV JUG (895).

879 BAC RAC. Crown Recreation Incorporated--East, 184-10 Jamaica Avenue, Hollis, N.Y. 11423; Crown Recreation Incorporated--West, 2640 East Del Amo Boulevard, Compton, Calif. 90221.

This is both a singles and doubles game for outdoors. Two steel poles with a twenty-foot long net stretched between them five feet above the ground, twenty-one inch rackets, and a soft ball are used. Back boundaries can be placed anywhere one wants.

880 BING-IT TENNIS. Childcraft Education Corp., 20 Kilmer Road, Edison, N.J. 08817.

A soft ball, a shuttlecock, and two circular paddles that give off a sound (bing!) when hit are used in this game.

881 COMPUTAMATIC TENNIS. Electronic Data Controls Corp., Computer Games Division, 715 North Cherry Street, Winston-Salem, N.C. 27101.

This is a battery-operated push button game apparently devised by someone who did not play tennis, as it refers to rallies as volleys.

882 COURT TENNIS. The United States Court Tennis Association is the governing body, and it publishes an occasional newsletter. The address will vary as new officers are elected, but one may write to the secretary and newsletter publisher, George Mars, 611 Park Avenue, Baltimore, Md. 21201, for information.

It is court tennis in the United States; it is tennis (as opposed to lawn tennis), real tennis, or royal tennis in England. The royal name is appropriate; this is the game played by Louis in France, the Henrys in England, and Napoleon and the Duke of Wellington, as well. Many of the modern games descended from it and its French equivalent, jeu de paume. It was not only popular among kings; in his book THE RACQUET GAME (New York: Macmillan, 1930) Allison Danzig tells us on page 14 that "it was said there were more tennis players in Paris during the reign of Henry IV than drunkards in England."

Even though there are very few courts in the United States, the game is played there by a hard corps of devotees, and, indeed, the 1976-1977 annual report of the United States Court Tennis Association even spoke of a court crunch--a crunch not likely to improve since the cost of construction of a court is considerable. It is an extremely complicated game to understand. The clearest explanation of how it is played is the one by Dick Squires in his book THE OTHER RACQUET SPORTS (see 17), or one may try George Plimpton's exposition in his introduction to the book by Etchebaster (annotated below.

An important book on court tennis is by Evan B. Noel and J.O.M. Clark, A HISTORY OF TENNIS. 2 vols. Oxford: Oxford University Press, 1924. A copy can occasionally be found in an antiquarian bookdealers store.. Two shorter works are annotated below (see 883,884).

883 Etchebaster, Pierre. PIERRE'S BOOK: THE GAME OF COURT TENNIS. Barre, Mass.: Barre, 1971. 51 p. Photos., dgrms. ISBN 0-8271-7126-9. LC 71-163883.

> Etchebaster was the outstanding professional court tennis champion; he never lost a match on even terms from 1928 through 1954. This is an instruction book by him and a tribute to him by some of his fellow players. An introduction by George Plimpton explains the game and gives a short biography.

884 Marshall, Julian. THE ANNALS OF TENNIS. London: "The Field" Office, 1878. Reprint. Baltimore: Racquet Sports Information and Services, 1973. 226 p. Dgrms., dwgs. ISBN 0-914934-01-5. LC 74-79109.

> A thorough history of and instruction book for court tennis that originally appeared as a series of articles in the English sport magazine THE FIELD (London: Harmondsworth Press, 1853--). Several untranslated passages in French and Latin are in the book; Marshall undoubtedly assumed that anyone reading it would be able to understand them, an assumption probably correct in 1878. When one reads of the early great player Biboche that "he once played a match fully equipped . . . with knapsack, musket, shako, cross belts . . . His antagonist was of course, only a moderate player," (p. 49), one realizes that Bobby Riggs has been around for some time.

885 DECK TENNIS

> No official organization appears to exist for this shipboard game, and while there is an official size court--forty feet by twelve feet for singles and forty feet by eighteen feet for doubles--one may well find that "Usually the court is bounded on the north by a lifeboat, on the south by the kennels, on the east by the aft funnel and on the west by a bevy of bars and stanchions which will send you spinning unless you watch your step."[1] A rubber ring or quoit is tossed across a net, caught with one hand, and tossed back until it either falls outside the boundaries or is missed.

886 15 LOVE. House of Games, Inc., P.O. Box 374, Elk Grove, Ill. 60201.

> In this dice board game, points are scored by rolling dice to advance a counter across a board marked like a tennis court. Singles or doubles can be played with tennis scoring.

887 FISHER-PRICE TENNIS. Fisher Price Toys, 636 Girard Avenue, East Aurora, N.Y. 14052.

---

1. John R. Tunis, SPORT FOR THE FUN OF IT (New York: A.S. Barnes, 1940), p. 63.

This is a board game played with a table tennis ball and two pinball machine-like flippers at each end of the board.

888 FRAHA. THE NEW GAMES BOOK. San Francisco: New Games Foundation, 1976.

889 KADIMA. Land Distributors, Plaza 1 Building, Norfolk, Va. 23510.

890 MACABEE. Seville Products, 5101 Unruh Street, Philadelphia, Pa. 19135.

891 SMASHBALL. Matkok Co., 1825 Jefferson Place, Washington, D.C. 20036.

The four games above are listed together because they are essentially the same game. A large round wooden paddle and a soft rubber ball are used by two or more players to hit the ball back and forth on the fly--or players can make up their own rules.

892 FRONTENIS. U.S. Fronton Athletic Association. c/o The Princeton Club, Box 1415, West Forty-third Street, New York, N.Y. 10036.

This is a game played in a three-walled cement court with a tin similar to a telltale in squash racquets on the front wall. The three walls are front, left side, and back; the racket is a nylon-strung tennis frame; the ball is smaller than a tennis ball and rockets around the court. For an amusing description by Dick Squires of the United States frontenis team in the 1968 Olympic games, read chapter 13 of his book, THE OTHER RACQUET SPORTS (see 17).

893 HOT TENNIS. Obtainable from Sportpages, 3373 Towerwood Drive, Dallas, Tex. 75234. Sportpages is not the manufacturer.

Small paddles, "hot birds" (in effect, modified shuttlecocks), and a net suspended in a frame across which players bat the birds are used in this game.

894 JOKARI. Jokari/U.S., Inc., Four Lemmon Park East, Dallas, Tex. 75204.

There are no walls, court, or net for this one; just two wood-end paddles and a rubber ball attached to an anchor block with an elastic band. A fifteen-by-thirty foot hard surface area is necessary for play.

KADIMA.

See 889.

895 LUV JUG. Game Gauge Co., 5395 Ravenswood Road, Fort Lauderdale, Fla. 33312.

> A jug is weighted by adding water, and then a loop is placed on top. A ball is attached to the loop with an elastic cord. Hit the ball with anything from hand to any racket; it bounces and returns to the hitter for another whack. Similar to Anchor Tennis (see 878).

MACABEE.

See 890.

896 NUTTSY TENNIS. Toomy, 901 East 233d Street, Carson, Calif. 90745.

> In this table game a ball is attached to a wire above a net, and push buttons control the spring activated rackets that hit it.

897 PADDLE SET. Cosom, P.O. Box 701, Lakeville, Minn. 55044.

> This game uses a plastic ball (about the size of a baseball) with holes in it. Two foam polypropylene paddles are used to hit the ball against a wall, to play solo, or over a net or string with a partner.

898 PADDLE TENNIS. (1) American Paddle Tennis League, 259 McCarty Drive, Beverly Hills, Calif. 90212. (2) The United States Paddle Tennis Association, 189 Seeley Street, Brooklyn, N.Y. 11218.

> Paddle tennis began in Michigan in 1898 as a game for children in playgrounds, but its real growth can be said to have begun in 1959 when most of the present rules and court dimensions were published and publicized by the United States Paddle Tennis Association. The large centers for the game are around Los Angeles and New York City. Both associations (given in citation) work to publicize and encourage participation in the sport, but there have been areas of disagreement. The rules for the New York game indicate that the underhand serve used can either be hit on the bounce or out of the hand provided the server uses the same pattern throughout the set. California allows the bounce serve only.

> While some books have sections on paddle tennis--the Diagram Group's ENJOYING RACQUET SPORTS (see 7), George Sullivan's PADDLE (see 113), and the best one, Dick Squire's THE OTHER RACQUET SPORTS (see 17)--there is no book devoted solely to the game. One may purchase from the United States Paddle Tennis Association a handbook which is planned to be part of a future book by Murray Geller. The unfortunate confusion between platform tennis and paddle tennis, typified by the title of Sullivan's book (see 113) persists today.

The whole story is told in some detail in Geller's handbook. For here, it is enough to say that court dimensions, net height, ball used, and service rule all differ, and that does not cover the greatest variation--the use of and necessity for a surrounding screen in platform tennis. With a few changes necessitated by the smaller court dimensions, paddle tennis is a cut down version of tennis. Platform tennis is not; the screens make it a new ball game.

899   PICKLE-BALL. Pickle-Ball, Inc., 3131 Western Avenue, Seattle, Wash. 98121.

This is a game played on a badminton size court using a tennis net with an enlarged table tennis bat and a whiffle ball (a perforated plastic ball about baseball size). A longer account is given in Dick Squires's book THE OTHER RACQUET SPORTS (see 17). It is very popular in Seattle, and the corporation would love to have it go national.

900   PING PONG TENNIS. c/o Terry Dillman, 6 Widmann Circle, State College, Pa. 16801.

This game is a mixture of table tennis and tennis played on a table which is wider than the five-foot table tennis table, and which is lined as a tennis court is lined. It uses rubber paddles, table tennis balls, five-point games, nine-game sets, with tennis serving and volleying allowed.

901   PRO TENNIS. Athol Research, 200 Fifth Avenus, New York, N.Y. 10010.

902   PRO TENNIS. Gamesman, Inc., Box 15008, Atlanta, Ga. 30333.

These are two different board games with the same name. The Athol game is not available separately; it comes as part of a group of sports games sold together under the title of Sports Spectacular. A board is laid out like a tennis court, and dice and strategy cards are used to advance a yellow chip (the ball) back and forth across the net. The Gamesman version also has a tennis court board, dice, and cards called "player profiles." Doubles and singles can be played under Gamesman rules, singles only for Athol.

903   RACQUETBALL WITHOUT THE WALLS. Jokari, 4 Lemmon Park East, Dallas, Tex. 75204.

This game has two racquetball rackets, and a ball attached by a stretch band to a base. Players hit the ball alternately after one or two bounces.

904   RACQUETS. The North American Racquets Association is the governing body, and it publishes an occasional newsletter. Write to the secretary

and newsletter publisher, George Mars, 611 Park Avenue, Baltimore, Md., 21201, for information.

It is not "racquets," it is "rackets," says Dick Squires in his THE OTHER RACQUET SPORTS (see 17) on p. 38; it is an English game and should have the English spelling. But because the official organization calls it "racquets" and because Robert Henderson in his BALL, BAT AND BISHOP (New York: Rockport, 1947. Reprint. Detroit: Gale Research Co., 1974) goes into the reasons for the spelling variations and comes out in favor of "racquets" on page 92, that spelling will be used here. Literary references to the game can be found as far back as 1500. In the eighteenth century it was played by prisoners in the Fleet Street Prison, and a century later Charles Dickens referred to its continued existence there near the end of chapter 45 of PICKWICK PAPERS. Popularity it had; it needed only respectability, and it got that with its introduction to the English public schools in the nineteenth century. William Surtees, recent world champion, in a conversation with the editor, said that the game today suffers from that very fact. There are ten courts still in existence in those schools so the boys learn it at a perfect age, but when they go on to the wider world they find only four other courts in all of England, which are not enough for continuing development and interest. In North America there are ten courts (Chicago has three of them), but no one here gets to those courts at an early enough age. Like court tennis (see 882), the expense of construction of the large rectangular concrete block on which the modern game is played will prevent more from being built. The incredible speed at which the very hard plastic ball is hit--up to 150 miles per hour in championship matches--would make television coverage impossible, said Surtees, so even though the game impresses people when they see it (unlike court tennis it is not difficult to comprehend) not enough people have seen it or are likely to see it to have it make much headway.

905   SCORCH.   Scorch Enterprises, 353 East Eighty-third Street, New York, N.Y. 10028.

Two paddles, two tape baselines set twenty-one feet apart, and two balls (experts can use the faster one) are the basic ingredients of this game. There's no net; just set up anywhere, hit back and forth on the fly, and score as in table tennis.

906   SHOTBALL.   Norca Industries, 235 Montee de Liesse, Ville St. Laurent, Montreal H4T 1P5.

This game is played on badminton courts with small perforated balls and loosely strung rackets that look like badminton rackets. The ball flies somewhat like a shuttlecock, but on-the-

bounce hitting is allowed, and the game can be played inside
or outside by using a different class of ball.

SMASHBALL.

See 891.

907 SOFTBALL TENNIS. Obtainable from the Writewell Co., 2 Transit Building, Boston, Mass. 02115. (Writewell is not the manufacturer.)

A twenty-inch long strung racket, foam rubber softball, and
net are the essential elements of this game. The ball is soft
enough so that it will not break glassware.

908 SOLO TENNIS. Dynamic Classics, 9 Stewart Place, Fairfield, N.J.
07006.

A ball is attached to a racket by a long elastic cord. Hit
it and it will return to the hitter.

909 SQUASH TENNIS. National Squash Tennis Association, 50 Vanderbilt
Avenue, New York, N.Y. 10017.

Squash tennis originated in New York in the 1890s as an
American adaptation of squash racquets. Why it did not succeed, while the other did, might be a subject for a physical
education major's master's thesis. It is still played, still has
its corps of devotees, still runs an annual tournament at the
Yale Club in New York City, and still gets a one-sentence
paragraph every year in the NEW YORK TIMES, that reports
the results of the finals of that tournament. But outside the
greater New York area the game is hardly known. The big
difference between it and squash racquets is the size and
speed of the ball; the one used for squash tennis is larger and
faster. Two books previously referred to should be consulted
for past and present history--Allison Danzig's THE RACQUET
GAME (New York: Macmillan, 1930), Part III, and Dick
Squires's THE OTHER RACQUET SPORTS (see 17), chapter 5.
Read them one after the other; it is interesting to note
Squires's uncredited "borrowings" from the older book.

910 TABLE BADMINTON. Obtainable from the Miles Kimball Co., 41 West
Eighth Avenue, Oshkosh, Wis. 54901. (Miles Kimball is not the manufacturer.)

Plastic shuttlecocks are placed on plastic rackets and flipped
over a net onto a board to score points.

911 TENNIS. Parker Brothers, 190 Bridge Street, Salem, Mass. 01970.

This card game consists of a serve deck and a play deck with
instructions on each card, as well as a board court and a ball
marker.

912 TENNIS ANYONE? Franklin Merchandising Co., 333 West Lake Street, Chicago, Ill. 60606.

This game uses a court of felt and foam padding with a net, plastic rackets, and discs. The rackets snap the discs back and forth across a net.

913 TENNISETTE. c/o Huntington Hartford, 1 Beekman Place, New York, N.Y. 10022.

This game, playable indoors or outdoors, combines elements of table tennis and tennis. The ball is of urethane foam rubber four inches in diameter weighing one ounce, and there are short (seventeen-inch) rackets. Two pentagon shaped tables are used with the points of the pentagons facing each other. The space between the tables is covered by an underneath netting (there is no standard net). The rules are essentially those of tennis with overhead serving and volleying allowed.

914 TENNIS TRAINER. Childcraft Education Corp., 20 Kilmer Road, Edison, N.J. 08817.

Twenty-inch nylon-strung rackets hit a foam ball back and forth across a portable twenty-inch net.

915 TENNI STRATA BOARD. J.R. Songman, Fossil, Oreg. 97830.

A board tennis court divided into three-quarter inch squares which are numbered and lettered, with four stylized players scaled to represent a person five feet nine inches tall, and a ball and net are used to play this game, developed to teach concepts of strategy.

916 TENNIWALL. United States Tenniwall Association, c/o Lyman Appleby, 519 East Seventy-eighth Street, New York, N.Y. 10021.

This game could be characterized as "one-wall handball played with a tennis racket." Originally called wall tennis, it has been played in New York City since the late 1950s. Rules are available from the association, which will also supply the book about the game annotated below.

917 Appleby, Lyman. HOW TO PLAY TENNIWALL. New York: United States Tenniwall Association, 1977. 61 p. Dgrms., dwgs. Paperbound.

Instruction on how to play the game is given along with chapters on equipment and court conduct. Standard stroke instruction is given with drawings illustrating these strokes. Regrettably, the drawings are separated from the textual description. There is some discussion of strategy, and the rules are given.

918   VIDEO TENNIS.

Video Tennis is a generic name that is often applied to the various racket games played on home television sets. It consists of a dotted net, a white representation of a ball, and oblong bars representing rackets. The bars are moved along the two sides of the set to block the ball back and forth. The games made NEWSWEEK (9 August 1976, p. 61), TIME (13 December 1976, p. 80), TENNIS (November 1977, p. 42), and CONSUMER REPORTS (November 1977, p. 630). The last is the most informative.

919   WINNING TENNIS.   P.O. Box 3125, Princeton, N.J. 08540.

This is a board game with two subsections, amateur and professional. The former is for beginners and consists of a board with tennis court markings, miniature players and ball, and dice. The ball is served and goes back and forth across the net line depending on the roll. The professional game uses the same equipment but is more complicated with net play featured.

920   ZIMM ZAMM (also known as ZIMM ZAMM SWINGBALL).   Fonas Corp., P.O. Box 759, Latrobe, Pa. 15650.

A metal pole is put in the ground, and there is a spring at the top to which a tennis ball is attached on a four-foot nylon cord. Players with paddles whack the ball around the pole.

Chapter 10

RECOMMENDED PURCHASES FOR
LIBRARIES AND INDIVIDUALS

The criteria for selecting the best books, in order of importance, are as follows: (1) The book is thorough: it covers all aspects of its topic; (2) It is written clearly so that style does not get in the way of substance; (3) For instruction books, (a) there are good sequence photographs for the strokes, and those photographs are well placed so the text describing the stroke is close to the illustrations, or (b) it presents an alternative theory to "standard instruction" that is important enough and/or popular enough to be represented; (4) For non-instruction books, the book makes a contribution to the literature that should be represented on library shelves.

The bulk of racket sport literature is, of course, instruction, and criticism of such books is not uncommon. Al Laney in his COVERING THE COURT (see 455) says of his early days as a reporter: "I had not at this time read any tennis instruction books, which I rate a most fortunate circumstance, since I was able to observe without being misled by their fallacies and errors."

The attitude that one cannot learn by reading but only by doing, under the guidance of an experienced professional, is fairly common. The reply can only be that there are three ways people learn--from observation, description, and performance. The importance of each of those methods will be mixed in varying proportions in the racket sport learning population, and certainly performance is the most important. For some, however, a good guide can be useful, and this chapter is written for those persons and for libraries wishing to purchase such books.

RACKET SPORTS IN GENERAL

The Squires book, THE OTHER RACQUET SPORTS (see 17) is the essential item. The author finely summarizes the basics and gives a feel for the games, and his informed predictions on the future of each one are worth reading. Individuals who play more than one of the games in this book will find RULES OF THE GAME: RACQUET SPORTS (see 15) a useful purchase to settle inevitable arguments. Libraries should purchase the book from which it was taken, RULES OF THE GAME (see 15). That book, the Squires book, and three or four of the tennis books recommended below should be the minimum purchases for libraries with limited budgets.

BADMINTON

The prime book is Davidson and Gustavson's WINNING BADMINTON (see 66). Published in 1964 it is still the best available; it is clear, thorough, and useful for all levels from beginner through advanced. Second place is shared by Davis's BADMINTON COMPLETE (see 68) and Brown's THE COMPLETE BOOK OF BADMINTON (see 61). Davis does have the faults mentioned in the annotation in this book, and it was written for an English audience--readers will need to know what terms such as "tramlines" mean. It is a good book and is particularly thorough on the serve and in the section of leading faults and how to correct them. Brown uses drawings rather than sequence photographs, but his sections on tactics and points on anticipation are excellent. Jim Poole's BADMINTON (see 79) is written in a style that will irritate women (he uses "men" and "girls"). But his emphasis on hitting the shuttle with forearm rotation and not wrist snap--points that were supported and extended in an article by Norma Harris entitled "Requiem for a Wrist Snap," in the March 1978 issue of RACQUETS CANADA, pages 81-84--makes his book another that libraries should consider.

PADDLEBALL

For the one-wall game there is only Hammer's PADDLEBALL (see 95); fortunately it is a good book. For the multiwalled varieties Fleming and Bloom's PADDLEBALL AND RACQUETBALL (see 94) is the choice. While it does cover both games it keeps distinctions clear.

PLATFORM TENNIS

First choice is Russell and Chu's WINNING PLATFORM TENNIS (see 110) with its emphasis on the modern aggressive game. A second choice is Sullivan's PADDLE (see 113). Occasional humor--the correct strategy when one lobs too short is "cowering"--provides an added bonus to an excellent book. Iseman's PLAY PADDLE! (see 108) with its admirable clarity, and Callaway and Hughes's PLATFORM TENNIS (see 106) with full-page sequence photographs, are worthy books.

RACQUETBALL

For individuals who dream of being champions and for libraries, MARTY HOGAN'S POWER RACQUETBALL (see 136) is an essential book. With the helpful analysis of top player Charlie Brumfield, Hogan presents a new theory of how the game should be played. Steve Keeley's COMPLETE BOOK OF

RACQUETBALL (see 137) has the most detail and, in spite of a clever writing style that might irritate some, would be the second choice for individuals but not for libraries, since the paper in this paperback is of poor quality. Other good books: Brumfield and Bairstow's OFF THE WALL (see 133), Reznik's RACQUETBALL (see 145), and Strandemo and Bruns's THE RACQUETBALL BOOK (see 157). The first and third of these have excellent sequence photographs and diagrams, and Reznik is second only to Keeley in its detailed coverage. The two books by Victor Spear (see 154,155) are both delightfully and dogmatically written, with the first especially offering much sound strategic advice. Racquetball is a sport in which books and interest are rapidly increasing, and libraries will need more of the former in the 1980s. Because it is one of the easiest games to learn at the elementary level, a final recommendation is Sauser and Shay's TEACHING YOUR CHILD RACQUETBALL (see 149) for public libraries in particular--and for parents interested in a good family game.

SQUASH RACQUETS

Two books are indispensable: Barnaby's WINNING SQUASH RACQUETS (see 182) and Truby's THE SCIENCE AND STRATEGY OF SQUASH (see 205). Barnaby's discussion of grips, spin, and shots is unequaled. He makes his usual dogmatic statements--"The return of any decent service should always be aimed high and deep along the wall."--and backs them up with sound analysis. His description of the Ace bandage ploy in the gamesmanship section is sheer delight. The book will be most useful to the intermediate and advanced player. Truby is good for all levels, is clear and thorough, and has the best sequence photographs. Khan and Randall's SQUASH RACQUETS: THE KHAN GAME (see 193) and Molloy's WINNING SQUASH (see 196) are two other worthy purchases, with the latter being especially useful on the changes the 70+ball has made in the game. Finally, Satterthwaite's THE THREE-WALL NICK AND OTHER ANGLES (see 199) with its informed commentary on the game and its players is highly recommended.

TABLE TENNIS

There is no outstanding table tennis instruction book but a noteworthy selection is Reisman's THE MONEY PLAYER (see 236), with a fascinating life story and portrait of the world of big time hustling. The problem with instruction books is that none of them goes into detail on the penholder style of play. Most books describe it briefly, say that it is inferior to the Western style, and leave it at that. The most satisfactory book on penholder play is Leach's TABLE TENNIS FOR THE SEVENTIES (see 232), which is fine in its text but which has many photographs that serve no useful instructional purpose and are only fair on the sequence shots. Miles's THE GAME OF TABLE TENNIS (see 233) has good sequence drawings and is the most clearly written, but has nothing on the doubles game or on the loop. Boggan's WINNING TABLE TENNIS (see 227) is best on the modern game, but the sequence photographs are inadequate. The same is true for every other book annotated in chapter 7. There are many good points, but no really complete job has been done. In Dick Squires's THE OTHER RACQUET

Recommended Purchases

SPORTS (see 17), he indicates that Dan Seemiller, the U.S. champion for several years, also feels there is no good book on the current market and thus is writing one himself. The advice here for individuals and libraries is to get Reisman and wait for the reviews of Seemiller.

TENNIS

Autobiography, Biography, History

There is no tennis equivalent of Franklin or Boswell. Two good books are Ashe and DeFord's ARTHUR ASHE: PORTRAIT IN MOTION (see 429) and DeFord's BIG BILL TILDEN (see 443). (DeFord is eminent in the biographical areas; his magazine article portrait of Jimmy Connors, "Raised by Women to Conquer Men," SPORTS IL-LUSTRATED, 28 August 1978, pp. 90-103, is better than any book biography annotated here.) Libraries do not need any of these, but they should have tennis history. Grimsley's TENNIS: ITS HISTORY, PEOPLE AND EVENTS (see 447) is the best general survey in print, but it does skim over the early years in too rapid fashion. For those years libraries should hold onto their copies of Potter's KINGS OF THE COURT (see 462) or put it on their desiderata lists, or get Alexander's LAWN TEN-NIS: ITS FOUNDERS AND ITS EARLY DAYS (see 427), which is delightfully written and takes a thorough look at the Outerbridge versus Davis controversy on who first brought tennis to the United States and when. For the modern period, two items are essential. Koster's THE TENNIS BUBBLE (see 453) with its survey and explanation of the various power groups is the first, and Wind's GAME, SET, AND MATCH (see 474), offering informed and finely written reflections on the game during the years of the tennis explosion is the second. Finally, Jack Kramer's THE GAME (see 454), with its details on the years before open tennis is recommended as an opinionated, fascinating portrait.

Fiction

Some may think it unusual to place a work of fiction on a list of recommended books for a subject such as tennis. An old examination question provides a justification. "One can learn more history of Victorian England from the novels of Dickens than from the histories of Trevelyan. Discuss." Art Hoppe's THE TIDDLING TENNIS THEORUM (see 503), while not as apt as the Dickens-Trevelyan example, is included as desirable not because it is great literature but simply as a charming fable by a knowledgeable enthusiast that other players cannot read without a "wince of recognition" at the types of people who inhabit the tennis world.

Instruction

There are many good instruction books, and before choosing the top ones it can be said that a library holding any book by Gonzales, King, Metzler, Chet and/or Bill Murphy, or Talbert has fine material on its shelves. The two books by TENNIS magazine based on their instructional series, TENNIS: HOW TO PLAY, HOW TO WIN and TENNIS STROKES AND STRATEGIES (see 706,709) are both good, as is the one by TENNIS USA when it was a magazine, WINNING TENNIS (see 720). People who like technical explanations of what is being done will respond to Jones's IMPROVING YOUR TENNIS and TENNIS: HOW TO BECOME A CHAMPION (see 624,626) or Plagenhoef's FUNDAMENTALS OF TENNIS (see 674). The less technically oriented can learn a lot from Gordon's IMPROVING YOUR TENNIS GAME (see 605). Kramer and Sheehan's HOW TO PLAY YOUR BEST TENNIS ALL THE TIME (see 636) and Kraft's TENNIS INSTRUCTION FOR FUN AND COMPETITION (see 635) are both good. The former is a fine one for the intermediate player who wants to raise her or his game a notch, and the latter will be helpful to nonconfident beginners who need encouragement.

For the most outstanding books, libraries should have a good representation of standard instruction books, as well as one or two books that offer a different approach. For standard instruction, three titles are recommended--Braden and Bruns's VIC BRADEN'S TENNIS FOR THE FUTURE (see 569), Barnaby's ADVANTAGE TENNIS (see 563), and Faulkner and Weymuller's ED FAULKNER'S TENNIS: HOW TO PLAY IT--HOW TO TEACH IT (see 592). The first is the most exhaustive instruction book on the market and is a good choice for libraries that can afford only one book. Duggan and Scott comment on Barnaby's book in THE TENNIS CATALOG (see 797) and their words are apt: "You may or may not become a convert [to Barnaby's thesis that racket skills are the most important element in learning the game] but you're sure to learn a lot from this particular work on the subject."[1] Faulkner's book is not as complete as the other two; only one serve is taught, and doubles is not covered; but text is so clear, the sequence photographs so good (in the unabridged version; in the abridged book they're hard to follow) that a top rank is deserved; it is the recommended choice for absolute beginners.

The above are all large books. For individuals wanting briefer presentations to carry along in a tennis case, Devereux's NET RESULTS (see 583) and Gould's TENNIS ANYONE? (see 606) are the recommended choices. For last minute cramming before the big match, Sonneman's THE COMPLEAT POCKET TENNIS STRATEGIST (see 698) offers sound strategic advice.

The subject of tennis strategy deserves major treatment of its own and gets two good ones in Segura and Heldman's PANCHO SEGURA'S CHAMPIONSHIP STRATEGY (see 689) and Harman and Monroe's fine book for the average player USE YOUR HEAD IN TENNIS (see 613). The doubles game receives full treatment from Charles (see 577); Doerner, Doerner and Ozier (see 584); Durr (see 587); Graebner, Graebner and Prince (see 607); Harman (see 612); Lott and Bairstow (see 649); Metzler (see 659); Smith, Lutz, and Sheehan (see 693); Talbert and Old (see 704); and Trabert and Hyams (see 713). Talbert's was first in the field, has long been the classic, and is a fine book. Even so, Metzler is the first choice with Lott a close second. All the books recommend that partners be together--both up at the net whenever possible or both in the backcourt when forced there, but never one up, one back. (Vic Braden's amusing film GO FOR A WINNER [see 325] makes the same point.) If one goes to a local pub-

---

1. Moira Duggan and Eugene Scott, THE TENNIS CATALOG (New York: Macmillan, 1978), p. 214.

lic court, however, and observes what is going on, what is most likely to be seen is one up, one back, or "singles on a doubles court" as doubles authors contemptuously call it. The average player has neither the serve nor the nerve to follow that serve in to the net, and even if that serve is a pat-ball lob, the average receiver has even less gumption and is not likely to follow the return in. Metzler (and to a lesser extent Barnaby [see 563] in his chapter on doubles) is the only author who has a substantial section on one up, one back, and his book will be of most use to the average player. It should be noted that Metzler does not recommend one up and one back; he agrees with all the others on the superiority of side by side.

Since most instruction books are written for beginners and intermediates, the advanced player may sometimes wonder if there is anything for her or him. Segura's book on strategy (see 689) has been referred to on the previous page, and the sections on advanced play are worth reading. Of the books entirely devoted to the topic--Jones (see 625), Metzler (see 655), Murphy (see 664), and Tilmanis (see 712)--the choice would be the Jones book. He tends to strive for the rich, beautiful prose prize on occasion, but when he gets down to the subject he has worthwhile things to say.

Left-handers are a breed unto themselves on the courts, and Schwed's SINISTER TENNIS (see 688) comments in detail on what they can do and what right-handed players can do to counteract. It is a good book that could have been better with grip photographs and sequence shots. For too long, left-handers have had to contend with either "hold the book up to the mirror" or "reverse all directions" statements. They deserve a text of their own.

Several books are aimed at tennis teachers. Faulkner and Weymuller's (see 592) remains number one. Other good ones are Brent's PATTERN PLAY TENNIS (see 572), Leighton's INSIDE TENNIS (see 645), the Murphys's TENNIS FOR THE PLAYER, TEACHER AND COACH (see 665), and Tilmanis's ADVANCED TENNIS FOR COACHES, TEACHERS AND PLAYERS (see 712). The Murphys recommend the graduated length method of learning for children. The founding mother of that method, Elaine Mason, (the founding father is Dan Halperin) believes in it for adults as well, and her book TENNIS (see 652) is worth looking at for that reason.

For nonstandard instruction there is one indispensable name--Gallwey. His first book, THE INNER GAME OF TENNIS (see 597) has been the all-time best selling instruction book, and his second book, INNER TENNIS (see 598), summarized the first and then moved toward a philosophy of life. Get one, both if possible, and also Shawn Tully's article "Inside the Inner Game," WORLD TENNIS, April 1977, pp. 43-47. Insert that in whichever book is bought; it contains commentaries on the Gallwey method, as well as his response to those commentaries.

Both libraries and coaches should consider two other nonstandard instruction books, Brent's PATTERN PLAY TENNIS (see 572) and Bradlee's INSTANT TEN-NIS (see 570). Brent supports teaching the volley before teaching groundstrokes and also believes that strokes should be taught as a series of patterns. Brad-lee's claim is that for years leading professionals have taught one way but played another. The feet sideways to the net and the weight shift theories are wrong, and pictures taken of leading players prove it, he says with some vehemence.

By this point the reader and the acquisitions librarian may feel swamped with recommendations. Some worthwhile books have been left out--Lenz's interest-ing UNISEX TENNIS (see 646) for example and Bill Tilden's MATCH PLAY AND THE SPIN OF THE BALL (see 711). Supporters of Tilden as the greatest of them all (among whom Don Budge is not included--see 436) may be upset that his best book is not here. If libraries have it they should certainly keep it; his discussion of spin is excellent, but so is that of the other authors recom-mended above, and their more modern books remain first choices. Lenz has a good discussion on the topic of the difference between the sexes in terms of tennis. There are a number of tennis for women books that begin by saying that women are not the same as men, and then go on to present instruction that hardly differs from that found in the standard books.

Juvenile

Biographies and instructional works comprise most of the juvenile section. None of the instructional works listed are recommended. A child who has reached a physical state at which he or she can master the complexities of movement that tennis requires, and who has had his or her curiosity aroused both by trying the game and by seeing great players live or on television, does not need a Deegan (see 736-738), Leighton (see 760), or Hopman (see 752) juvenile in-struction book. Such children cannot understand Plagenhoef (see 674) but they can comprehend Gould (see 606) or any of the adult texts that are clear. As stated earlier in the annotation for Barbara Harrah's guide to sports literature for children (see 9), many books are listed in her book that are annotated here in the adult instructional section.

Biographies are different, and the two by Frayne (see 742, 743; the latter is the better), all of those by May (see 763-766), Robinson's ARTHUR ASHE, TENNIS CHAMPION (see 784), and Sullivan's QUEENS OF THE COURT (see 791) are good books for the younger reader. For tennis history, good drawings are found in Ravielli's WHAT IS TENNIS? (see 782) and excellent text in Reardon's MATCH POINT (see 783).

Reference

A good encyclopedia is normally a recommended library reference purchase. It is useful to have a tennis results summary, as well as a guide to famous whos and whats. Unfortunately, neither of the two leading candidates, Robertson and Kramer's THE ENCYCLOPEDIA OF TENNIS (see 805) and the United States Tennis Association's OFFICIAL ENCYCLOPEDIA OF TENNIS (see 811) is an outstanding example of a reference book. Robertson does not have an index and needs one; the United States Tennis Association has one but it does not include personal names, and its table of contents is run on so the user cannot find material easily. Since it is the more recent of the two and does contain more information, the latter is given a qualified recommendation.

A useful item for individuals is Nick Powel's "THE CODE" (see 803). Libraries don't really need it, and its small size and paperback format make it an easy candidate for loss or theft.

Research libraries collect bibliographies, and the bibliography for early tennis materials is that compiled by Robert Henderson in 1932 that appears in Whitman's TENNIS: ORIGINS AND MYSTERIES (see 473). Of the other books annotated in the reference section of the tennis chapter, the recommendation is that libraries ought to have one of the tennis handbook guides, with the choice lying between Duggan and Scott's THE TENNIS CATALOG (see 797) and Tennis Magazine's THE TENNIS PLAYER'S HANDBOOK (see 809A). The former is more specific (discussing brand names), the latter more up-to-date (it includes all levels of the rating program discussed on pp. 185-86 of this book). Both are good, and price may be the deciding factor.

Miscellaneous

In the area of miscellaneous works, libraries in affluent suburbia ought to have one of the tennis court construction books, and either Anderson's HOW TO BUILD YOUR OWN TENNIS COURT (see 819) or Neal's BUILD YOUR OWN TENNIS COURT (see 848) will do. The latter is the most complete and has the added bonus of its chapter on platform tennis court construction, while the former is the easiest to understand.

The two best books on tennis psychology are LOVE AND HATE ON THE TENNIS COURT (see 822) and PSYCHODYNAMIC TENNIS (see 831). A new book seen by this editor in galley form is TOTAL TENNIS by M. Barrie Richmond (New York: Macmillan, 1980) and it will also make a worthy contribution. Billie Jean King's TENNIS LOVE (see 840) has sound words on tennis mothering and fathering and is also recommended.

Most tennis books have a chapter with exercises for conditioning for the game, but Hines and Morgenstern's QUICK TENNIS (see 835) is definitive. The exercises they offer are not easy, but they are good, and the thorough coverage of court mobility is a strong bonus.

Two final suggestions are offered in this category of miscellaneous. Both individuals and libraries should get McPhee's LEVELS OF THE GAME (see 845). Part biographical, more sociological, it and the previously recommended book by Wind (see 474) are the best "tennis as literature" contributions. Finally, here is the outstanding coffee table book. Friends and strangers are coming to your party, and you wish to let the latter know (and remind the former) that you are a discriminating player. The book to carelessly leave open on the table is Eugene Scott's TENNIS: GAME OF MOTION (see 857). This book can often be found at remainder sales. It contains fine pictures and informed text.

APPENDIX

An alphabetical list of names and addresses of distributors of audiovisual materials follows. These addresses were correct as of the date of publication. For updates consult the following publications: (1) AUDIO-VISUAL MARKET PLACE (New York: R.R. Bowker, 1969-- . Annual.); (2) EDUCATIONAL FILM LOCATOR OF THE CONSORTIUM OF UNIVERSITY FILM CENTERS AND R.R. BOWKER COMPANY (New York: R.R. Bowker, 1978-- . Biannual[?]); (3) UNITED STATES TENNIS ASSOCIATION. TENNIS FILM LIST (Princeton, N.J.: 1971-- . Annual.)

AAHPERD. American Alliance for Health, Physical Education and Recreation and Dance
1201 Sixteenth Street, N.W.,
Washington, D.C. 20036.

Aetna. Film Librarian,
Public Relations and Advertising Department,
Aetna Life and Casualty,
Hartford, Conn. 06156.

AIMS. Instructional Media Services,
626 Justin Avenue,
Glendale, Calif. 91201.

American Platform Tennis Association.
52 Upper Montclair Plaza
Upper Montclair, N.J. 07043.

AMF Head. Marketing Department,
4801 North Sixty-third Street,
Boulder, Colo. 80301.

AMF Voit. Orange County Film Service,
2040 South Grand Avenue,
Santa Ana, Calif. 92705.

Arizona. University of,
Bureau of Audiovisual Services,
Tuscon, Ariz. 85721.

Association Films.
866 Third Avenue,
New York, N.Y. 10022.

AstroVideo, Inc.
90 Golden Gate Avenue
San Francisco, Calif. 94102.

Athletic Institute.
200 North Castlewood Drive,
North Palm Beach, Fla. 33408.

Atlas Health Club.
901 Hotel Circle South,
San Diego, Calif. 92138.

Australian Information Service.
Australian Consulate General,
636 Fifth Avenue,
New York, N.Y. 10020.

Appendix

Australian Information Service.
First Secretarion (Information),
Embassy of Australia,
1601 Massachusetts Avenue, N.W.,
Washington, D.C. 20036.

Australian Information Service.
Press and Information Officer,
Australian Consulate General,
360 Post Street, Union Square,
San Francisco, Calif. 94108.

A.W. Peller and Associates.
Educational Materials,
13-00 Plaza Road,
Fair Lawn, N.J. 07410.

Bergwall Productions.
839 Stewart Avenue,
Garden City, N.Y. 11530.

BFA. Educational Media,
Division of CBS,
2211 Michigan Avenue,
P.O. Box 1795,
Santa Monica, Calif. 90406.

Boston University. Film Library,
765 Commonwealth Avenue,
Boston, Mass. 02215.

Brentwood Productions.
P.O. Box 49956,
Los Angeles, Calif. 90049.

California, University of,
Extension Media Center,
Berkeley, Calif. 94720.

Carousel Films.
1501 Broadway,
New York, N.Y. 10036.

Champions on Film.
745 State Circle,
Ann Arbor, Mich. 48104.

Chevron U.S.A.
575 Market Street,
San Francisco, Calif. 94105.

Churchill Films.
662 North Robertson Boulevard,
Los Angeles, Calif. 90069.

Cloud 9 Films.
P.O. Box 24181,
Minneapolis, Minn. 55424.

Coaching Association of Canada ·
333 River Road,
Ottawa, Ontario K1L 8B9.

Coca-Cola U.S.A.
Communications Support Unit,
P.O. Drawer 1734,
Atlanta, Ga. 30301.

Colonial Films.
4315 North East Expressway Road,
Doraville, Ga. 30340.

Colorado, University of,
Educational Media Center,
Stadium Building,
Boulder, Colo. 80309.

Connecticut, University of,
Center for Instructional Media
and Technology,
Storrs, Conn. 06268.

Converse.
Sporting Goods Division,
1454 Ormandy Drive
Baton Rouge, La. 70808

Educational Audio Visual.
Pleasantville, N.Y. 10570.

Educational Enrichment Materials.
110 South Bedford Road,
Mount Kisco, N.Y. 10549.

Encyclopedia Britannica.
Educational Corp.,
425 North Michigan Avenue,
Chicago, Ill. 60611.

Eye Gate Media.
146-01 Archer Avenue,
Jamaica, N.Y. 11435.

Film Comm.
One Main Place
Dallas, Tex. 75250.

Films, Inc.
733 Green Bay Road
Wilmette, III. 60091.

Fisher/Feld.
888 Seventh Avenue
New York, N.Y. 10019.

Forest Hills Productions.
Box A619,
Madison Square Station,
New York, N.Y. 10010.

General Mills Film Center.
P.O. Box 1113,
Minneapolis, Minn. 55440.

Golden Door.
2748 Ninth Street,
Berkeley, Calif. 94710.

Idaho, University of.
A/V and Photo Center,
Moscow, Idaho 83843.

Idaho State University.
Audio Visual Services,
Campus Box 8064,
Pocatello, Idaho 83209.

Illinois, University of.
Visual Aids Service,
1325 South Oak Street,
Champaign, III. 61820.

Imperial International Learning Corp.
P.O. Box 548,
Kankakee, III. 60901.

Indiana University.
Audio Visual Center,
Bloomington, Ind. 47401.

Inner Game Resources.
P.O. Box 4206,
Malibu, Calif. 90265.

Iowa, University of.
Audio Visual Center,
C-5 East Hall,
Iowa City, Iowa 52242.

Iowa State University.
Media Resources Center,
121 Pearson Hall,
Ames, Iowa 50010.

Ivy Films.
165 West Forty-sixth Street,
New York, N.Y. 10036.

Johnson-Nyquist Productions, Inc.
23854 Via Fabricante,
Mission Viejo, Calif. 92691.

Kansas, University of.
Audio-Visual Center,
Film Rental Service,
746 Massachusetts Street,
Lawrence, Kans. 66044.

Kent State University.
Audio Visual Services,
330 Library Building,
Kent, Ohio 44242.

KOCE TV Foundation.
P.O. Box 2476,
Huntington Beach, Calif. 92647.

Lord and King Associates.
P.O. Box 68,
Winfield, III. 60190.

McManus/Wilson Films.
2128 Fillmore Street
San Francisco, Calif. 94115.

Macmillan Films.
34 MacQuesten Parkway South,
Mount Vernon, N.Y. 10550.

Maryland Center for Public
Broadcasting.
Owings Mills, Md. 21117.

Mason Distributing Co.
7531 Robertson Lane NW,
P.O. Box 7146,
Roanoke, Va. 24019.

Michigan, University of.
Audio-Visual Education Center,
416 Fouth Street,
Ann Arbor, Mich. 48109.

Minnesota, University of.
Audio Visual Library Services,
3300 University Avenue SE,
Minneapolis, Minn. 55414.

Modern Talking Picture Service.
5000 Park Street North
St. Petersburg, Fla. 33709.

National Film Board of Canada.
P.O. Box 6100, Station A,
Montreal, Quebec H3C 3H5.

National Film Board of Canada.
1251 Avenue of the Americas,
New York, N.Y. 10020.

Nebraska, University of. Lincoln.
Instructional Media Center,
Nebraska Hall 421,
Lincoln, Nebr. 68588.

9200 Film Center.
P.O. Box 1113,
Minneapolis, Minn. 55440.

Northern Illinois University.
Media Distribution Department,
De Kalb, Ill. 60015.

Oklahoma State University.
Audio Visual Center,
Stillwater, Okla. 74074.

Ontario Badminton Association.
559 Jarvis Street,
Toronto, Ontario M4Y 2J1.

Paramount Communications.
5451 Marathon Street,
Hollywood, Calif. 90038.

Pennsylvania State University.
Audio-Visual Services,
7 Willard Building,
University Park, Pa. 16802.

Phoenix Films.
470 Park Avenue South,
New York, N.Y. 10016.

Public Television Library.
Public Broadcasting Service,
475 L'Enfant Plaza, S.W.,
Washington, D.C. 20024.

Richard J. Reilly.
P.O. Box 1052,
Danbury, Conn. 06810.

Rolex Watch U.S.A.
665 Fifth Avenue,
New York, N.Y. 10022.

Sales and Marketing Associates.
207 West Main Street,
Durant, Okla. 74701.

Scholastic Coach Athletic Services.
50 West Forty-fourth Street,
New York, N.Y. 10036.

SCOPE.
P.O. Box 206
Ahwahnee, Calif. 93601.

Service Press.
Department B4,
6369 Reynolds Road,
Haslett, Mich. 48840.

Society for Visual Education. (SVE).
1345 Diversy Parkway,
Chicago, Ill. 60614.

South Carolina, University of.
Audio Visual Services,
Columbia, S.C. 29208.

Southern Illinois University.
Learning Resources Services,
Carbondale, Ill. 62901.

South Florida University.
Division of Educational Resources-
Films,
Tampa, Fla. 33620.

Sportlite Films.
20 North Wacker Drive,
Chicago, Ill. 60606.

Sports Films and Talents.
7431 Bush Lake Road,
Minneapolis, Minn. 55435.

Sports Investors.
120 East Fifty-sixth Street,
New York, N.Y. 10022.

Sports World Cinema.
P.O. Box 17022,
2367 Murray Holladay Road,
Salt Lake City, Utah 84117.

Star Film Co.
79 Bobolink Lane,
Levittown, N.Y. 11756.

Sterling Educational Films.
241 East Thirty-fourth Street,
New York, N.Y. 10016.

SVE.
See Society for Visual Education.

Syracuse University.
Film Rental Center,
1455 East Colvin Street,
Syracuse, N.Y. 13210.

Tennessee, University of.
Teaching Materials Center,
R-61 Communications,
Knoxville, Tenn. 37916.

Tennis Films International.
44 Puritan Road,
Newton Highlands, Mass. 02161.

Texas, University of.
Film Library,
Box W,
Austin, Tex. 78712.

Time-Life Multimedia.
100 Eisenhower Drive,
Paramus, N.J. 07652.

Trans World International
1800 Century Park East
Los Angeles, Calif. 90067.

Travelers Film Library.
One Tower Square,
Hartford, Conn. 06115.

Troll Associates.
320 Route 17,
Mahwah, N.J. 07430.

United States Squash Racquets
Association.
211 Ford Road,
Bala Cynwyd, Pa. 19004.

United States Table Tennis
Association (USTTA).
P.O. Box J
Bridgeton, Mo. 63044.

United States Tennis Association
(USTA). The association has a
central film library at 729 Alexander Road, Princeton, N.J.
08540. It also has twenty-three
sections and film district libraries,
whose addresses change frequently.
Persons seeking USTA films are
urged to write or telephone the
central library (609-452-2580) to
obtain the name, address, or
phone number of the closest section
or district film library.

USTA
See United States Tennis Association.

USTTA.
See United States Table Tennis
Association.

Utah, University of.
Educational Media Center,
207 Milton Bennian Hall,
Salt Lake City, Utah 84112.

Utah State University.
Audio Visual Services,
Logan, Utah 84321.

Vantage Communications.
P.O. Box 546,
Nyack, N.Y. 10960.

Video Tape Network.
115 East Sixty-second Street,
New York, N.Y. 10021.

Walt Disney Films.
500 South Buena Vista Street,
Burbank, Calif. 91521.

Washington State University.
Instructional Media Services,
Pullman, Wash. 99164.

Welling Motion Picture Service,
454 Meacham Avenue,
Elmont, N.Y. 11003.

West Glen Communications.
565 Fifth Avenue,
New York, N.Y. 10017.

Wisconsin, University of. La Crosse.
Film Rental Library,
127 Wing Communications Center,
1705 State Street,
La Crosse, Wis. 54601.

Wisconsin, University of. Madison.
Bureau of Audio Visual Instruction,
1327 University Avenue,
Madison, Wis. 53706.

WTT.
See World Team Tennis.

Wyoming, University of.
Audio Visual Services,
Box 3273, University Station,
Room 14, Knight Hall,
Laramie, Wyo. 82071.

AUTHOR INDEX

This index includes authors, compilers, editors, illustrators, translators, and other contributors to works cited in the text. Authors cited in footnotes, authors of periodical articles, or narrators of audiovisual material are excluded. This index is alphabetized letter by letter. Numbers refer to item numbers unless they are preceded by a "p.", in which case they refer to a page.

Author Index

Brecheen, Joel 571
Breen, James 60
Brennan, Dan 480A
Brennan, Peter 481
Brent, R. Spencer 572
Bright, James 820
Brinkley, William 482
Brown, Edward 61
Brown, Jim 573-74
Brown, Virginia 59
Brumfield, Churles 133, 136
Brundle, Fred 62
Bruns, Bill 157, 569
Budge, Don 436
Burchard, Marshall 730-31
Burchard, Sue 731-32
Burke, Jim 437
Burris, Barbara 63
Buxton, Angela 627

C

Callaway, Bob 106
Campbell, K. Gordon 821
Campbell, Ottis 159
Canadian Badminton Association 64
Cantin, Eugene 575
Carr, Jack 228
Carr, John Dickson 483
Carrington, Jack 229
Casewit, Curtis 576
Cath, Stanley 822
Champion, Rick 823
Chapin, Kim 452, 630
Chapman, Claire 184
Chappell, Annette 739
Charles, Allegra 577
Chase, Edward 578
Christopher, Matt 484
Chu, Ernest 109-10
Church, Carol 733
Clark, J.O.M. p. 188
Clavering, Molly 485
Claymore, Tod. See Clevely, Hugh
Clerici, Gianni 438
Clevely, Hugh 486-87
Cobb, Nathan 822
Cohen, Joel 235
Collins, Bud 446, 456, 641-42
Collins, Ed 579

Conroy, John 580, 634, 834
Consortium of University Film Centers
    p. xvi, p. 205
Constable, Betty 185
Cook, Joseph 734
Cooke, Sarah Palfrey. See Palfrey,
    Sarah
Coombs, Charles 735
Cosby, Bill 824
Court, Margaret 439
Courtier, Sidney 488
Cowan, Glenn 230
Cox, Mark 581, 681
Cox, William 489
Crossley, Ken 65
Curtis, Bruce 793
Cutler, Burt 825
Cutler, Merritt 582

D

Daalen, Nicholas Van. See Van
    Daalen, Nicholas
Danner, Fred 231
Danzig, Allison 440, p. 49,
    p. 188, p. 194
Daveson, Mons 490
Davidson, Kenneth 66
Davidson, Owen 441-42
Davis, Pat 67-69
Deegan, Paul 736-38, 761
DeFord, Frank 429, 443, 454
Delman, David 491
Delson, Rod 142
Demers, Ralph 491A
der Meer, Dennis Van. See Van
    der Meer, Dennis
Devereux, Rick 583
Devlin, J. Frank 70
Diagram Group 7, p. 191
Dickmeyer, Lowell 739
DiGiacomo, Melchior 858
Doerner, Cynthia 584
Doerner, Peter 584
Dolan, Edward, Jr. 740
Dowell, Linus 133B
Downey, Jake 71-73
Driver, Helen 585-86
Duggan, Moira 797
Duroska, Lud 741

Author Index

Harrah, Barbara 9
Harris, Peter 502
Harrison, J. Rufford 226
Harrison, June 433
Hasegawa, Sam 749
Hashman, Judy 76
Hawk, Dick 603
Hawkey, Richard 189-92
Haynes, Connie 834
Hedges, Martin 799
Heldman, Glcdys 689
Heldman, Julius 447
Hendershot, Claude 10
Henderson, Robert p. 69, p. 193,
    p. 204
Herda, D.J. 750
Herzog, Billy Jean 614
Hevener, Jim 105
Higdon, Hal 751
Hines, Henry 835
Hoffman, Greg 448, 840
Hoffman, Marshall 21
Hogan, Marty 136
Hopman, Harry 615, 752
Hoppe, Art 503
Hovis, Ford 708
Howorth, Beckett 836
Huang, Bob 616
Hughes, Michael 106
Hull, Gordon 837
Humphries, Rod 469
Hunt, Lesley 617
Huss, Sally Moore 618
Hutto, Nelson 504
Hyams, Joe 604, 631, 713

I

Iseman, Jay 108

J

Jackson, Caary 505
Jacobs, Helen 449, 506-8, 620
Jacobs, Linda 509, 753-57
Jaeger, Eloise 621
Janoff, Murray 450
Johnson, Joan 622
Joint Committee of the United States
    Lawn Tennis Association and the

American Association for Health,
    Physical Education and Recreation
    623
Jones, Ann 451
Jones, C(larence). M(edlycott).
    76, 441-42, 624-27, 758
Jungle, Hank 716

K

Kahn, Alvin 822
Kaufman, Axel 838
Keane, Bill 839
Keeley, Steve 137-38
Kelly, Julie 800
Kenfield, John 628-29
Khan, Hashim 193
King, Billie Jean 452, 630-31,
    840
Kirwan, Nancy 800
Kleiman, Carol 632
Klein, Jerome 801
Klein, Norma 511
Koster, Rich 453
Kozar, Andrew 96
Kraft, Eve 580, 633-34, 834
Kraft, Steven 707
Kraft, Virginia 635
Kramer, Jack (racquetball) 139
Kramer, Jack (tennis) 454, 636,
    805

L

Lambert, Derek 512
Laney, Al 455, p. 197
Lardner, Rex 70, 201, 637-39,
    841-42
Larson, Charles 97
Laver, Rod 456, 640-43A
Lawrence, A. Paul 11, 140
Lawrence, Andrew 759
Leach, Johnny 232
Leary, Don 644
Leedy, Jack 843
Leigh, Roberta 513
Leighton, Harry 621, 760
Leighton, Jim 645
Lenglen, Suzanne 514
Lenz, Bill 646

Author Index

Olsen, James 777
Olson, Arne 63
Orantes, Manolo 668
O'Shea, Mary Jo 779
Owens, Eleanor 802
Ozier, Dan 584

P

Palfrey, Sarah 669
Parrish, Marlene 849-50
Patterson, Jeff 611, 670
Paulson, Gary 780
Paulson, Jack. See Jackson, Caary
Pearce, Janice 671
Pearce, Wayne 671
Peck, Norman 185
Pelton, Barry 78, 672
Peters, Ludovic 529
Peterson, James 133A, 146
Petrocelli, Orlando 530
Petty, Roy 673
Philip, David 235
Phillips, Betty 781
Pici, J.R. 531
Plagenhoef, Stanley 674
Platt, Don 675
Platt, Kin 532
Plimpton, George 883
Pollard, Jack 643A, 676
Pons, Fred 677
Poole, James 79
Poppenberg, Mary 849-50
Porter, Mark 533
Potter, Edward 461-62
Potter, Jeremy 534
Powel, Nick 803
Pray, Rick 14
Prince, Kim 607
Professional Tennis Registry--USA 678

R

Ralston, Dennis 679
Ramo, Simon 680
Randall, Richard 193
Ravielli, Anthony 782
Ray, Robert 535
Reach, James 558

Reardon, Maureen 783
Reisman, Marty 236
Remsberg, Charles 74
Reznik, John 133A, 145-46
Rhame, M. LeVan 852
Rich, Jim 147
Richards, Gilbert 804
Richmond, M. Barrie p. 204
Riessen, Clare 681
Riessen, Marty 463
Riggs, Bobby 464
Riskey, Earl 96
Roberts, Jack 853
Robertson, Max 805
Robinson, Louie, Jr. 725, 784
Robinson, Ruth p. 2
Robison, Nancy 785
Robyns, Gwen 854
Rogers, Wynn 80
Rosenbaum, Helen 806
Rosewall, Ken 682-83
Ross, David 792
Rowland, Jim 197
Rowley, Peter 465
Roy, Harcourt 684
Rudulph, Bob 237
Russell, Doug 109-10
Rutledge, Abbie 81
Rutler, George 198

S

Sabin, Francene 786-87
Sanderlin, Owenita 536
Sanderson, J.D. 855
Satterthwaite, Frank 199
Sauser, Jean 148-49
Scagnetti, Jack 142
Scharff, Robert 685
Schayer, E. Richard 537
Schickel, Richard 466
Schmitz, Dorothy 788
Schulman, Janet 538
Schultz, Nikki 686
Schulz, Charles 856
Schwed, Peter 440, 687-88
Scott, Eugene 150, 797, 857-58
Scott, Leroy 539
Scott, Thomas 143A
Seewagen, George 789

Author Index

TITLE INDEX

Titles of audiovisual materials, books, and periodicals when they are used as a separate item number are included in the index. All the first named are distinguished by the symbol (AV), all the last by the symbol (P). Subtitles are not included except when they are needed to clarify the title (for example, "Smashing: Jimmy Connors"), or to distinguish between materials having the same title. For books with the same title where there is no subtitle, or when title and subtitle are identical, the author's name in parentheses following the title is used as the means of differentiation.

Symbols have also been employed following some of the titles to indicate what sport is being covered. A title such as "Basic Strokes," for example, could refer to any game discussed in this book. To clarify which game is being referred to in all such cases of doubt the following are symbols used: (B)-- Badminton, (C)--Court tennis, (R)--Racquetball, (T)--Tennis, (TT)--Table Tennis.

This index is alphabetized letter by letter. Numbers refer to item numbers unless they are preceded by a "p.", in which case they refer to a page.

D

E

SUBJECT INDEX

Persons as subjects and subjects proper are included in this index. For persons, entries have been made when they wrote autobiographies, have biographies written about them, have entire chapters in books devoted to them, or appear in audiovisual presentations. Those last two are not complete--persons appearing in tennis histories or who are subjects of statements such as "Highlights of earlier matches are shown," are normally not included here. In many audiovisual instances the names of subjects will not be found in the annotation itself. For instance, the annotation for item 127, 1977 U.S.R.A. NATIONAL RACQUETBALL CHAMPIONSHIP, does not mention the name Davey Bledsoe, but a subject entry under his name in this index refers to 127 because he was the winner of the 1977 championship and there is substantial footage of him in the videocassette. Forms of names used were determined arbitrarily by the editor with cross-references from alternate forms. Thus Helen Wills was chosen as the entry for that player with cross-references from Helen Moody and Helen Roark.

For subjects proper, entries have been made without using the qualifying sport. Thus "Drills" is used rather than "Tennis drills;" "Equipment" rather than "Racket sport equipment" and so on. All of the "Other Games" listed in chapter 9 will also be found here.

This index is alphabetized letter by letter. Numbers refer to item numbers unless they are preceded by a "p.", in which case they refer to a page.

Subject Index

Subject Index

ASSOCIATION INDEX

This index is alphabetized letter by letter. Numbers given refer to item numbers unless they are preceded by a "p.", in which case they refer to a page.